Control of Federal Spending

Control of
Federal Spending

Proceedings of
The Academy of
Political Science

Volume 35
Number 4

ISSN 0065-0684

Edited by C. Lowell Harriss

New York, 1985

Contents

* With excerpts from the Grace Commission reports.

IMPROVING MANAGEMENT

Preface

Federal government spending continues to rise — from already high levels to alarming new heights. Both the level attained and the rate of increase are causes of concern. In many respects the problems are long-standing. Yet some new elements have complicated the problems.

Whether the problems remain unsolved from the past or result from recent developments, they demand continuing attention. Expenditure control bears on the size of the Federal deficit, in itself a subject of increasing concern. The problems involve real resources — and taxes and borrowing — in large amounts. The trends foreshadow even higher expenditures and more reason for making a determined effort to understand and to act constructively, and act sooner rather than later.

This volume presents discussions on a variety of specific topics. The authors draw on a wide diversity of contacts with the problems. The reader will gain many insights into the difficulties of reducing the rates of growth and will find suggestions for achieving progress.

The views expressed are those of the authors and not necessarily those of any organizations with which they are associated. The Academy of Political Science serves as a forum for the development and dissemination of opinion on public-policy questions, but it does not make recommendations on political and social issues.

The Academy expresses its appreciation to the John M. Olin Foundation, Inc., and the Robert Schalkenbach Foundation, Inc., for financing this project. It is also grateful to William Farr, David Ordan, and Deuward Bultman for editing the manuscripts and supervising the production of this volume.

C. LOWELL HARRISS
Executive Director

Contributors

CHARLES F. BINGMAN, formerly Deputy Associate Director (Management), Office of Management and Budget, is Distinguished Practitioner in Residence, National Academy of Public Administration.

MILTON FRIEDMAN, a Nobel Prize Laureate in Economics, is Senior Research Fellow at the Hoover Institution, Stanford University, and Professor of Economics Emeritus at the University of Chicago.

ROSE FRIEDMAN, Ph.D. in economics, collaborated with her husband, Milton Friedman, on *Capitalism and Freedom* and the best-seller *Free to Choose.*

STEVE H. HANKE, formerly Senior Economist, President's Council of Economic Advisers, is Professor of Applied Economics, The Johns Hopkins University. He is the author of *Studies in Water and Wastewater Economics.*

C. LOWELL HARRISS is Professor Emeritus of Economics, Columbia University; Executive Director, the Academy of Political Science; Economic Consultant, Tax Foundation, Inc.; and Associate, Lincoln Institute of Land Policy.

ROBERT W. SCHLECK, Senior Research Analyst, Tax Foundation, Inc., is the author of *Federal Employee Retirement Systems* and *Employee Pension Systems in State and Local Government.*

KENNETH A. SHEPSLE is Professor of Political Science and Research Associate, Center for the Study of American Business, Washington University, St. Louis, Missouri. He is the author of the forthcoming *Giant Jigsaw Puzzle,* a book on the congressional committee assignment process.

FRED THOMPSON is Associate Professor, Graduate Program in Public Policy and Administration, Columbia University. He is the editor of *Managing Public Enterprises.*

AL ULLMAN, President of Ullman Consultants, Inc., served in the U.S. House of Representatives from 1957 through 1980. He was Chairman of the House Ways and Means Committee from 1975 through 1980.

MURRAY L. WEIDENBAUM, former Chairman of the Council of Economic Advisers, is Director of the Center for the Study of American Business, Washington University, St. Louis, Missouri. He is the author of *Business, Government, and the Public.*

BARRY R. WEINGAST is Assistant Professor of Economics and Business and also Research Associate, Center for the Study of American Business, Washington University, St. Louis, Missouri.

AARON WILDAVSKY, President Elect of the American Political Science Association (1984–85), is Professor of Political Science and Public Policy, University of California, Berkeley. He is the author of *How to Limit Government Spending* and *The Politics of the Budgetary Process*.

BENJAMIN ZYCHER, formerly Senior Staff Economist, Council of Economic Advisers, is Economist, Rand Corporation.

Blueprints for Cost Control: Recommendations of the Grace Commission

C. LOWELL HARRISS*

Experience as governor of California led President Reagan to ask a group from the private sector to study Federal government operations. It was headed by J. Peter Grace, chairman of the W. R. Grace & Co. He recruited 161 executives from business, the professions, and nonprofit organizations. They then obtained the services of approximately 2,000 officials from corporations, legal and accounting firms, and other private organizations; these men and women made detailed, on-the-spot studies of specific agencies and activities. (A 591-page volume, *War on Waste*, available in paperback from Macmillan, consists of the two volumes of the *Report to the President*. The other forty-seven volumes listed in table 1 supply evidence, commentary, and the specific recommendations.) The next essay in this volume explains the group's methods of operation.

The group has come to be known as the Grace Commission, and that term will be used in this volume. The official title was the President's Private Sector Survey on Cost Control (PPSS).

The commission made, by its own count, 2,478 specific recommendations. It supported them with masses of evidence and commentary. Its reports also contain data on the need for cost control and discussions about conditions and procedures for controlling Federal spending. Cost reductions would eventually exceed $100 billion a year; increases in receipts would be more than $20 billion a year. Many proposals offer prospects of improving government services; the potential benefits, therefore, should exceed those with identifiable monetary effects.

The major findings and recommendations show the need for attention and responsive action. This essay presents, often in the commission's own words (or those of its chairman), some results of its massive efforts. A few of the following essays also include materials from the reports.

* With excerpts from the Grace Commission reports.

The findings include statistics measuring the size of the expenditure problem. The directive establishing the group assumed that there was a real need for more effective restraint of the growth of Federal spending. This belief undoubtedly had broad and deep support throughout the country. But how big a need? The commission engaged Data Resources, Inc., a leading professional forecasting organization, to make estimates beyond the normal five-year span of budget projections. Although the future of Federal finances involves many uncertainties, one thing is certain — the power of compounding. Even amounts that may seem "small" for one year — perhaps a few tens of billions in Federal fiscal affairs — cumulate over fifteen or twenty years to formidable totals. Therefore, even apparently modest annual expenditures — or continuing reductions — soon build up to large amounts, whereas procrastination only adds to later interest costs.

Estimates of cost reductions are usually in amounts for three years rather than annual rates or cumulative totals for, say, the rest of the decade or the century. The three-year concept applies, not to possibilities in any immediate or defined calendar period — say, 1985–87 — but to three years of fully implementing a recommendation. In many cases complete implementation would require considerable time even if a start were made at once. In reality, the best possible beginnings might be relatively small; cost savings in the first three years would often be considerably below the eventually realized amounts. Examples of savings that might be expected relatively soon were cited by Mr. Grace on 8 February 1984 in congressional testimony when he identified

possible near term savings of $59 billion which could result from the implementation of PPSS recommendations. These possible savings, achievable over three years, are in the areas of:

	Three-Year Savings ($ billions)
(1) Inventory Management	$13.404
(2) Loan Management	11.080
(3) Tax Collections	10.746
(4) General Management	8.048
(5) Cash Management	6.389
(6) Reduced Error Rates	5.852
(7) User Charges	3.187
(8) Total	58.706

Under Inventory Management, more than $7 billion could be saved over three years by more selective use of military specifications in the procurement of commercially available hardware. More than $6 billion in additional savings would result from inventory reductions reflecting improved management techniques.

Revenue Enhancement

Recommendations go beyond cost savings as such. Approximately 15 percent of the net deficit reduction would come from increased receipts. The PPSS recommended greater use of charging, fees, and prices. One test of the desirability of a process or an activity is whether those who ask for it will pay the cost. Government, however, performs some activities — such as national defense — for which prices cannot be charged, and requiring beneficiaries of other activities to pay for the results may be neither desirable nor possible. Whether it is best to raise revenue through taxes or through prices will depend on the specific case. The recipient of a passport, for example, can be charged for it; he cannot be charged, however, for his part of each day's diplomatic representation abroad.

Most of the opportunities for charging identified by the Grace Commission have long been recognized. The potentials have not been exploited, because those who would be required to pay prefer to get benefits free of charge or priced below cost. Such objections will not be overcome easily.

Proposal Groupings

Table 1 lists the reports and the three-year estimates of cost reduction, from the largest down. Many proposals can be implemented by the agency. Others, especially those of large amounts, would require congressional action.

TABLE 1

PPSS Reports
Savings and Revenue Enhancement Opportunities
Three-Year Totals (Duplicated)
($ Millions)

Reports	(1) Savings	(2) Revenue	(3) Total
1. Program subsidies	$58,900	$ 0	$58,900
2. Federal retirement programs	58,100	0	58,100
3. Defense-OSD	44,500	300	44,800
4. Personnel management	39,300	0	39,300
5. Federal health care costs	28,900	0	28,900
6. Privatization	11,200	17,200	28,400
7. Air Force	27,600	0	27,600
8. Financial asset management	13,800	9,700	23,500
9. Procurement	20,300	0	20,300
10. Automated data processing/OA	19,100	0	19,100
11. Beyond PPSS	10,800	5,200	16,000
12. Army	13,400	0	13,400
13. Health and Human Services/HCFA/PHS	12,700	600	13,300
14. Agriculture	12,200	600	12,800
15. Research and development	12,100	0	12,100
16. Federal hospital management	9,200	2,700	11,900
17. Wage-setting laws	11,700	0	11,700
18. Treasury	2,400	9,100	11,500
19. User charges	0	10,200	10,200
20. Banking	1,600	7,800	9,400
21. Health and Human Services/SSA	8,400	1,000	9,400

continued on next page

TABLE 1–*continued*

Reports	(1) Savings	(2) Revenue	(3) Total
22. Congressional encroachment	7,700	1,100	8,800
23. Navy	7,200	0	7,200
24. Low-income standards	5,900	0	5,900
25. Federal construction	5,400	0	5,400
26. Transportation	2,700	1,700	4,400
27. Energy	2,800	1,300	4,100
28. Labor	3,700	0	3,700
29. Business	2,400	900	3,300
30. Veterans Administration	2,100	1,000	3,100
31. Education	2,800	0	2,800
32. Housing and Urban Development	2,500	300	2,800
33. Real property	2,400	0	2,400
34. EPA/SBA/FEMA	1,700	200	1,900
35. Travel and Transportation Management	1,900	0	1,900
36. Publishing, printing, and audio visual	1,400	300	1,700
37. Interior	300	1,000	1,300
38. Justice	200	700	900
39. State/U.S. Information Agency	400	300	700
40. Commerce	200	500	700
41. Land and facilities management	200	400	600
42. Health and Human Services/other	600	0	600
43. Federal feeding	300	0	300
44. Information gap	0	0	0
45. Federal financial management	0	0	0
46. Federal management systems	0	0	0
47. Anomalies	0	0	0
Totals: Duplicated	$470,800	$74,200	$545,000
Less: Duplicated amounts	(112,800)	(7,800)	(120,600)
Totals: Unduplicated	$358,000	$66,400	$424,400

NOTE: Columns do not add up to totals because figures were rounded to nearest $100 million.

Volumes grouped as Management Office Selected Issues deal with a variety of topics, as follows:

    I. Publishing, Printing, Reproduction, and Audiovisual Activities
    II. Travel and Traffic Management
    III. Financial Management in the Federal Government
    IV. Wage Setting Laws: Impact on the Federal Government
    V. Anomalies in the Federal Work Environment
    VI. Federal Retirement Systems
    VII. Information Gap in the Federal Government
    VIII. The Cost of Congressional Encroachment
    IX. Federal Health Care Costs
    X. Opportunities Beyond PPSS
    XI. Federally Subsidized Programs

These volumes are concerned with problems and with issues that are common to many agencies and programs or to the entire government. Several volumes draw on private-sector practices to suggest possibilities for cost reduction and service improvement. The examination by leaders from the private sector has produced substance of solid value, as well as concrete recommendations. They are included in the commission's total of 2,478 along with proposals for the various agencies. The authors, recognizing the complexity of many issues, recommend additional study in some cases. Yet the dominant tone is a sense of urgency, the need for prompt action that the authors believe can rest on the evidence and analyses in the reports.

The appendixes (pages 6–26) present three selections related to the Grace recommendations. Appendix 1 is the letter sent with the reports to President Reagan. Although it does not presume to summarize the results of the massive undertaking, it presents highlights that the commission wished to emphasize.

Appendix 2 is a portion of the analyses of the Grace recommendations by two official agencies, the Congressional Budget Office and the General Accounting Office. These two organizations established by Congress to serve on a nonpartisan basis were asked to evaluate the PPSS proposals. That request resulted in a 397-page volume submitted in February 1984. In itself it is a substantial study of many Federal government activities. To varying degrees it draws on knowledge (and judgments) throughout the government as the CBO and the GAO used the many sources available to them.

The two agencies selected for review those proposals that the PPSS estimated to involve three-year budget reductions of $1 billion or more – 397 grouped into 90 sets. These "recommendations account for almost 90 percent of the potential three-year savings as estimated by the Grace Commission." Because of the budgeting schedule for fiscal year 1985, the needs of the committee required the CBO and GAO to work under considerable time pressures. The CBO concentrated on quantitative budgetary effects. It expressed no opinion on the merits or probable results of recommendations.

A complex situation can never be summarized either accurately or adequately. Such is certainly true regarding the CBO's estimates of the budgetary effects of the PPSS recommendations. It made estimates for sixty-seven out of ninety sets of Grace proposals. In some cases the CBO results cast doubt on the reliability of PPSS estimates. A study of the reasons for differences reveals the complexities of the problems. The CBO estimated for the three budget years 1985–87, whereas the PPSS concept is for three years of full implementation. Some of the proposals, however, cannot even begin within three fiscal years, and some could not be fully implemented in this century. The CBO estimates rested on its budget-baseline concept. Some PPSS proposals had been implemented by the time the CBO made its study and thus had already been incorporated into the CBO baseline estimates; no additional expenditure reduction was counted. Lack of precision in specification of the Grace proposals prevented the CBO from making estimates in some cases. Other technical factors also complicated comparison.

The GAO evaluated the substance of proposals, drawing on more than a decade of objective examinations of government programs and operations.

Rudolph G. Penner, director of the Congressional Budget Office, and Charles A. Bowsher, comptroller general of the United States (head of the General Accounting Office), testified before the Senate Committee on the Budget on 28 February 1984. Parts of their testimony are followed by selections from the joint CBO-GAO study. These excerpts do not reflect the sweep of the project, but they do suggest the substance of the CBO and GAO analyses.

Appendix 3 presents selections chosen from among numerous recommendations of somewhat general scope — endorsement of the item veto, a proposal that has a long record of support. Although the prospects of adopting this spending control device seem slight, the commission's discussion throws light on some of the forces involved in decisions about Federal spending.

APPENDIX 1

January 12, 1984

The Honorable Ronald Reagan
President of the United States
The White House
Washington, D.C.

Dear Mr. President,

Following your directive to identify and suggest remedies for waste and abuse in the Federal Government, the President's Private Sector Survey (PPSS) offers recommendations which would save:

- $424 billion in three years, rising to
- $1.9 trillion *per year* by the year 2000.

These proposals would transform the Federal debt situation as follows:

	Federal Debt ($ trillions)		Annual Interest on Federal Debt ($ billions)	
	Without PPSS	With PPSS	Without PPSS	With PPSS
1990	$3.2	$2.0	$252.3	$89.2
1995	6.2	2.2	540.9	62.3
2000	13.0	2.5	1,520.7	75.1

You asked the American people to help you get the Government "off their backs." If the American people realized how rapidly Federal Government spending is likely to grow under existing legislated programs, I am convinced they would compel their elected representatives to "get the Government off their backs." In our survey to search out ways to cut costs in the Government, great emphasis was placed on the spending outlook, which is as follows:

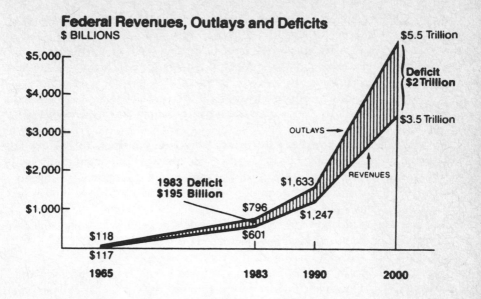

Federal Revenues, Outlays and Deficits
$ BILLIONS

If fundamental changes are not made in Federal spending, as compared with the fiscal 1983 deficit of $195 billion, a deficit of over ten times that amount, $2 trillion, is projected for the year 2000. . . . In that year, the Federal debt would be $13.0 trillion ($160,000 per current taxpayer) and the interest alone on the debt would be $1.5 trillion per year ($18,500 per year per current taxpayer).

Mr. President, these projections are the result of a joint effort between PPSS and a leading U.S. economic forecasting firm. They are the result of a very careful study and drove us to seek out every possible savings opportunity, "like tireless bloodhounds," as you requested.

In the course of the search by our 36 Task Forces, chaired by 161 top executives from around the country and staffed by over 2,000 volunteers that they provided, we came up with 2,478 separate, distinct, and specific recommendations which are the basis for the carefully projected savings. For practical purposes, these savings, if fully implemented, could virtually eliminate the reported deficit by the 1990's versus an alternative deficit of $10.2 trillion in the decade of the 1990's if no action is taken.

Equally important, the 2,478 cost-cutting, revenue-enhancing recommendations we have made can be achieved without raising taxes, without weakening America's needed defense build-up, and without in any way harming necessary social welfare programs.

Because we are starting from a deficit of $195 billion, every dollar we can stop spending is a dollar that the Government does not have to borrow. With future Government borrowing costs at 11 percent (versus 10.75 percent now and 14.5 percent when you took office) and inflation taken at 6 percent per year over the longer run, these savings compound quickly.

Applying these interest and inflation rates, the result is that a dollar saved today accumulates to $32 over 12 years and $71 over 17 years. Thus, any potential saving made, as compared to not making the saving, translates into a difference in cumulative spending of 32 times that amount through 1995 and 71 times that amount through the end of the century. . . .

This is, of course, a horrendous prospect. If the American people understood the gravity of the outlook, they would not, I believe, support representatives who might let it happen.

Mr. President, you have been so correct in resisting attempts to balance the budget by increasing taxes. The tax load on the average American family is already at counterproductive levels with the underground economy having now grown to an estimated $500 billion per year, costing about $100 billion in lost Federal tax revenues per year.

The size of the underground economy is understandable when one considers that median family income taxes have increased from $9 in 1948 to $2,218 in 1983, or by 246 times. This is runaway taxation at its worst.

Importantly, any meaningful increases in taxes from personal income would have to come from lower and middle income families, as 90 percent of all personal taxable income is generated below the taxable income level of $35,000.

Further, there isn't much more that can be extracted from high income brackets. If the Government took 100 percent of all taxable income beyond the $75,000 tax bracket not already taxed, it would get only $17 billion, and this confiscation, which would destroy productive enterprise, would only be sufficient to run the Government for seven days. . . .

Our survey studied the small as well as the major items of cost savings, items of broad national impact as well as those of a more localized nature. I believe you will be interested in a few random examples of what we found:

- In the Northwest, the Federal Power Marketing Administration is selling subsidized power at one-third of market rates. If the Federal power were priced at market, there would be a three-year increase in revenues of $4.5 billion, which equates to the three-year personal income taxes of 676,000 median income American families who are thus subsidizing a discrete group in one part of the country.
- The Civil Service and Military Retirement Systems provide to participants three times and six times the benefits, respectively, of the best private sector plans. The Government's civilian and military employees retire at an earlier age, typically age 55 and 40, respectively, versus 63 to 64 in the private sector, with substantially more liberal benefit formulas than their private sector counterparts. In addition, the pensions of Federal retirees are fully indexed for inflation — a rarity in the private sector. Modifying major Federal pensions to provide benefits comparable to those of the best private sector plans, slightly better in the case of military pensions, would result in three-year savings of $60.9 billion, equivalent to the three-year income taxes of 9.2 million median income families.
- A relatively small item in the overall, but representative of many, is the prohibition of competitive bidding on the movement of military personnel household

goods to and from Alaska and Hawaii, despite a DOD test showing that competitive bidding would reduce costs by as much as 26 percent. Elimination of this provision would save $69.5 million in three years, equivalent to the three-year income taxes of 10,400 median income families.

- We found Congressional interference to be a major problem. For example, because Congress obstructs the closing of bases that the military wants to close, the three-year waste is $367 million. In total, PPSS recommends three-year savings of $3.1 billion by closing excess military bases, equivalent to the three-year income taxes of 466,000 median income families.

Mr. President, these are just a few of the absurd situations that we found throughout the Government that add up to billions of dollars per year and where the opportunities for savings are clearly available.

Some of the recommendations made by PPSS have been made before. Others are entirely new. Regardless of their origins, the focus must now be on implementation. The current economic trends are simply too serious to delay action any longer.

PPSS has submitted 36 major Task Force reports and 11 studies on special subjects such as subsidies and retirement. In total, these reports substantiate three-year ongoing savings of $424.4 billion, plus cash accelerations of $66 billion. These are all analyzed and supported in great detail. Capsuled in terms of the functional problems to which they relate, the savings are as follows:

PPSS Savings Recommendations

	$ Billions	% of Total
Program Waste	$160.9	37.9%
System Failures	151.3	35.7
Personnel Mismanagement	90.9	21.4
Structural Deficiencies	12.7	3.0
Other Opportunities	8.6	2.0
Total	$424.4	100.0%

These data confirm our findings that system failures and personnel mismanagement together comprise well over one-half, 57.1 percent, of the total savings possibilities. They are at the foundation of inefficiencies in the Federal Government. Program waste, which accounts for 37.9 percent of the savings recommendations, would also be substantially eliminated if proper systems and personnel management were in place.

The above underscores one of our most important recommendations, which is the establishment of an Office of Federal Management in the Executive Office of the President. This Federal Government top management office would include OMB, GSA and OPM and have Government-wide responsibility for establishing, modernizing, and monitoring management systems.

If it is set up and staffed properly, it could go a long way to avoid in the future the thousands of deficiencies and examples of waste that we have identified. We would not feel our task complete if we just identified past deficiencies without recommendations for a management and organizational structure that would be best suited for preventing the errors of the past.

Additionally, the establishment of this new office would be beneficial in the implementation process of the PPSS recommendations.

In this regard, we believe that your Cabinet Council on Management and Administration, working in concert with the Office of Cabinet Affairs, is uniquely suited to lead a Government-wide effort to restore sound principles of management and efficiency to the Federal Government. While the Cabinet Council already has taken a leadership role in this regard, we urge you to call upon it to make implementation of the PPSS recommendations Government-wide its highest priority. . . .

Respectfully,

J. Peter Grace
Chairman

APPENDIX 2

CONGRESSIONAL BUDGET OFFICE
(STATEMENT OF RUDOLPH G. PENNER*)

POTENTIAL BUDGETARY IMPACT

For purposes of analysis and discussion, our report groups the 396 Grace Commission recommendations selected for review into 90 separate sets of proposals. It was possible to develop estimates of potential budgetary impact for 67 of these 90 sets. For the other 23 sets of proposals reviewed, budget estimates could not be prepared because either the proposals were too vague or the available information too scant.

[Assuming that] those Grace Commission proposals that we could measure against our baseline projections for fiscal years 1985-1989 . . . are implemented by October 1, 1984, we estimate that they could result in unified budget deficit reductions of about $15 billion in 1985 and nearly $70 billion by 1989. The cumulative five-year reductions from CBO's baseline projections amount to $194 billion, including lower net interest costs of $34 billion as a result of lower deficits. Reductions in off-budget spending would add another $7-$8 billion annually during the next five years. The total deficit reduction effect for 1985-1989 is projected to be $233 billion. . . .

* Senate Committee on the Budget, *Hearing on Efficiency in Government*, 98th Cong., 2d sess., 28 Feb. 1984, 12-26.

Although the majority of the Grace Commission recommendations can be characterized as management proposals to achieve greater efficiencies or to operate on a more business-like basis, the bulk of the cost savings estimated by both the CBO-GAO study and by the commission are associated with often very dramatic proposals to change policies or to restructure programs. Many of these policy-change proposals go far beyond any recently contemplated by the Congress, and all of them would require Congressional action.

National Defense Programs

The budgetary savings that we could identify for national defense programs are small — only $14 billion over five years — because the budget impact for most of the 112 recommendations could not be estimated. The Grace Commission gave considerable attention to reviewing defense programs. . . . But the bulk of the recommendations were not sufficiently specific to develop a good budget impact estimate. . . .

This does not mean that the commission's recommendations for defense program savings lack merit or are ill conceived. Indeed, the task force recommendations generally are based on widely accepted principles of good management and efficiency. Many of these recommendations have been previously proposed by the General Accounting Office and also cover many of the same areas that were included in the so-called Carlucci initiatives announced by the Defense Department in 1981. . . .

The Survey task force estimates of potential savings for most defense recommendations, at best, are illustrative and are not founded on historical data, detailed analyses, specific budget proposals of programmatic changes. Many of their estimates are based on judgmental assumptions based on industry experience that we could not validate. While their cost estimates may be adequate for illustrative purposes, more programmatic information is needed for purposes of making budget estimates. . . .

Entitlements and Other Mandatory Spending Programs

The Grace Commission advanced an array of proposals for cutting spending on entitlement programs, based on a judgment that many program benefits may be too generous or available to too many people. Accordingly, the commission recommends policy changes that would reduce either the size or the availability of benefits, or both. While other proposals in this area seek to improve program administration, by far the greatest savings potential lies in revising policies and restructuring programs.

We analyzed 43 different Grace Commission recommendations for entitlement and other mandatory spending programs. The estimated budget savings for the next three years is relatively modest, but over five years could exceed $50 billion. The largest saving would be in the area of federal health care programs, where the commission recommends limiting the growth of health care expenditures to the annual change in the gross national product (GNP). In conjunction with this expenditure cap, it also proposes a dramatic restructuring of federal health care programs. Though the specifics of the commission's plan are not fully developed, it apparently would apportion federal health funds among geographical regions on a per capita basis that also reflected regional variations in health care costs. Monies would go to private, state, and local bidders competing for service contracts. What services would be provided are not clearly outlined. The CBO budget estimate for this proposal assumes that such a major program restructuring would take at least two years to put into place. By 1989, CBO projects that limiting health care expenditures to GNP growth would reduce Medicare-Medicaid outlays by 10 percent from baseline projections of current law, and produce total savings of $29 billion during 1987–1989. . . . Almost all of the potential savings would require Congressional action. . . .

By far the largest five-year savings in this entire spending area would result from the proposal to replace certain direct loan programs with loan guarantees. The commission proposes to convert the direct loan programs of the Farmers Home Administration and the major business loan programs of the Small Business Administration into guaranteed loan programs, with the government guaranteeing no more than 75 percent of the principal amount. This would transfer more responsibilities and risk to the private sector and encourage more careful selection of loan recipients. On the other hand, such a shift would increase borrowers' costs in those programs that currently have subsidized interest rates, thus reducing the programs' ability to serve households and businesses with limited financial resources.

CBO estimates that this change alone would reduce total government outlays — both on and off budget — by more than $40 billion over the 1985–1989 period, largely because loan disbursements averaging about $9 billion per year would be forgone. Long-term savings would be appreciably less, however, because the federal government would also forgo the repayments, which currently stretch out as long as 50 years. . . .

Revenues

The Grace Commission reports offer several revenue-raising proposals that could help to narrow the long-term federal deficit. The revenue proposals include four tax policy recommendations — one of which has already been enacted — and several initiatives that could mean more efficient management of the federal government's cash flow. Of the tax policy recommendations, the most far-reaching is the proposal calling for the taxation of federal subsidy payments. The management initiatives include shortening tax deferral periods allowed some taxpayers and accelerating the government's deposit of tax and other receipts. CBO estimates that the overall increase in revenues from these proposals — not counting one proposal that CBO could not estimate — could amount to more than $40 billion during the next five years.

The scope of the Grace Commission proposal to tax federal subsidies is very broad, ranging from cash benefits under Social Security or Aid to Families with Dependent Children (AFDC) to in-kind goods and services such as food stamps and Medicaid. In particular, the commission sees poor targeting and duplication of benefits to individuals qualifying for several means-tested programs as giving rise to substantial waste of federal dollars. Besides the potential increase in tax receipts, the commission sees improved targeting of means-tested benefits as an important effect from taxing federal subsidies. Although the Survey report on Federally Subsidized Programs discusses the inclusion of all federal subsidies in taxable income, the estimated savings in the report result solely from the taxation of means-tested benefits. CBO estimates that taxation of means-tested benefits could raise as much as $15 billion over the 1985–1989 period.

A second major revenue raiser recommended by the Grace Commission would be derived by augmenting the Internal Revenue Service's staffing for collection of delinquent taxes and examination of tax returns, and from the accelerated disposition of tax cases brought before the U.S. Tax Court. CBO estimates revenue increases amounting to $13 billion over the next five years. The commission's proposal to limit the use of tax-exempt bonds for private purposes would add another $9.5 billion during 1985–1989. . . .

CONCLUDING REMARKS

Most of the Grace Commission recommendations involve various management improvements that could be implemented administratively. The bulk of the potential savings, however, relate to recommendations that would require significant changes in current laws and policies. The federal spending generated by the policies and programs studied by the Grace Commission has been subject to close scrutiny before and should continue to be reviewed for possible savings. The magnitude of the savings projected by the Grace Commission for its purposes in these areas, however, is much too large to be attributed simply to eliminating waste and inefficiency. Rather, the commission's proposals should be characterized for the most part as possible changes in public policy that could help reduce mounting federal deficits.

These proposals all represent tough decisions with difficult trade-offs. The CBO-GAO analysis reveals that the Grace Commission has not found an easy solution to the federal deficit problem, although it has helped to focus attention within the Administration and the Congress on some ways to control the rising cost of government.

GENERAL ACCOUNTING OFFICE
(STATEMENT OF CHARLES A. BOWSHER*)

RESULTS OF OUR ANALYSIS

Before presenting the details of our analysis let me underline two fundamental concerns we have about the results of the Grace Commission's work. First, we share CBO's finding that many of the Commission's savings estimates are considerably higher than can reasonably be expected. Our fear is that action on many worthwhile Commission recommendations will be jeopardized by widespread recognition that the associated savings estimates are significantly overstated.

Second, we are concerned that the Commission, in its final report and elsewhere, characterized its proposals as actions needed to reduce waste, abuse, and inefficiency in the federal government, when much of its work and identified savings potential more precisely concern policy and legislative readjustments. . . . It is our hope that the Commission's efforts to promote its work will not be counterproductive and detract from the cost cutting and management improvement proposals presented.

These concerns notwithstanding, we found a good deal to agree with in the 400 Commission recommendations we examined. In fact, we found that nearly two-thirds of the individual recommendations have overall merit. For about one-third of the recommendations we examined, GAO had made a related recommendation in the past.

It is important to note, however, that our general agreement with about two-thirds of the individual recommendations does not translate into agreement with a proportionate amount of the estimated savings. A number of the proposals with the largest associated savings estimates were those we could not support. . . .

Of the recommendations we examined, we found that about one half could be accomplished by executive branch action with the remainder requiring congressional action. In this regard, we agreed with the Commission's assessments of implementation authority in all but about ten percent of the cases. Areas where we disagreed were about evenly split between cases where the Commission said congressional action was required while we believed only executive action was required and vice versa. . . .

DEFENSE

In the area of national defense, GAO examined 21 sets of proposals. We identified 8 proposals that we could generally support on their merit, 7 proposals which we could not support, and 6 others where we had to qualify our support or had no strong opinion. . . .

* Senate Committee on the Budget, *Hearing on Efficiency in Government*, 98th Cong., 2d sess., 28 Feb. 1984, 37–48.

Improved weapons system acquisition was one of the Commission's major thrusts in the defense area. We agree that improved weapons system procurement practices would result in savings, and just as importantly, in better quality weapon systems. GAO has performed considerable work on the effectiveness of the weapon system acquisition process. GAO reports have emphasized areas where the Commission also found problems, particularly in the need to affirm requirements, reduce cost, improve program management, and improve disclosure to Congress.

We also agree that inefficient weapon production rates result in higher unit costs, reduce DOD's purchasing power, and result in program instability. It is not practical, however, to produce all weapon systems at the most economical production rate because of many competing requirements for defense dollars. We believe that, for each weapon system, it is important to establish the various levels at which economies can be achieved so congressional and DOD decisionmakers are aware of the economic impacts when they alter program funding.

GAO further agrees with the Commission that commonality of subsystems, equipment, and parts holds the promise of reducing life cycle logistics costs and many maintenance problems which can impair military readiness. Standardization of equipment, however, is not a panacea and each case needs to be considered on its own merits. Generally, GAO has found over the last decade that DOD could and should increase its efforts to improve commonality of equipment, parts, and subsystems.

We are concerned about a number of the Commission's defense proposals. For example, the Commission recommended that biennial budgeting be instituted for major weapons systems procurement. We support efforts to alleviate problems of planning and budgeting for major weapons systems, which the Commission believes biennial budgeting will accomplish. We believe, however, that the results of adopting biennial budgeting without other needed improvements in the financial management structure of the government as a whole would be disappointing.

We also have concern over the Commission's military retirement system proposals. There is widespread agreement that the system is expensive. Beyond this, however, there is less agreement on whether the system benefits are too generous. Many of the Commission's proposals to revise military retirement pay are new and go far beyond the scope of previous recommendations to reform retirement pay. Our basic concern is that the proposals focus exclusively on one element of the total life cycle cost of military manpower, i.e., retirement pay. The Commission did not estimate the specific manpower force profile changes that would result from its recommendations, whether these profile changes would adversely affect military effectiveness, or whether offsetting costs would be incurred to maintain a militarily effective force profile. Looking at the retirement system in isolation, and making cost reduction recommendations without knowing what effect such changes will have on the force profile and life cycle manpower costs, could result in a less effective and/or a more costly military force, even though the retirement account may be less.

ENTITLEMENTS

In the entitlements area, almost all of the cost saving potential identified by the Commission involves policy initiatives designed to reduce benefits to individuals or businesses, and to redefine the federal role in health care. . . .

Specifically, of the 16 sets of proposals in the entitlements area, we generally agreed with 10, generally disagreed with 4, and had to qualify our support or had no strong views on 2. For those 10 proposals that we could support, CBO estimated potential savings totalling about $6 billion.

The most significant savings estimate proposed by the Commission in the entitlements area involved limiting the growth in federal health care costs to the growth in the gross national product (GNP) — a fundamental change in the federal role in health care. . . . In GAO's opinion, it is not appropriate to implement the Commission's proposals at this time because (1) limiting federal health care cost to the growth in the GNP could require dramatic changes in the way medical care is provided, (2) the level of health care provided to most people would have to be lowered or beneficiaries would have to pay more for their health care, and (3) the ability of at least some Medicare and most Medicaid beneficiaries to pay the additional cost is questionable. . . .

NONDEFENSE DISCRETIONARY

We also addressed a wide variety of proposals in the broad area of nondefense discretionary spending and offsetting receipts. Proposals in this area include cash management, debt collection, housing, energy, and others. We found 20 of the 30 sets of proposals generally to have merit, generally disagreed with only 2 proposals, and had to qualify our support or had no basis for an opinion on the 8 others. For the 20 proposals we found to have overall merit, CBO's estimated savings potential totalled nearly $10 billion.

The Commission made numerous recommendations for federal agencies to develop and use good management practices in collecting debts owed the government, and we have long endorsed stronger federal management in this area. However, some of the Commission's recommendations are for actions already in progress and already addressed by the enactment of the Debt Collection Act of 1982. Nonetheless, we agree that savings opportunities still exist.

One opportunity involves offsetting delinquent debts against federal tax refunds due debtors. We have supported the use of IRS offset, and the Commission acknowledged that the use of IRS offset is a viable means of collecting debts owed the government. Our support of the IRS offset, however, should not be interpreted as a recommendation that IRS become a debt collection "clearinghouse." Debt collection is primarily the responsibility of each federal agency.

One area where we can only partially support the Commission's positions concerns the federal power marketing administrations. The Commission proposes reducing the costs associated with the power marketing administrations by (1) requiring them to repay federal investments on a timely basis and at market interest rates; (2) charging a user fee for water used to produce electricity; and (3) eventually selling the PMAs to nonfederal entities. While we have strongly supported the first recommendation over the last several years, we have reservations about the second because of recent changes that have significantly increased the power marketing administrations' power rates.

With respect to selling the PMAs to nonfederal entities, we note that the Commission based its analysis only on electricity production and did not address the actions needed to assure that other purposes of these facilities, such as irrigation, navigation, flood control and fish and wildlife protection will continue to be met. We also note that federally generated power, sold in 38 states, is generally lower in cost than other alternatives and changing the preference rights to this power of public bodies and electric cooperatives would represent a significant policy change.

FEDERAL CIVILIAN EMPLOYMENT

In the area of federal civilian employment and compensation, we addressed 12 sets of proposals. We generally agreed with 5, disagreed with 3, and either qualify our support or had no strong views on 4. . . .

The largest Commission savings estimate involves a proposal to reduce civil service retirement benefits. . . . The Commission proposed sweeping changes in the system based on its view that prevailing retirement benefits in the private sector are much less liberal. . . .

We cannot agree with the Commission's conclusions nor endorse its recommendations as being representative of private sector practices. In our opinion, adopting the Commission's proposals could result in lower benefits for federal employees than those received by their private sector counterparts. Moreover, some of the proposals would reduce the amounts now being paid to retirees and the benefits that active employees have already earned. We question the equity of such retroactive cuts and believe they could be subject to question in the courts.

A major shortcoming in the Commission's analysis was that it limited its benefit comparison to pension plans and social security. It did not consider the capital accumulation plans that many private employers sponsor to provide additional retirement income to their employees. Some of the proposals would deserve consideration if the federal retirement package were reconstructed to include all three elements of retirement income available in the private sector, but the Commission did not recommend that this be done.

In addition to its proposals to change the retirement system's benefit structure, the Commission recommended that the system's accounting practices be changed to achieve better recognition of accruing costs. We endorse this recommendation. It is consistent with our long-held position that current practices cause accruing costs to be understated.

REVENUE ENHANCEMENTS

. . . In this area we either qualify our support or have no basis for an opinion on 7 of the 11 proposals. We generally agreed with 2 proposals and generally disagreed with the remaining 2. CBO's savings estimate for the 2 proposals we supported totalled about $500 million.

One of the proposals with which we disagree — taxing means-tested benefits — represents $59 [billion] of the total $76 billion in revenue enhancements estimated by the Commission. The Commission indicated that its proposal was necessary because many federally subsidized programs, especially means-tested programs, have not been effective in reducing the poverty gap and they serve individuals who have incomes above the poverty level. However, we believe that the means-tested programs included by the Commission were not primarily intended to reduce the poverty level and we question whether they should be included. For example — Medicaid — is designed to meet health needs for people without sufficient resources or income to pay for medical health services. In addition, the Medicaid payment goes to the provider, not to the beneficiary.

Notwithstanding the merits, implementation of the Commission's proposal in this area would be difficult because many means-tested programs are jointly administered by the federal government and the states. The Commission also did not resolve the problem of how to determine the cash value to a beneficiary of an in-kind benefit, such as medical services under Medicaid, which would be essential for the purpose of taxation. For these reasons, we believe it may be inappropriate to consider that the government could achieve any dollar savings in this area when drafting legislation.

On the other hand, we generally support the Commission's proposal to improve federal administration of our tax laws by increasing the number of IRS staff auditing tax returns.

CONCLUSION

. . . Based on our assessment of 90 Commission proposals, we are able to endorse 45, or half, on the basis of their conceptual merit. The Commission's estimated savings for these proposals totalled $128 billion over a 3-year period. CBO was able to develop 3-year budget impact estimates for 32 of these proposals totalling $17 billion. The other 13 proposals with which we agree were valued at $53 billion by the Commission, but neither CBO nor GAO could develop a budget reduction estimate.

Additional savings may be possible by adopting some or all of the 27 Commission proposals for which we had to qualify our support or had no basis to offer an opinion. The Commission's estimated savings for these proposals totalled $126 billion.

In closing, I believe congressional and administrative action is necessary to reduce the federal deficit and the Commission's report serves a useful purpose in focusing attention and stimulating necessary debate on some of the possible actions. GAO is prepared to assist the cognizant congressional committees in analyzing further any of the Commission's recommendations not covered by the CBO/GAO report. . . .

EXCERPTS FROM THE CBO-GAO JOINT STUDY*

Management Proposals

The majority of the Grace Commission recommendations selected for review are concerned with management issues, such as financial management, procurement practices, management of real property, and management of research and development programs. Approximately 40 percent of the three-year cost savings estimated by the Grace Commission for the 396 recommendations examined by CBO and GAO can be attributed to proposed management improvements. GAO has previously recommended many of these management improvements, and some are currently being implemented. About half of the PPSSCC estimated three-year savings could be achieved by administrative measures without further action by the Congress. The other half of the management savings would require Congressional action. . . .

The largest management saving would derive from augmenting the Internal Revenue Service's (IRS) staffing for collection of delinquent taxes and examination of tax returns, and from the disposition of tax cases brought before the U.S. Tax Court. CBO estimated savings amounting to $3.7 billion for 1986–1987 (and $13.0 billion over the five-year period 1985–1989) for this set of proposals, compared to $10.7 billion in three-year savings estimated by the PPSSCC. These proposals were among those suggested by Mr. Grace as appropriate for quick action. The CBO savings estimate is lower mainly because the goal of halting the growth of backlogged tax collections has largely been accomplished through IRS staff increases provided by the Congress in 1983 appropriations. GAO agrees with the recommendations for further staff increases for the collection of delinquent taxes and the examination of returns, but not with the recommendation to establish an appellate tax board. Rather, GAO has recently made alternative recommendations to the Tax Court that, when implemented, should achieve the PPSSCC's objectives at a lower cost.

One of the largest three-year management savings projected by the Grace Commission was associated with a number of recommendations to improve federal work force productivity. The PPSSCC contends that the federal government, like any other employer, can improve productivity by changing its methods of opera-

---

* Congressional Budget Office and General Accounting Office, *Analysis of the Grace Commission's Major Proposals for Cost Control* (Washington, D.C.: GPO, 1984), 13–17, 23, 107–8.

tions, raising employees' skill levels, and investing more than it does now in work-facilitating equipment. CBO has tentatively estimated that the PPSSCC management proposals could lead to a federal productivity rise over four years of an extra 4.4 percent, which could yield net annual long-term compensation savings of some $1.8 billion. But because of the time required to accomplish changes, the near-term outlay savings would amount to only $0.5 billion for 1985-1987, compared to the PPSSCC three-year savings estimate of $17.1 billion.

Despite considerable federal activity and interest in improved productivity over the past 12 years, GAO has found agency efforts ill-prepared and poorly directed, disjointed, short-lived, and hence ineffective. Potential government-wide improvements in labor productivity, according to GAO calculations, would come mainly from five categories of federal work: compliance and enforcement of regulations, natural resource and environmental management, education and training, administration of loans and grants, and health-related services.

In four separate reports, the Grace Commission recommends more contracting out to private firms for certain support services, including maintenance, security, and data processing. Current Executive Branch policy, as set forth in OMB Circular A-76, requires the government to contract for these services unless federal workers can perform them at less cost. Reliance on the private sector for support services has been federal policy since 1955, but without effective implementation in GAO's view. The CBO estimates long-term savings from contracting out at $1.1 billion annually, about one-fifth of the PPSSCC estimate of $5.6 billion. The CBO estimate assumes no change in the current statutory restrictions on contracting out for certain services in the Veterans Administration and the Defense Department, and much smaller average savings per conversion to contract.

Under an accelerated A-76 program, CBO estimates that as many as 165,000 federal jobs, mostly blue-collar, could shift to private firms, with most of the job shifts occurring in defense agencies. In the near term, however, savings would be much smaller than the estimated long-term amounts because the proposals would have to be implemented gradually and there would be costs associated with transferring functions to the private sector, including payments to laid-off federal workers. CBO estimates that outlay savings for 1985-1989 would accumulate to about $0.7 billion. Additional outlay savings approaching $0.4 billion would occur over the same period if restrictions on contracting out at DOD and the VA were lifted. While Circular A-76 can be carried out administratively, GAO believes that effective implementation will not occur unless the Congress legislates a national policy on contracting out.

In another management proposal, the Grace Commission proposed various administrative steps for tightening the enforcement of the statutory Social Security earnings test provisions to reduce overpayments. Mr. Grace singled out this proposal as one of those appropriate for achieving $4.0 billion in savings during 1985-1987 in his recent testimony before the Senate Finance Committee. CBO estimates, however, that little or no savings would result from these recommendations over the next five years, although savings could occur in later years. GAO reports that the Social Security Administration (SSA) has already accelerated its enforcement efforts, and that further reductions in overpayments are likely only after SSA's computer system is upgraded. The PPSSCC report on the Social Security Administration acknowledges that a new computer system would not be available until 1989 at the earliest.

The Grace Commission made a number of other management proposals for which CBO was not able to estimate budget savings against its baseline projections. Either the proposals were so general in nature that estimating assumptions could not be made, or there were insufficient data available to use for preparing a savings estimate. These proposals included a number of recommendations for improving government procurement practices and real property management, especially in defense programs. Examples of such recommendations include making greater use of multiyear procurement of major weapons systems, increasing the practice of acquiring weapons from dual sources, establishing and maintaining more efficient production rates for weapons systems, improving defense inventory management, and increasing the use of common parts and standards. Conceptually, these proposals make good sense, some have been recommended before, and are endorsed by GAO on the basis of their merit, and others need further study. Many, in fact, were included as part of the so-called Carlucci initiatives announced by the Defense Department in 1981. Undoubtedly, significant savings are possible, but these generally cannot be calculated in terms of budgetary impact for 1985–1989 without more specific proposals.

Similarly, the PPSSCC task forces made a number of proposals for improving the management of research and development (R&D) programs, both in the Defense Department and for civilian programs. Some of the R&D recommendations were too general to permit measurement of possible budgetary impact. One recommendation relating to independent R&D charges to defense contractors could increase costs to the government. The commission also proposed that the Veterans Administration develop and utilize a hospital resource allocation and planning model based on diagnosis-related groups to achieve estimated savings of $4.9 billion over three years. CBO and GAO expect that the savings are overstated but do not consider an accurate estimate feasible, because any savings would depend upon policy decisions that were not specified by the PPSSCC and cannot be predicted.

Consistent with the results of many GAO reports, the Grace Commission also recommends a major increase in the acquisition of computers in order to replace obsolete hardware and to achieve greater efficiencies and productivity. CBO and GAO point out that budgetary savings in this area are heavily dependent upon effective management and acquisition strategies. The budget impact cannot be determined, however, because it is not known whether the added equipment would be leased or purchased. If new equipment were leased, immediate budget expenditures would go down. But if the new equipment were purchased — which would lead to even greater savings over its life cycle — the immediate budget impact would be higher expenditures.

Repealing Wage-Setting Laws

The Grace Commission believes that three major federal wage-setting laws — the Davis-Bacon, Walsh-Healy, and Service Contract Acts — are no longer necessary or productive, and should be repealed. The commission projects savings of $11.65 billion over three years if these acts were repealed. The CBO estimate of possible savings for 1985–1987 is somewhat lower — $5.3 billion — because it would take several years before the savings would have a major effect on budgetary outlays. GAO agrees that the Davis-Bacon and Service Contract Acts should be repealed. But if the Davis-Bacon Act is repealed, GAO believes that the Secretary of Labor should consider periodically reviewing construction contracts awarded by the government to assess whether any egregious situations occurred affecting the employees working on the contracts. Also, if the Service Contract Act is repealed, GAO recommends that the administrator of federal procurement policy monitor the impact of repeal and, if he determines that repeal had an adverse impact on service workers, develop administrative policies or legislative remedies to correct the problem. GAO has not taken a position on repeal of the Walsh-Healy Act, but it agrees with the Grace Commission's recommendation to eliminate the act's requirement for overtime pay for workdays exceeding eight hours.

PPSSCC Proposal [on Health-Care Costs]

During 1975–1983 federal health expenditures grew at 14 percent annually compared with an annual increase of 10 percent in GNP during the same period. Although some of this difference can be accounted for by higher inflation in health-care prices compared with general inflation, most of the increase in health-care cost over general inflation has been due to increased usage. The PPSSCC attributes much of the rapid increase in federal health-care costs to lack of competition because of the low out-of-pocket expenses incurred by beneficiaries of federal health programs. The PPSSCC accepts the recently legislated diagnosis-related group (DRG) prospective payment system for Medicare only as a short-term solution that will not work in the long term.

The PPSSCC proposes limiting the growth in the Medicare and Medicaid program costs to the rate of growth of the GNP. This growth limit would determine the amount of federal money available for Medicare, Medicaid, and other federal health programs. Based on the total number of Medicare and Medicaid beneficiaries, the funds would be divided on a per capita basis. The funds would be distributed to regions according to the number of beneficiaries within each region and regional variations in health care costs. Based on the established per capita spending rates, private-sector and state and local health-care systems would submit competitive bids to the federal government to provide health-care services. Beneficiaries would have a choice of plans with varying degrees of coverage and benefit levels.

The PPSSCC proposal is not specific with respect to which federal programs are included in the proposal or how the plan would be implemented for the different federal programs. Medicaid is administered by states while Medicare is administered by the federal government. The Department of Defense (DOD) and the Veterans

Administration (VA) both run nationwide systems of hospitals and clinics for their beneficiaries. Although federal health programs provide health care through a great variety of institutional arrangements, the PPSSCC did not tailor its proposal to the different agencies. . . .

APPENDIX 3

GRACE COMMISSION'S RECOMMENDATIONS FOR AN ITEM-VETO POWER*

This Report has focused on the growing involvement by Congress in day-to-day program management, which in part results in unnecessary and excessive Federal spending, prevention of program and operational efficiencies by agency managers, and skewing of national program priorities aid mandates to fit demands of local interests. This Report recognizes that much of such involvement by Congress reflects pressures brought to bear by constituents concerned for their own local interests perhaps without sufficient regard for the cumulative impact of their actions on national programs and the national interest.

With the national debt, Federal deficits and Federal spending at all time highs, it is imperative that the Executive Branch and the Congress begin to work together to correct the problems described in this and the other PPSS reports. . . .

Much of the unnecessary and wasteful spending identified by PPSS was embodied in legislative riders attached to appropriations bills. A rider is language inserted into a bill which has no direct bearing on the main thrust of the measure, and so merely "rides" along with it. The rules of both the House and the Senate supposedly prohibit this practice, but those rules are often ignored. The President's principal recourse to unwanted legislation from Congress is the veto. But, if a President disagrees with a rider, that disagreement can be expressed only by vetoing the entire bill. In practical terms, then, a President usually must accept these spending riders unless they are egregious, or he is prepared for a major confrontation with Congress.

As a part of the cooperative process necessary to enable Congress to enact the corrective legislation so vital to regaining control of Federal spending, PPSS recommends that the President submit to Congress a proposal to confer on the Chief Executive item veto authority over appropriations bills.

This would enable the President to reject specific spending provisions without

* Vol. 8, 109–14.

affecting the entire measure, and any veto would still be subject to an overriding veto by Congress.

Moreover, for every legislative rider actually enacted, executive agencies jump countless times at such less formal commands of Congressional committees. They would not do so but for the availability of non-vetoable legislative riders pointed like a "gun at their head." Item veto authority would "unload" this gun.

In attempting to evaluate the effects of an item veto, it is perhaps instructive to review the substantial experience that states have had with item veto authority. . . .

Massachusetts became the first state to confer its governor with a veto power in 1780. The first government on American shores to constitutionally provide an item veto authority was the Confederacy. The item veto spread steadily among the states following the Civil War and by 1892, 14 had adopted it. By 1950, 38 states had the item veto and today the constitutions of 43 states provide such authority to their governors. In all but one of these states, Washington, that authority is limited to appropriations bills. Only Indiana, Maine, Nevada, New Hampshire, North Carolina, Rhode Island and Vermont do not provide their governors with item veto authority. No state adopting such authority has subsequently withdrawn it.

Congress had vested the territorial governors of Hawaii and Alaska with item veto authority in 1900 and 1912, and for the territorial governors of the Philippines in 1916, Puerto Rico in 1917, Guam in 1950, and the Virgin Islands in 1954. It has yet to accord similar authority to its own President. . . .

States actually have two general types of selective veto authority—item veto authority and line-item veto authority. The latter is more restrictive, allowing the governor only to veto line item figures, i.e., appropriation levels in appropriation bills. Item veto authority, on the other hand, allows the governor to veto separate legislative provisions, including riders or restrictions, as well as appropriation figures.

PPSS is recommending item veto authority in the Federal Government because it alone would allow the President to veto objectionable legislative riders whose inclusion by Congress in appropriations bills might be subject to question.

Almost every President since the Civil War has complained about legislative riders on appropriations bills, and at least six—Grant, Hayes, Arthur, Franklin Roosevelt, Truman and Eisenhower—have called for item veto authority to counter the practice.

Congressional supporters have included leaders of both major parties, both liberals and conservatives. . . .

The concept is also supported by organizations ranging from the League of Women Voters to the American Farm Bureau Federation to the U.S. Chamber of Commerce.

The Gallup Poll, in 1979, found that 70 percent of the American public, including a solid majority of those claiming membership in both major parties, supported giving item veto authority to the President.

The complaint most often heard against the item veto is that it would confer too much power on the President, upsetting the balance between the Executive and Legislative Branches.

"It would give the President dictatorial powers," said a senior Congressional leader. . . .

The experience of 43 state governments does not support that view. Quite the contrary, the state legislators have been among the strong supporters of that authority. The steady increase in states which have voluntarily conferred such authority on their governors indicates this may be an idea whose time has come for Congress to address.

PPSS has no desire to become embroiled in Constitutional issues. However, it would appear that item veto authority over appropriations bills could provide the "effectual" veto power intended in Article I of the Constitution which provides that:

> Every bill which shall have passed the House of Representatives and the Senate, shall, before it becomes a law, be presented to the President of the United States; if he approves he shall sign it, but if not he shall return it, with his objections. . . .

The drafters of this provision envisioned the term "bill" in a much narrower sense than it is now employed. In the early stages of our Government, each bill was concerned with a single, specific subject, which had to be clearly identified in the title. During this period, a President could singularly veto all the proposed legislation on a single subject, by vetoing a "bill."

Over succeeding years, Congress enlarged the number and scope of unrelated subjects lumped together in a bill, until a single appropriations bill today may cover several unrelated cabinet departments, agencies and programs. Thus the President is deprived of the authority to selectively veto proposed legislation on a single subject.

Former Speaker of the House William B. Bankhead stated in a letter in 1937:

> The word "bill" . . . should have a construction not more narrow than the separable items . . . which might have been the subject of separate bills. . . . The purpose and plan of the Constitution would be carried out by the constriction of which I have indicated. . . . Permitting official approval by the President of that which is agreed to and disapproval of that to which he objects would be in harmony with the plan and purpose of the applicable provision of the Constitution. Any construction of the word "bill" which compels the President officially to approve that which he does not approve in order to avoid striking down the whole bill, or, on the other hand, to strike down the whole bill in order to reach items he does not approve, is a construction contrary to this plan.

Since Congress will probably never revert to the practice of confining bills to a single subject, item veto authority may be the best way of restoring the selectivity and scope originally intended for the veto power it provided.

The Supreme Court has reaffirmed that neither Congress nor its committees can take any "legislative action" except through those procedures involving presentment and veto authority prescribed in the Constitution. Since committee directives do not follow such procedures, it becomes questionable whether they are "legislative actions."

A legislative action, according to the Court's opinion, is identifiable by its nature. By compelling executive agencies to do or not do something, committee directives accomplish the same thing as legislative action, not by binding legal force, but by the mere threat to enact legislation in the constituted manner which a President realistically may be unable to veto.

Item veto authority would remove that "gun to the head," thereby converting committee pronouncements to suggestions to executive agencies. This would be more in keeping with the Constitutional scheme of enabling both the Executive and the Legislative Branches to act independently in performing their separate, important functions.

Chief Justice John Marshall wrote: "It is the peculiar province of the legislature to prescribe general rules for the government of society; the application of those rules would seem to be the duty of other departments."

One of the positive aspects of item veto authority is that it does not entail reforming the nature of Congress. Congress would retain ultimate legislative authority through its powers to override a veto. Nonetheless, decreasing Congressional involvement with day-to-day management decision-making by reducing the impact of riders and similar actions will have a very favorable impact on cost-reduction and productivity programs. . . .

Organization and Operation of the Grace Commission

C. LOWELL HARRISS*

The President's Private Sector Survey on Cost Control (PPSS), better known as the Grace Commission, and its operations differed from those surveys familiar to most Americans. Previous studies at the Federal level included the Taft Commission (1910–12), the Brownlow Committee (1936–37), two Hoover Commissions (1947–49 and 1953–55), the Ash Council (1969–71), and the Carter Reorganization Project (1977–79). Hundreds of state and local commissions have served over the years. The groups have often had specific legislative authorization and complete or partial government financing. Typically, the selection of members has been the responsibility of more than one source — executive, legislative, and civic organizations. Deliberate efforts are usually made to achieve bipartisanship or nonpartisanship through representing various approaches, interest groups, and backgrounds.

The PPSS was established by executive order on 30 June 1982. It was not an undertaking that included congressional participation. It had no government financing. The president directed the group to:

• Identify opportunities for increased efficiency and reduced costs achievable by Executive action or legislation.
• Determine areas where managerial accountability can be enhanced and administrative controls improved.
• Suggest short- and long-term managerial operating improvements.
• Specify areas where further study can be justified by potential savings.
• Provide information and data relating to Governmental expenditures, indebtedness, and personnel management. [IV-4]

* With excerpts from the Grace Commission reports, chiefly volume 2 of a *A Report to the President*, 12 January 1984. The author has also drawn from interviews and other sources. The process of selection from a mass of material compels the omission of much that would contribute to an understanding of the procedures followed.

The executive committee consisted of 161 top executives from the business, professional, and nonprofit worlds – "individuals who had proven ability to effectively and efficiently manage their own enterprises." [VI-4]

About 80 percent were either chairmen, presidents, chief executive officers of the Nation's leading corporations. The rest were principals of top law, accounting, investment and management consulting firms; former high-level Government officials; the heads of foundations and trade associations; and leaders from other private sector fields, including education, medicine, labor, and the media. [VI-3–4]

A quarter of the *Fortune* top 100 industrial companies were represented, as were the largest commercial banks, insurance companies, retailers, transportation companies, and the biggest advertising agency. [VI-4]

This group then organized itself into thirty-six task forces. Four examined Defense. Eighteen examined other individual agencies, such as Treasury, Interior, and Commerce. The others studied functions that overlapped several agencies – such as data processing, personnel, procurement, research and development, user charges, and construction management. In addition, the Management Office studied other topics and issued eleven reports, resulting in a total of forty-seven reports.

The leaders of each task force enlisted the support of persons holding positions of responsibility in American business, accounting, law, management consulting, and nonprofit organizations. These people met with the heads of the agency to be studied, received briefings, and then proceeded with detailed investigations. Typically, a person spent several weeks or months in on-the-spot study. Guidance and coordination came from a Washington staff of the PPSS as well as from selected Washington-based business executives.

Approximately two thousand individuals participated in the survey. Many had some experience in a governmental operation – military service or employment in the civil service or with companies doing business with the government.

. . . A total of over 850 corporations, professional firms, and other private sector organizations contributed people, money, and/or services and equipment to the fulfillment of the President's mandate.

Because the numbers were so large, so varied in the skills represented, and stem from so many private sector sources, it seems safe to say that there is very little in the way of economic, social, financial, and managerial capabilities and experiences which did not exist somewhere in the Survey's reservoir of talent. [VI-4]

It was not the principal purpose of PPSS to examine basic public policy, which reflects the major goals of the people as expressed through the democratic process. For example, PPSS did not focus on whether the Federal Government should concentrate its resources on defense, education, highways, health and welfare, or nutrition, nor did it address the question of what priority should be accorded each of these endeavors. PPSS concentrated, instead, on overall Government operations as distinguished from policy but included an examination of the execution of policy. Its primary concern was the degree of efficiency in the expenditure of tax resources and whether those expenditures achieved the desired public purpose at an acceptable cost through workable mechanisms and organizations equipped with the proper tools.

PPSS concentrated first and foremost on operations. At times, however, it was extremely difficult to draw a precise line clearly separating operations and policy. Indeed, there were numerous instances where a very significant overlap existed between operations and policy, with Task Forces unable to look at one without the other. It is interesting to note that many of the historical initiatives which preceded PPSS, particularly Hoover I and Hoover II, also found it difficult to make this differentiation. [VI-7-8]

Task forces varied in size from twenty to ninety members. They divided their review of departments and agencies into four distinct phases: organization and start-up, diagnostic survey, in-depth survey, and report preparation.

The work of the Task Forces was monitored and coordinated by the Survey Management Office. Reporting to the Chairman, the Management Office consisted of a Director, Deputy Director (the sole Government employee designated as the Government liaison by the White House), Chief Operating Officer, and a staff of about 50 office personnel. Of particular importance were 12 "desk officers," most of whom were senior Washington-based executives with broad experience in working with the Federal Government. Each desk officer was responsible for the orientation of three to four Task Forces, guiding their efforts toward the most productive areas of review; coordinating planning and communications, monitoring progress, and assuring the quality of final Task Force reports. The work of this group supplemented and expanded upon that of a Government resources group, which included the Inspectors General offices, the Office of Management and Budget (OMB), the General Services Administration, and the Assistant Secretaries for Management. These two groups acted as a bridge between members of the Task Forces and the departments and agencies they reviewed. [VI-7]

Government and governing differ from business. Successful business experience may not always transfer readily to the operations of government. Within business, of course, activities vary widely. Within government, too, jobs and responsibilities differ enormously. Some of the difficulties of applying the skills of business to government may be obvious, but others are somewhat obscure. The Grace Commission reports recognize the reality of doubts about the transferability of experience. The group faced the issue and asked, "What experience [do] businessmen have that qualifies them to examine the Federal government?" It cited similarities of jobs and presented fifty examples to indicate differences found in the costs of what it believed to be essentially similar activities. Presumably, such differences suggest the potential for improvement in Federal performance. Four are shown in table 1.

Conflict of Interest

Potential conflict of interest presented problems in manning the various groups. Highest qualifications might be expected to lie with persons who knew about an operation. However, their firms may have had business dealings with the agency

TABLE 1

Potentials for Improving Federal Performance

Function	Federal Government	Private Sector	Federal Government Failure Relative to Private Sector
Lending money	$765 billion loans outstanding	$1,500 billion loans outstanding	HUD makes only 3 attempts to collect loans versus 24 to 36 tries in the private sector; 41% delinquency rate on current Federal receivables.
Hospital management	177,000 beds	1,481,000 beds	VA Hospital in the Bronx cost $153,000 per bed, about 1.5 times the $97,400 per bed spent constructing the comparable Duke University Hospital.
Automated data processing	250,000 ADP employees	2,000,000 + ADP employees	Half the government's computers are so old that manufacturers no longer service them. Additional personnel expenses amount to $600 million annually.
Pension fund assets	$96 billion Civil Service Retirement System (CSRS)	$481 billion	CSRS rate of return in 1980 was 7.4% compared to 14% and over for a majority of private sector plans.

or have some expectation of future orders. The report summarizes the actions taken to deal with the problem:

> Because of the understandable need to call upon people knowledgeable in the functions to be studied, the Survey was highly sensitive to possible conflicts of interest and took every reasonable step to avoid them, including the establishment of internal rules and standards that went beyond the requirements of the law. It is the Survey's view that it brought the best expertise of the private sector into the public analysis of Government, while avoiding compromise of the public trust.

> Specifically, all members of the Executive Committee were cleared for appointment to that Committee by the White House Office of Legal Counsel. In addition, members of the Executive Committee who were asked to serve as Co-chairs of individual Task Forces were cleared for those assignments, not only by the White House Office of Legal Counsel, but also by the respective departments and agencies. In addition, Task Force members, who were not subject to the same conflict of interest statutes as were appointees to the Executive Committee, were subjected to an internal review for purposes of identifying and, if necessary, eliminating any potential or perceived conflicts of interest. [VI-5]

In short, selections and assignments were made with care to avoid conflict of interest. (We have no way of knowing what loss of competence and experience may have resulted.) Yet the Nader group's criticism of the final report cited conflict of interest and identified some cases of potential conflict.

The commission's report states:

Private sector management is driven by the need to ensure the enterprise's continued economic survival. This is a precondition for profit or any other measure of success and the satisfaction of this precondition requires constant attention to managerial efficiency and the effective use of resources in a competitive arena. The unforgiving tests of both the balance sheet and the marketplace must be met. Failure to meet the demands of either will, in time, bring the enterprise to an end, with the attendant consequences not only to management but to the investors, employees, suppliers, customers, and the community as well. In short, the private sector cannot operate with a continuing and growing deficit. Failure to operate efficiently and to ensure a satisfactory return to investors will cause the private sector enterprise to fail, with devastating effects on all its components — particularly its employees.

Government has no such incentive to survive, let alone succeed, nor any such test to meet. The Government, unlike private sector enterprise, is not normally managed as if it were subject to the consequences of prolonged managerial inefficiency or persistent failure to control costs. Such consequences have historically been avoided in the public sector — or, more accurately, postponed — by Government's propensity to increase tax revenues, engage in deficit spending, and spend yet more money on failed programs with the result of masking their ineffectiveness.

The members of the President's Private Sector Survey on Cost Control (PPSS) believe that the disciplines necessary for survival and success in the private arena *must* be introduced into Government to a far greater degree than previously has been the case. It is that belief which motivated the PPSS effort. A government which cannot efficiently manage the people's money and the people's business will ultimately fail its citizenry by failing the same inescapable test which disciplines the private sector: those of the competitive marketplace and of the balance sheet. [VI-2]

The outsiders who came to study on the spot brought various kinds of experience. Their freshness of approach in itself could be valuable. Complete understanding of an agency, however, would require the familiarity of the government staffs, the law, and the conditions of operations. The task force reports frequently make explicit acknowledgment of excellent cooperation from the civil servants and express respect and admiration for the government staffs.

Civil servants close to the operations were often well aware of opportunities for improvement. Prior studies of promising proposals were examined. The Grace Commission reported:

The fact of the matter is that the press of business, at both the departments and agencies and OMB, simply precludes an in-depth, comprehensive survey, such as that conducted by PPSS. That certainly does not mean that the departments and agencies and OMB are not doing their job; it simply means that because of immediate needs departments and agencies and OMB find it difficult to address more than the issues "of the moment." Additionally, the value derived from a "fresh look" by outsiders with the capability to evaluate and recommend adoption of proven and cost effective private sector systems, techniques, and management tools could not be realized by an "in house" study. [VI-8]

Some PPSS recommendations were based on those that agency staffs had been making or wanting to make. The Grace Commission offered an opportunity for civil servants to voice their proposals. Experienced civil servants have been acutely aware of defects, deficiencies, and possible methods of improvement.

The PPSS quotes (VI-9) a General Accounting Office report: "Most agency contacts viewed the task forces as positive attempts to identify cost savings. They generally viewed task force members as very talented experts who provided free advice and an objective viewpoint. Given these perceptions, most agencies surveyed were willing to help the task forces and had an open mind on the findings." Guidelines were provided to the task forces to standardize calculations. At the beginning of the project, an inflation rate of 10 percent was suggested by OMB, although the current rate of inflation has turned lower. The authors note: "Although PPSS has tried to be consistent and technically accurate in its calculations, its figures are, of necessity, of a *planning* rather than a *budget* quality. Emphasis, first and foremost, should be on the specific opportunity reported, with exact dollar savings and/or revenues to be a secondary effort and determined in concert with the departments and agencies and OMB." [VI-9]

Public discussions preceded final conclusions. To a considerable extent, each task force's report used a format that led to general uniformity. Where possible, the findings and recommendations were "priced," i.e., figures for the magnitudes involved were estimated. PPSS made 2,478 recommendations, which if implemented would reduce government spending by $424.4 billion over three years. All reports used a three-element classification system based on the estimated degree of certainty about potential dollar savings and the desirability of adoption. The categories were divided, as indicated in table 2.

Financing the Survey

No congressional appropriations were requested or supplied. The entire cost of the project was borne by the private sector (except for one Federal employee and the time of Federal employees who assisted PPSS personnel). The business community and private foundations were asked to contribute funds. In addition, of course, many paid the salaries and expenses of employees who worked on the task force projects. The total cost to the private sector was estimated at around $76 million in people, services, travel, and supplies.

Follow-up Efforts

Prior studies of many types—some by the government and some by outside groups—have produced masses of valuable work that was never implemented. Proposals that would have served constructively to improve government performance and to get the job done less expensively have been wasted.

Mr. Grace and his associates have been well aware of the need for more than study and reporting. President Reagan and his staff know of the need for follow-up if potential benefits are to be realized. Both groups are convinced of the importance of reducing the growth of Federal spending and of improving efficiency. Support for action as against "file and forget" stems also from concern about Federal

TABLE 2

Categories of PPSS Recommendations

Category	Degree of Supportability
I	Fully substantiated and defensible. Recommendations in this category are, in the opinion of the task force, convincing and deserving of prompt implementation.
II	Substantially documented and supportable. Recommendations in this category may not be fully rationalized or documented in the report, but all indications point to the desirability and defensibility of proceeding with their implementation.
III	Potentially justifiable and supportable. Recommendations in this category, while meritorious, are not regarded as fully supported in the report, due to time, personnel resources, and other constraints, but are deemed worthy of further analysis to determine the full extent of their merit.

NOTE: The figures in table 1 of the previous essay include only amounts in categories I and II.

budget deficits. Year after year they have been large, and for the near future even prosperity and achievable economic growth will not balance the budget.

Public opinion polls show widespread concern about the budget deficit. One hope for improvement lies in better control of spending, and that is what the Grace Commission offers. Considerable momentum had been built before the final report went to the president in January 1984. Before summarizing the continuing efforts of Mr. Grace and his group, it will be helpful to see what is being done in government.

Executive Branch

By all accounts the follow-up procedures in the executive branch have firm presidential support, not merely lip service. This support reflects conviction about the merits of the goals, a determination to get results, and general confidence in the Grace Commission's recommendations. The Cabinet Council has organized and is monitoring a systematic examination and follow-through. Every Grace recommendation will get attention. Though not every recommendation will be adopted, some action must be taken. As of November 1984, the White House had deliberated 1,153 of the 2,478 recommendations and had agreed to implement 81.5 percent of them. Of these, 680 totaling $103.5 billion in three-year savings have either been included in the budget baseline for 1983, 1984, or 1985, or targeted for short-term adoption.

The review process presents an opportunity for reexamining each proposal. Modifications can be made to reflect new evidence, changing circumstances, and responses of agency representatives or other executive-branch entity, such as the Office of Management and Budget (OMB). Refinements and constructive modifications can result. So also can resistance and bureaucratic obstruction. In the latter half of 1984, the reviews are tied in with preparation of the 1986 budget to be presented in January 1985.

For those Grace recommendations not being implemented, some explicit statement of the reasons for the decision must be available. And, it appears, the statement must convince a senior official. At the White House there is a strong but, of course, not conclusive presumption that Grace recommendations deserve presidential support.

All of the recommendations involving national defense are being considered as part of a special process. This process includes other initiatives that have also been established to improve military procurement and operations. The Grace proposals are treated as a respected element of a complex process but not one to override all others, nor one assumed to embrace all that should be used.

In July 1984 President Reagan held a White House reception for the Grace Commission. Some 1,500 of the participants appeared to receive his thanks and to hear him say:

> Ultimately, I believe history will record that the American people's biggest victory over bureaucracy and big Government began with the work of you who are here today.
>
> *We will continue to press for reduced growth in spending* by adopting the kind of commonsense, overdue measures you . . . proposed.
>
> *Your work was courageous and daring.* You didn't seek approval of the Washington establishment, but produced a report that shook the foundations of the establishment.

The Commission's Continuing Efforts

To carry on the work of informing and persuading, Mr. Grace and his associates set up the Foundation for the President's Private Sector Survey on Cost Control, Inc., a nonpolitical and nonpartisan group to raise funds and to finance speakers and publicity. The first issue of its *Newsletter*, dated June 1984, includes the following:

> *The big news is that an impressive momentum has been building* among members of the public, in Congress, and the business community.
>
> *The PPSS report has drawn a striking response from voters*, coming as it did just when attention was focusing on the huge deficit. The hope opened up by the PPSS report for Government savings caught the public's imagination and Congress has been feeling the heat.
>
> *It is now becoming clear that Congress cannot sidestep action*, certainly not indefinitely. Members are being told this by voters in back-home meetings and one-on-one talks, plus their letters.
>
> *Here is how the PPSS agenda is being advanced:*
>
> *The Foundation for PPSS picks up where the Executive Order left off*, erecting an educational campaign that reaches across the country. *A speakers bureau* has been organized which includes members of the PPSS Executive Committee, Project Managers, and top PPSS officials.

Besides this newsletter, several publications have been produced — including a 16-page summary brochure on PPSS recommendations titled "We Can Blow the Whistle on Waste." The final PPSS report to the president, *War on Waste*, published by Macmillan, is available in paperback. Macmillan has also published a hardcover book titled *Burning Money: The Waste of Your Tax Dollars*, Mr. Grace's own account as chairman of PPSS.

The July 1984 issue of the *Newsletter* reported, among other things, that the Treasury Department had accepted 92 out of 110 recommendations in two reports. Other successes were also noted. Evidence of determination to sustain pressure was clear. Proposals for waterway user charges, however, had encountered formidable opposition from operators and shippers of coal and grain.

An organization formed in the summer of 1984, Citizens Against Waste (CAW), has a clearly bipartisan board. Jack Anderson, the syndicated columnist, is cochairman along with Mr. Grace. Although on many issues of public policy the members have positions that undoubtedly differ widely, they agree on the desirability of supporting PPSS recommendations.

The approach of Citizens Against Waste seeks to direct attention toward substance and to downplay any partisan political elements. Controversy, however, must arise from the nature of many of the proposals. The weight that the Grace Commission designation carries will have influence but cannot be expected in itself to override the power of special interests, some of which will deserve respect.

The PPSS brochure cites forty-seven examples of waste. The first reads: "Social Security paid $14.6 billion in error between 1980 and 1982. Delays in retrieving wrong payments cost the government $128 million in added interest expense in 1983." The last reads: "About 50% of postal workers receiving disability could perform some type of work, according to an Assistant Postmaster General. Unnecessary government-wide disability benefits cost taxpayers $189 million over three years." The other forty-five examples reinforce the conclusion that "waste and inefficiency" demand action. The brochure includes many other examples of things that PPSS found wrong and opportunities for improvement.

What do the commission's follow-up efforts propose that the public do? The organization, of course, needs financial support. The public is urged to do more. It can indicate support by writing—in petition form and letters to Washington, especially to members of Congress. Local organizations can focus pressure on lawmakers. The foundation's educational materials can be distributed at meetings of service organizations, professional associations, taxpayer associations, and political groups. A Speaker's Bureau will provide speakers upon request.

The commission's publicity refers repeatedly to waste, abuse, fraud, and inefficiency. Striking examples illustrate the distressing folly and waste, some apparently long-standing and still, despite publicity, continuing.

The clear cases of waste, especially those that seem to be readily correctable, provide a basis for motivating an audience. Support for change should result. These obvious examples, however, do not reflect all of the waste, abuse, and inefficiency. Nor do they relate systematically to the tens or hundreds of billions of dollars of cost reductions that the commission's reports cite as achievable over a few years. It would be quite misleading to imply that a solution of the relatively easy cases of obvious waste would yield $100 billion or so a year of savings.

Most of the "big money" lies in changes that would not be easy. Nor can things that seem obviously not worth the taxpayers' money always be eliminated by merely bringing facts into the open. Cases that most persons would identify as waste may be highly prized by certain recipients and their supporters in Congress and the bureaucracy. Mr. Grace cited an example in the *New York Times* on 27 September 1984: "[Congress in 1984 extended the] subsidized rates for electric power from western Federal generating facilities . . . for thirty years at a time when the nation faces its worst fiscal crisis ever. How can Congress justify preferable power rates ranging from 7 to 25 percent of the rates paid by 85 percent of the taxpayers—a subsidy not for the poor or needy, but the lucky?"

The motivation, the sense of purpose that must impress any close observer of the process, showed convincing evidence of continuing public support.

Congressional Role

The Grace report refers to the problems and actions that had been taken up to the time of its submission. It reads in part:

> Congressional support for PPSS cost control efforts is . . . critical if the full savings impact is to be realized.
>
> At the same time, projections of annual budget deficits of $200 billion a year . . . have helped prompt the Congress as a body and members as individuals to take more than a passing interest in PPSS recommendations. . . .
>
> . . . Numerous hearings and briefings have been held at which PPSS representatives have discussed their findings and recommendations and responded to questions from members of Congress and their staffs. These sessions have in nearly all cases been marked by expressions of willingness to give a fair hearing to the recommendations and to consider how Congress might be involved in their implementation. Coming across clearly was a deep-seated concern with the burgeoning costs of Government and consequent openness to initiatives that give promise of moderating the problem.
>
> The PPSS Chairman and his staff have provided testimony to both the Senate and House Budget Committees and other committees as well. Other senior Survey officials have appeared before [congressional committees].
>
> Representatives of many of the PPSS Task Forces have also briefed Committees and Subcommittees in both houses of Congress. . . .

In the *New York Times* on 27 September 1984, Mr. Grace also stated: "The commission estimated that 73 percent of the [dollar reductions] would require direct Congressional approval and that Congress would influence an amount closer to 85 percent in one way or another," often the authorizing legislation. In some cases, such as modernizing the data-processing systems, appropriations will be needed. PPSS did not itself include members of Congress or their staffs. To some extent the process was a rival to Congress, and to some extent its recommendations will provide support for spending control that members of Congress know the budget deficit requires though they are politically distasteful.

Political rivalries will affect congressional responses. Although PPSS was non-partisan, its origins during a Republican presidency can be expected to exert some influence. The continuing processes of government had already involved several of the recommendations by the time the initial report was presented, and more were considered as Congress met in 1984.

Many of the programs and practices that the Grace Commission criticized exist because influential groups in Congress and in the voting public want them. The programs are not the result of poor administration. Legislation and influence from Capitol Hill brought them into being. These forces play a role in the continuing life of expenditures. Some programs may have more merit than judged by the Grace review. The fact that a group from the private sector recommended change does not necessarily establish a conclusion. At the very least, however, it does establish the desirability of more consideration.

As the White House seeks to implement the many Grace proposals that it supports but that require new legislation, it will send Congress requests for action. A new process of examination will begin. On their own, members of Congress have supported legislation based on Grace Commission reports, and more cases will arise.

The proposals and the efforts to arouse public concern appear at a time when large Federal budget deficits are much in the news. The need for cost reduction was quite generally acknowledged to be of continuing, not merely passing, importance. The testing of the Grace proposals that involve the largest amounts lies ahead. Further evaluation of their merits and shortcomings will extend over several budget years. So will the balancing of political forces that will determine the final actions.

Federal Spending and
the Budget Crisis

AL ULLMAN

While it goes without saying that the growth of Federal spending and its control is a timely subject for discussion — especially given the massive Federal deficits — it might be best to begin by clarifying exactly what "the growth of Federal spending" means. Too often in the current political debate, the tendency of some political and fiscal conservatives is to demonize the growth of government, as if it were an independent entity, expanding according to its own internal momentum without relation to objective need or reality. Frequently accompanying such thinking is a nostalgic desire to halt its growth, perhaps even to roll it back to past levels.

It is undeniable that the expansion of government has been significant, particularly in recent years. It is also undeniable that this growth has led to some urgent problems whose resolution demands immediate action. Nonetheless, it would be counterproductive to approach this issue from a simplistic, backward-looking perspective, or to focus on the growth of government without examining the reasons for that growth — the Federal government's assumption of new responsibilities that are a natural result of the growth of American society.

Although occasional excesses have occurred as the Federal government has mistakenly acquired new roles better left to state and local levels or to the private sector, people should not thereby conclude, as many have, that any expansion into new areas of involvement is inherently suspect. Quite to the contrary, political entities *should* evolve and grow as necessary to address new circumstances and problems. A government that did not respond to changing times and exigencies by broadening its functions to meet the emerging needs of its citizens would be worthy of suspicion indeed.

To illustrate how a democratic government gradually acquires new responsibilities as the economy and society change, it may be useful to review briefly the primary areas of Federal expansion over the last half-century. Such an examination suggests that the similar growth of needs and demands in the future will be equally legitimate and continuous and that any workable fiscal system for the coming decades must therefore accept and incorporate it as a given.

The Great Depression and the New Deal programs were probably more responsible than any other factors for the development of a "social conscience" in this country. Stemming from Roosevelt's implementation of Keynesian economic theory to reconstruct the shattered American economy, the New Deal demonstrated that government could successfully assume an activist role in ensuring the basic well-being of its citizens, instead of relying on the workings of the unrestrained marketplace. The precedent that the government should provide for Americans in times of need was set through the establishment of social security, mass public employment, and other economic reconstruction programs.

Along with the "social conscience," this growth of Federal responsibilities was also spurred by the increasing vitality of participatory democracy in the United States. The powerful pressures exerted on the political process by various constituencies was rarely met with less than an enthusiastic desire on the part of Congress to accommodate them. As American society grew, along with an awareness of the developing gaps in its social fabric, the basic mandate of the New Deal was logically extended to areas where the resources of state and local governments were incapable of responding to emergent needs. Federal involvement thus gradually came to encompass the areas of health care, employment security, housing, education, lower-income assistance, agricultural and rural aid programs, economic development assistance, and veterans' care, among others.

This explosion of public demands on government was not confined to the provision of basic social services. In time the Federal government was called on to involve itself in a wide array of areas, including environmental protection, transportation, national infrastructure-building, and the equal-employment program, to name but a few.

In addition, recent spending growth has been due not to public demands per se, but rather to a variety of impersonal economic and political causes:

• Prime among these has been the rise of inflation, which precipitated tying work income as well as social security, retirement, welfare, health, and other entitlement benefits to the cost of living.

• The United States military involvement in Southeast Asia, though indirectly, was another contributor to spending growth; the creation of the "volunteer army," largely because of the divisive national controversy over the draft, resulted in massive increases in pay and benefits to military personnel. More recently, the prodefense climate has added still more to the growth of the military budget through the acquisition of phenomenally costly high-technology and other expensive weapons systems.

• The rise in the past few years of interest rates has led not only to hikes in the cost of most government programs but also to massive increases in the burden of financing the national debt. Especially given the magnitude of the Federal deficit in recent years, the current net interest component of the budget is only a pale forerunner of the crushing debt load the Federal government will face in the outyears as more and more is borrowed to cover the shortfall.

Finally, though they do not presently account for a large proportion of Federal spending relative to other categories, one cannot ignore the future impact of program increases in areas with enormous growth potential — programs that open up "new horizons" of Federal endeavor whose surfaces have only been scratched. Space exploration, particularly with the advent of the space shuttle and the expansion of orbital military applications, and energy, especially with global political instability endangering the security of oil supplies and the concomitant need to develop reliable alternative energy sources, are just two of these fields. Just as only a few decades ago government planners would have found it impossible to anticipate the nearly geometric increases in the scope of government that were to take place, so must current policymakers assume that there will be largely or even totally unimagined frontiers of future Federal effort that will have to be reckoned with as they search for workable solutions to the growing fiscal crisis.

A brief statistical analysis will illustrate some of these growth trends. In the recent postwar period, Federal expenditures in the income-security category (including social security and other entitlements) of the budget as a share of gross national product (GNP) — not merely in absolute dollar terms — have grown astronomically. In the fiscal year 1947–80 period, these outlays expanded more than sixfold, from 1.2 percent to 7.3 percent of GNP. Another example is that of Federal spending in the area of health care, where growth was quicker and even sharper. In the fiscal year 1960–80 period, for instance, outlays in this budget category — again, as a share of GNP — grew by a factor of 14 from 0.15 percent to 2.1 percent. The period of steepest growth in this span came, as might be expected, in the late 1960s with the establishment of Medicare; in the five-year fiscal year 1965–69 period alone, health care outlays quintupled in proportion, rising from 0.24 percent to 1.2 percent of GNP. The statistics also reveal a number of other budget categories where growth was particularly striking, especially in recent years; these include commerce and transportation, education and manpower, natural resources and environment, and agriculture and rural development.

When viewed alongside other statistical indices, the figures are especially indicative. Although gross national debt as a percentage of GNP had been in a more or less steady decline since the 1960s, rapid growth in this measure due to the size of recent deficits is forecast for the outyears. The Reagan administration estimates that total national debt as a share of GNP will grow from 34.8 percent in fiscal year 1981 to 50.5 percent by fiscal year 1987 — a leap of over 15 percent in just six years. Meanwhile — as will be touched on later in this discussion — revenues as a share of GNP, after holding fairly steady since the late 1940s, are in the midst of a nosedive that began at the start of this decade. At the same time, Federal expenditures as a percentage of GNP, which similarly had stayed roughly level, are beginning a marked rise.[1]

The expansion in the functions of government briefly described here is only that which has occurred most recently; it is just one segment of the continual growth in the size and scope of Federal responsibilities that has characterized the entire history of the United States. As needs emerge and evolve, the democratic process powerfully facilitates the public demands that lead to their resolution; and once acknowledged, these new areas of involvement are rarely abandoned. Similarly, in the course of changing times, government may find itself faced with unforeseen and onerous yet necessary costs of coping with the fiscal effects of economic dislocations, and these too must be allowed for.

There is no reason to think that, as the nation matures and adapts to the challenges of the future, the need for the Federal government to take on new, unprecedented functions will somehow vanish or that the evolution of its responsibilities will come to an abrupt end at this point in history. But if a gradual broadening in the scope of these responsibilities is a legitimate and natural condition of political life, it follows that growth in their costs is likewise inescapable. To hope that the real level of government expenditures could be reduced or even simply kept constant would be the height of unrealism.

This is by no means to argue that Federal spending is totally "uncontrollable" or that it is fated to increase by leaps and bounds, as in the past few decades. Rather, the point is that necessary growth should be managed in order to minimize whatever negative effects it may have on the American economy.

Certainly, direct restraints on spending are part of the solution. Congress must scrutinize proposed spending levels across the board to ensure that inefficient or extravagant expenditures are pared away. And it must use all the tools at its disposal — most important, the budgetary disciplines contained in the Congressional Budget and Impoundment Control Act of 1974 — to force a tough yearly reassessment of national priorities and to put all spending in the context of total expenditures and the need for revenues.

The Budget Act was the result of congressional concern over two problems that were emerging in the early 1970s. First was the fact that Federal spending was getting increasingly out of control, with no adequate disciplines incorporated in the fiscal process. Second was the lack of coordination between congressional appropriations and tax-writing committees; whether expenditures would equal revenues each year was purely a matter of luck. Resulting from this chaotic situation was a growing dominance of the spending process by the executive branch. Since the president's annual budget submission was, by default, the sole unified statement of national priorities in existence in Washington, Congress's role had been reduced to that of making ad hoc additions to and subtractions from that document. In essence, Congress had abdicated its constitutional responsibility to set Federal spending priorities through its sole authority to set expenditure levels. But with the advent of the Budget Act, Congress was finally compelled to view any spending program in terms of the whole picture — total outlays as well as the need for revenues to pay for those outlays.

Recent critics of the congressional budget process have charged that this system is not working as intended, and they point to the existence of Federal deficits as evidence of this. Naturally, refinements in the process can be made. But it would be wrong to view it as a panacea for all fiscal problems, especially when political and economic forces external to it have created massive dislocations that no budget procedures could have fully dealt with. Moreover, those who support scrapping this system fail to recognize the very real successes it has brought about— the stringent budget cutback of 1981, for example (even though one can disagree with the areas in which those reductions were made) — and to realize that, without the disciplines afforded by that process, the current fiscal imbalance would in all likelihood have been far worse than it is now.

But even assuming that growth in government spending were to be severely restricted in all areas even further than at present, there would still be giant deficits in the budget. Particularly if one recognized that the deeper the spending cuts in social programs, the greater the danger of breaking the government's fundamental commitments to its citizens in the areas of health care, welfare, and other forms of income security. It is clear there are definite limits on how far this path can lead.

It is therefore increasingly clear that a true answer to the Federal fiscal crisis must account for both sides of the budgetary equation—revenues as well as spending. Yet—partly because of ideological political resistance to the notion that increased taxation of some sort is necessary to ensure the nation's fiscal integrity— the United States, instead of squarely confronting the need to reassess the present revenue system, has chosen to sit complacently on an eroding revenue base. This inaction comes when a fundamental restructuring of the tax system is imperative to the foundation of a revitalized economy that will carry the United States strongly into the world marketplace of the twenty-first century.

In particular, the concept of an amendment to the Constitution requiring a balanced budget has become something of a rallying point for conservatives. Yet this notion, when closely examined, proves to be grossly facile; to be workable, far too many loopholes would have to be incorporated into its implementation, and as a result such an amendment would be virtually unenforceable. The Constitution is not the place for that sort of uncertainty and inefficiency.

Another argument commonly used by political conservatives against generating new revenues as a means of reducing the deficit is that the government will simply use the increased revenues to fund new or enlarged programs. According to this view, lack of revenue —"starving government," so to speak— should have the effect of forcing the government to live within its means. But recent experience shows that a lack of revenue has little — if any— impact on the accumulation of huge deficits and continued spending increases. Since 1981, even though some of the most drastic tax cuts in American history were enacted by the president and Congress, deficits soared to their present record levels. While Federal revenues as a share of GNP were cut from 20.8 percent to 18.6 percent in the fiscal year 1981–83 period, Federal outlays in that time jumped from 22.8 percent to 24.7 percent of GNP. So, even as revenues were being slashed, exactly the opposite was happening to spending. The result was that the deficit's share of GNP shot up from 2.0 percent to 6.1 percent in those years. Obviously, there is nothing magical about "revenue restraint."

Thus it is clear that deficits cannot be eliminated simply by cutting spending. Restructuring the tax system so as to generate sufficient revenues to pay for government is absolutely essential in order to attain fiscal integrity.

Before discussing the necessary action on the revenue side, however, let us examine what can be done on the spending side. The most realistic strategy for restraining spending would be twofold: strengthening the existing congressional and executive budget processes and setting workable limits on total Federal spending in terms of percentages of GNP. Several improvements can be suggested to make the congressional budget process more effective. For instance, although it was initially envisioned to incorporate two budget resolutions per fiscal year, recent evolution in the use of the system has moved it toward being essentially a one-resolution budget process. Formally modifying the congressional budget schedule to utilize just one budget resolution with a generally binding effect would simplify and tighten up this important step in the process. In addition, the current "reconciliation" mechanism, which requires authorizing committees to bring their spending totals into conformance with those levels prescribed in the budget resolution, should be toughened still further by mandating stricter committee compliance to reconciliation instructions.

Another long-needed step taken recently by Congress is that of separating out the social security trust fund operations from the unified budget. Since it is self-financing and required by law to recoup sufficient revenues to cover its outlays, removal of the social security retirement and disability systems should allow the remainder of the budget, funded largely from general revenues, to be acted on with greater precision and equity.

Finally, although it is not feasible to prohibit the use of "budget-busting" continuing resolutions by Congress at the end of each fiscal year, Congress should nonetheless make every effort to limit their use to extraordinary and exceptional economic circumstances, not as a standard "end-run" means of circumventing budget requirements. Along with these congressional actions, the executive branch should contribute to greater fiscal discipline through the support and enactment of appropriate legislation to improve fiscal policy in the executive agencies.

As for a GNP-based limitation on total Federal spending, procedures should be instituted, via an amendment to the Budget Act, whereby neither house of Congress could adopt a budget resolution for any fiscal year if the total outlays surpassed a specific percentage of the estimated GNP for that year. Exceptions to this limitation could be made in only two cases: (1) if the president were to send to Congress, as part of a budget message, a request for a suspension of the limitation along with a detailed explanation and a designation of those spending programs involved; or (2) if there were two consecutive calendar quarters of negative real growth in the GNP (during the current calendar quarter and the three immediately preceding calendar quarters). In the first case, the budget committee of either house would have to review the president's request and indicate its findings and recommendations in its report on the resolution. In the second case, either the budget committee or the conference committee on the resolution would be able to include in its report a recommendation to suspend the GNP limitation along with a listing of the same specifics required in a presidential suspension request.

There are two primary virtues of a GNP-based spending limitation of this nature. First, assuming it were set at a fixed percentage level, such a limitation would permit appropriate adjustments in Federal spending proportional to the growth of the national economy—a commonsense and responsible way of allowing the expansion of Federal involvement necessary to keep pace with the needs of a growing society. Second, establishing a benchmark goal for the scope of government in terms of a percentage of GNP would constitute a clearcut point of reference for the actions needed on *both* sides of the fiscal balance to attain budgetary integrity.

It should be noted that, although the balance between outlays and revenues is an ideal means of assessing the fiscal soundness of the Federal budget, perfect balance may nonetheless be a goal that is not achievable in every conceivable economic situation. Flexibility to accommodate expansion or contraction in the economy, through either allowing revenues to exceed outlays or the reverse, may at times be appropriate to forestall impending periods of inflation or recession. In most circumstances, however, a balanced budget is a realistic and achievable goal and should be treated as such.

But when all is said and done, the inescapable requirement to meaningful reform of the fiscal structure is a fundamental reshaping of the tax system. Without such reform, this nation will not be able to surmount its own economic ills at home or survive in the international marketplace of the coming decades. To bring about the changes that are called for, this reassessment must be thoroughgoing and basic.

There is in the popular thinking of Americans—and in the thinking of many American academics as well—a notion that the income tax system is somehow integral to the principles of a democratic society. But this notion is far from the truth. The nation can no longer afford anything but a hardheaded, pragmatic analysis of this economic crisis.

To begin with, the corporate income tax has always lacked solid grounding in tax theory. And, in any event, since its institution it has become totally inequitable. Not only do businesses in many sectors of the economy pay no taxes at all, but those that do pay taxes face wide disparities in their effective tax rate that were never intended. Because of the legitimate need to maintain adequate incentives in the economic system and also because the purely political pressures for special treatment to one category of enterprises or another, all efforts to correct the inequities of the corporate income tax have been stymied.

Moreover, an examination of historical trends shows that even when it is viewed simply as a source of revenue the corporate income tax is nearing the point of losing all credibility. From a high of 48.2 percent in 1942, the share of the total

Federal revenues generated by the corporate income tax has steadily declined; in 1983, its share of revenues came to a meager 6.2 percent. In light of its obvious unfairness and the marginal amount of revenues it generates, it is clear that the time has come to abolish the corporate income tax.

As for the individual income tax, it too has grown increasingly unfair with the passage of time. The American middle class is shouldering a disproportionately heavy and still growing portion of this tax relative to either the lower or the upper ends of the economic scale. This system has been overtaken by a horrendous complexity, as year after year numerous revenue-losing special treatments, redounding mainly to the benefit of the wealthy, are written into the tax code. At the same time, despite the "supply-side" tax cuts of 1981, income tax rates continue to be far higher than they should be, largely because of the government's need for revenue. And, in penny-wise but pound-foolish fashion, personal savings are subject to taxation — hitting the middle classes the hardest and constituting a powerful disincentive for the investment and capital formation desperately needed to replace and modernize the United States's aging industrial base.

Indeed, it is clear that if the United States is to compete in the future world marketplace it must develop a tax system that harnesses and redirects the great energies of the economy — not one that suffocates them. Certainly, the United States cannot afford to continue much longer under the present tax structure — one that places a steep penalty on extra work effort, taxes savings, and encourages investments on the basis of their tax consequences rather than economic productivity, while its credibility is being sapped by the growth of loopholes and the "underground economy" of tax avoiders.

It is becoming increasingly clear that if revenue levels are going to be brought to an appropriate percentage of GNP to meet budget requirements without further imperiling the United States's capability to assume leadership in the international economic arena, it will be necessary to turn to some form of consumption-side taxation to meet a significant portion of our revenue needs. This should be accompanied by a simplification of the income tax system and a reduction of individual income tax rates to justifiable levels.

By far, the most effective and collectible tax of this nature would be a flat-rate tax on business transactions computed on the basis of added value. Such a means of revenue generation would comprise the second component of a responsible strategy for the management of Federal spending — a revenue system that can be counted on to satisfy its side of the budgetary equation.

The other virtues of a flat-rate transaction tax are manifold. Since it would fall only on consumption and not on savings, it would be a strong incentive to save and invest. Since it would discourage consumption, it would attack inflation at its source instead of forcing the use of restrictive, recession-oriented monetary policy; spendthrift consumerism would be replaced by thrift and frugality. It would slash the onerous income tax burden, eliminating the economic distortions caused by the consideration of tax consequences. And, by being imposed on imports while exempted from exports, it would provide a valuable — and GATT-legal — trade "subsidy" that would help to levelize the international playing field vis-à-vis Japan and our European competitors, who already employ this mechanism.

Though this essay is not the appropriate place to enter into a detailed description of how such a transaction tax would be instituted and administered, an illustration will show how it might be integrated into the current tax structure to achieve the goal of meeting budgetary requirements. Let us assume a significant reduction in income tax rates as a result of the more than offsetting revenues a transaction tax would bring in, as well as elimination of the corporate income tax. If a Federal spending limitation amounting to 25 percent of GNP were to be legislated, the supporting revenue mix might well break down roughly as follows:

Source	% GNP
Individual income tax	8.5
Flat-rate transaction tax	7.5
Social insurance taxes	6.5
Miscellaneous revenues, including excise taxes	2.5

Any regressive effects of the transaction tax would be mitigated by the significant reductions in individual income taxes shown above, which would bring about a major easing of the tax burden on lower and lower-middle income groups.

In sum, the true issue is not how to put an end to the growth in Federal spending; rather, it is the more realistic question of how to manage and cope with the necessary expansion in expenditures that characterizes a dynamic and responsive democracy. The proposal made here — prudent and reasonable spending restraints that allow a modicum of growth in the commitments of Federal government, coupled with a revitalized tax system that will generate sufficient revenues for government and pave the way for a future economic prosperity that the present system hinders — would constitute a responsible solution to the impending American economic crisis.

NOTE

1. Sources: U.S. Department of Commerce, Bureau of the Census, *Historical Statistics of the United States: Colonial Times to 1970*, 1975; idem, *Statistical Abstract of the United States, 1984*, 1983; Office of Management and Budget, Executive Office of the President, *The United States Budget in Brief, FY 1985*, 1984.

The Budget Dilemma and Its Solution

MURRAY L. WEIDENBAUM

The fundamental budget problem facing the United States arises from the failure to match the 1981 tax cuts with comparable spending cuts. While Federal revenues were reduced by about $700 billion during the five-year period 1982–86, civilian outlays were cut by only about one-half of that amount—and defense procurement was accelerated. The severe recession in 1981–82 temporarily worsened the deficit. However, the persistence of unusually large deficits in this current period of economic recovery demonstrates the long-term nature of the budget dilemma (see table 1).

Basically, deficits can be reduced by increasing revenues or cutting spending. There is no shortage of ways to raise taxes[1] — instituting a "temporary" surcharge, reversing the personal income-tax cuts, or postponing the scheduled indexing of the personal income-tax structure. Indirectly, the same objective may be achieved via "tax reform"— broadening the base of taxable income so that the public does not realize that the total tax burden is rising. Thus, most proposals for shifting to a flat or flatter tax structure focus on the rate reductions that would be achieved. They soft-pedal discussion of the great extent to which citizens would be paying Federal income taxes on items that they do not now report or even think of as taxable income. Examples include employer-paid medical and retirement benefits, veterans' benefits, social security and other government retirement payments, and unemployment compensation. Also, under a flat tax, no deductions would be allowed for state and local taxes, interest payments, or charitable deductions.

"Tax simplification" suggestions aside, a general tax increase would be misguided. Deficits are not so undesirable that the costs of proposals to reduce them should be ignored. There are ways of curbing the deficit that would do more economic harm than good. Tax increases that reduce saving and investment are prime examples. Such actions would signal to the advocates of more government spending that they now have a clear field. But, more basically, such tax increases would

TABLE 1

Baseline Federal Budget Projections
(By fiscal year)

Category	1983 Actual	1984 Base	Projections				
			1985	1986	1987	1988	1989
			In Billions of Dollars				
Revenues	$601	$663	$733	$795	$863	$945	$1,016
Outlays	796	853	928	1,012	1,112	1,227	1,342
Deficit	$195	$190	$195	$217	$248	$282	$326
			As a Percent of GNP				
Revenues	18.6	18.6	18.7	18.7	18.7	19.0	18.9
Outlays	24.7	23.9	23.7	23.8	24.1	24.6	24.9
Deficit	6.1	5.3	5.0	5.1	5.4	5.6	6.1

SOURCE: Congressional Budget Office.

reverse the beneficial effects of the 1981 tax cuts on saving, investment, and economic growth.

Unfortunately for the public dialogue, economists know much more about taxes than about government spending. Compare, for example, the extent of programmatic detail in the sections on taxation and government spending in current public-finance textbooks. Thus, most serious discussions of the deficit problem briefly pay lip service to the need for economy and efficiency in government spending but quickly pass on to examine the possibilities for increasing taxes. But to start the effort to reduce the deficit by focusing on revenue changes is a confession of failure to control government spending.

The more satisfying—though more difficult—response to the nation's budget problem is to proceed with a comprehensive round of budget cutting. Inspiration can be taken from the old motto of the budget office, "Good budgeting is the uniform distribution of dissatisfaction." The truth of the matter is that not enough of the spending agencies are dissatisfied. Far too frequently, pleas for additional spending cuts are dismissed by asserting that defense is too important to cut, entitlements are too difficult to change, and the "all other" category is too small to bother with. Yet opportunities for serious and careful budget pruning abound in every department, military and civilian, social and economic.

The nation must face the painful fact that the tax cuts have not been earned by matching spending cuts. While Federal revenues have been declining as a percent of GNP in recent years, Federal spending has been rising faster than the GNP. Despite all of the attention to some highly publicized budget cuts, the task of controlling the rapid growth of Federal spending lies ahead. Defense outlays, entitlement spending, farm subsidies, and interest payments continue to be growth areas of the Federal budget. The rapid increases in these four areas far more than offset cuts in food stamps, school lunch, college loans, and other "social" programs.

Controlling Defense Spending

Supporters of a substantial military buildup do not necessarily have to exempt the defense establishment from the rigorous budget review that civilian agencies undergo. A recent report on the Department of Defense's (DOD) budget problems by the General Accounting Office underscores this point. A typical quote from the report deals with operations and maintenance (O & M) spending: "Last year we also reported that DOD did not have a well-planned strategy and priority system for applying increased funding to O & M programs. As a result, funds were applied to some programs in excess of what could be absorbed efficiently and effectively. DOD still does not have a well-planned strategy for applying increased funding to O & M programs."[2] GAO went on to point out specifics:

At Fort Lee $2.7 million was received during September 1982 to be obligated before the fiscal year ended on September 30. The money was used to finance projects that had not been validated, were not in the approved backlog, and were not in the 1982 or 1983 work plans.

At Fort Stewart year-end funding amounting to $92,000 was used to construct a bicycle path while more mission-related projects were not funded.

At Little Creek Naval Amphibious Base, $300,000 was used to resurface tennis courts, widen sidewalks, and paint signs while roof repair projects went unfinanced.

Here is a sampling of other shortcomings found by GAO:

As much as 36 percent of the flying done by Navy tactical and patrol squadrons is for nontraining activities; however, the budget is based on training for primary mission readiness.

Each year millions of dollars "migrate" from mission-related programs to real property maintenance. Because much of these budget transfers occur in the last months of the fiscal year, projects of questionable need are sometimes funded in an attempt to spend the money before year-end.[3]

There are other and related grounds on which to question the size of planned increases in the military budget. The projected rates of expansion in the procurement of weapon systems are more rapid than were experienced at the height of the Vietnam War. The current upturn in the economy is rapidly using up the margin of excess capacity that characterized the earlier years of the present military buildup. Adjusting the flow of military production to a more moderate pace would make less likely the cost overruns and time delays that have so bedeviled the Pentagon in the past.

More recently, there have been reports of the Defense Department's rush to spend all its available money before the fiscal year ended on 30 September 1983. Hasty procurement moves included buying 57,600 softballs, a fourteen-month supply of paper, and piles of ice-cube makers and video-cassette players.[4] Tighter reins on defense spending would do more than contribute to a smaller budget deficit.

Such improved managerial controls would solidify the necessary public support for the continued high level of military strength required to keep the peace in a dangerous world.

The rationale for shifting from the target of 5 percent annual growth in real military spending, which was presented in the 1980 presidential campaign, to 10 percent or more has never been convincingly explained. Surely, the military posture of the United States has not deteriorated in these last three years. A return to the 5 percent target is now appropriate. Adopting a more measured attitude toward military preparedness avoids crash programs; it opposes the view that every nickel appropriated must be spent at all costs. National security is not promoted by showing the Soviets how fast the United States government can spend money.

There is, moreover, a serious national defense argument in favor of slowing down the rapid growth of military procurement. The most recently available data, covering 1980, demonstrate that weapon programs showing large cost overruns are precisely those whose unit volumes are cut back the most by a Pentagon forced to meet budgetary constraints. Table 2 shows that military procurements that stay close to outlay targets are more likely to be continued as planned. Most weapon-system programs with cost overruns under 40 percent were maintained without reduction. But each of the weapon systems with cost increases of more than 40 percent was cut back. The largest reductions occurred in the programs with the greatest overruns.

An implicit conclusion arises from these data: slowing the growth rate of de-

TABLE 2

Military Cost Overruns and Program Cutbacks in 1980

Weapon System	Cost Overruns	Unit Cutbacks
Major overruns		
Hellfire missile	322%	82%
Patriot missile	154	67
SSG-7 ship	79	75
AH64 aircraft	67	43
EA-6B aircraft	52	33
XM-1 tank	49	21
F-18 aircraft	44	40
P-3C aircraft	43	50
Minor overruns		
UH-60 aircraft	33	19
Phoenix missile	30	0
ALCM missile	27	8
EC-1300 aircraft	26	0
SN688 ship	20	0
Pershing II missile	19	0
Harpoon missile	14	0
F-14A aircraft	9	0

SOURCE: Congressional Budget Office analysis of 1980.

fense spending to conform more closely with production capabilities will both reduce the deficit and make more likely the successful completion of the military buildup. Rather than choosing between national security and economic factors, the two may go hand in hand.

Controlling "Entitlement" Outlays

The largest category of Federal spending is the "entitlements," which are dominated by social-security outlays (see table 3). Here it is useful to analyze the problem

TABLE 3

Baseline Federal Outlay Projections for Entitlements and Other Mandatory Spending
(By fiscal year, in billions of dollars)

	1983 Actual	1984 Base	Projections				
			1985	1986	1987	1988	1989
Social insurance programs							
Social security	$165	$173	$184	$197	$211	$227	$243
Medicare	56	64	74	83	94	106	120
Unemployment compensation	31	22	19	18	18	18	19
Railroad retirement	6	6	6	6	6	7	7
Subtotal	$258	$265	$283	$303	$329	$358	$388
Means-tested programs							
Medicaid	$19	$21	$23	$25	$27	$30	$32
Food stamps	12	11	11	12	12	13	13
Assistance payments	8	8	8	8	8	9	9
Supplemental security income	9	8	9	10	10	12	11
Veterans' pensions	4	4	4	4	4	4	4
Guaranteed student loans	3	3	3	3	3	3	3
Child nutrition	3	3	4	4	4	4	4
Other	2	2	2	2	2	2	2
Subtotal	$60	$61	$65	$68	$72	$77	$81
Federal employee retirement and disability							
Civilian	$21	$22	$24	$26	$28	$29	$31
Military	16	17	18	19	20	21	23
Subtotal	$37	$39	$41	$44	$48	$51	$54
Other programs							
Veterans' benefits	$13	$13	$13	$13	$13	$14	$14
Farm price supports	19	7	9	12	13	15	18
General revenue sharing	5	5	5	5	5	5	5
Social services	3	4	4	4	4	4	4
Other	6	6	6	6	6	7	7
Subtotal	$46	$35	$36	$40	$42	$45	$48
Total	$400	$400	$425	$456	$490	$530	$570

SOURCE: Congressional Budget Office.
NOTE: Figures may not total because of rounding.

in terms of three generations. The first generation is represented by retired workers who are now receiving social-security benefits. For most of their working lives, these people were told that they were earning a social-security pension. In fact, the government set up account numbers to record all of their contributions and those of their employers. However, those contributions, including the interest earned, do not begin to cover their monthly social-security checks.[5] The recipients do not know—nor do they want to hear—that bad news. The inescapable fact is that this nation has made a moral commitment to the people now on the social-security rolls to pay at least the current level of monthly payments and probably with some allowance to cover future inflation. Advocates of budget restraint must accept that.

But the working generation is very different. This generation still has the opportunity to adjust to changes in future social-security benefits—provided the shifts are phased in gradually. Many of these people are sophisticated enough to understand that retroactive benefits, by their very nature, must represent a hidden subsidy paid by someone else and thus are the economic equivalent of welfare outlays. Key long-term changes in benefit schedules are therefore feasible.

The most basic changes, however, can be made in the prospective benefit payments to the younger generation. Many of them are still in school, and others have only recently entered the work force. Retirement benefits are far from their minds. Provided that their taxes are not increased in the process, these young people are likely to go along with a variety of reasonable changes in the entitlement programs. This represents a long-term opportunity to reduce the welfare (or intergenerational transfer) aspect of this category of outlays.

Controlling Other Spending Programs

It has become fashionable to deduct defense and entitlement spending from the budget total and show that the remainder is either too small to bother with or already declining (see table 4). Such an approach is far too gross for a satisfactory analysis of the budget quandary. It ignores important cross-currents that are occurring within the "all other" category (see table 5). For example, the fastest growing area of spending in recent years is neither entitlements nor defense. Rather, it is a component of "all other"—farm subsidies. This category of Federal spending rose from $3 billion in 1981 to $21 billion in 1983. Moreover, recent congressional action on the dairy program ensures that the U.S. Department of Agriculture will continue subsidizing some of the wealthiest farmers at the expense of taxpayers and consumers.[6]

Sacred cows are not limited to the dairy industry. Take for example the National Endowment for the Humanities. One might assume that only the culturally ignorant would try to cut that agency's budget. But an examination of the details reveals that a portion of these outlays will finance a history of each of the fourteen branches of a municipal library.[7] A person does not have to be a Philistine to have the gumption to say that such expenditures show that the amount cut from civilian budgets is not too much but far too little.

By no means should Congress be let off the hook. After all, each Federal outlay is made pursuant to an appropriation enacted by Congress. According to a recent report, the House Rules Committee took action to eliminate a supposed inequity: the members of the committee were approving trips by members of other committees but had not gone on any themselves. The chairman proposed to remedy

TABLE 4

Baseline Federal Outlay Projections for
Major Spending Categories
(By fiscal year, in billions of dollars)

	1983 Actual	1984 Base	Projections				
			1985	1986	1987	1988	1989
National defense	$210	$235	$263	$295	$331	$372	$419
Entitlements and other mandatory spending	400	400	425	456	490	530	570
Nondefense discretionary spending	144	156	161	168	178	189	198
Net interest	90	108	127	145	168	194	219
Offsetting receipts	−48	−46	−49	−52	−55	−59	−64
Total budget outlays	$796	$853	$928	$1,012	$1,112	$1,227	$1,342
Off-budget federal entities	12	13	13	13	14	13	13
Total outlays	$808	$866	$941	$1,025	$1,125	$1,240	$1,355

SOURCE: Congressional Budget Office.
NOTE: Figures may not total because of rounding.

TABLE 5

Baseline Federal Projections for Nondefense
Discretionary Spending
(By fiscal years, in billions of dollars)

	1983 Actual	1984 Base	Projections				
			1985	1986	1987	1988	1989
Aid to foreign governments and international organizations	$9	$10	$11	$11	$12	$12	$13
Federal government operations	21	24	24	25	26	27	28
Infrastructure	40	47	46	48	49	51	53
Assistance to business and commerce	9	8	7	7	8	9	10
Research and development	17	18	19	20	21	22	23
Benefits and services to individuals	48	50	52	55	58	60	63
Civilian agency pay raises	—	1	1	3	5	7	9
Total	$144	$156	$161	$168	$178	$189	$198

SOURCE: Congressional Budget Office.
NOTE: Figures may not total because of rounding.

this discriminatory state of affairs — at the expense of the taxpayers, of course — by a bus tour across the Potomac to Alexandria, Virginia. That suggestion failed to win sufficient support, but the chairman persevered and succeeded in gaining approval for a trip to South America, Costa Rica, and Jamaica.[8]

Tax-writing committees should not be ignored either. In late 1982, the Congress adopted the "love-boat" bill. Professionals who like sunbathing and shuffleboard while attending floating "seminars in the Caribbean" can now write off those so-called business expenses — provided they take one of the four cruise ships that fly under the American flag.[9] Such displays of patriotism are truly touching.

A far larger example of low-priority expenditures is the list of new public-works projects recently approved by the Senate Committee on Environment and Public Works.[10] At a time when the Treasury is paying about 13 percent for its long-term money, the committee and the Corps of Engineers are using the unrealistically low interest rate of 7.875 percent in evaluating these projects. The practical effect is to show a higher ratio of benefits to cost than would result from using a more realistic interest rate. Nevertheless, even with the subsidized interest rate, projects totaling more than $1 billion generate such extremely marginal ratios of benefits to costs as 1.2, 1.1, and 1.0 (see table 6). In plain English, Congress is scraping the bottom of the pork barrel.

Conclusion

Victor Hugo once wrote, "The budget, strange fish and monster vast,/To which from all sides the hook is cast." Surely the present budget dilemma is of vast proportions and the size of the budget reflects the successful efforts of so many parts of the society to get their "hook" into the Treasury. Yet a search for villains is not helpful, because there is plenty of blame to go around. It is the president who submitted the $200 billion deficit budgets, and it is the Congress that is going along with them. The much-ballyhooed "first installment" of deficit reduction will do little to change that. Very few of the cuts will take effect in fiscal 1985. Much of the estimated reductions have already been incorporated into the Reagan administration's estimates of the deficit.

The basic reason for the persistence of the budget problem, however, is that the average citizen generates the pressure for more government spending when he or she says, "I'm all for economy in government . . . but don't cut the special project in my area or the one benefiting my industry, because that is different." The author vividly recalls his meeting with an interest group pleading for a bailout from the government. When he said, "That's just a form of welfare," the group protested vehemently: "Welfare is for poor people."

This is no forecast of doom or gloom. With an expanding economy and a rising pool of savings, the budget deficits will, over time, shrink in importance. Meanwhile, if the Federal Reserve System is forced to maintain excessive monetary stimulus, the deficits will contribute to another round of inflation. If the Fed does not so monetize the deficits, the competition of Treasury borrowing and private

TABLE 6

Proposed Water Resources Development Act of 1983
Corps of Engineers Project

Project	Cost ($ millions)	B/C Ratio at 7.875%
Redbank and Fancher Creeks, Calif.	$ 75.2	1.2
Fountain Creek, Pueblo, Colo.	7.8	1.2
Rock River, Rockford, Ill.	27.9	1.1
Green Bay Levee, Iowa	6.3	1.1
Perry Creek, Iowa	40.9	1.1
Halstead, Kansas	7.5	1.1
Bushley Bayou, La.	42.8	1.1
Quincy Coastal Streams, Mass.	25.3	1.1
St. Paul, Minn.	7.9	1.2
South Fork Zumbro River, Minn.	87.7	1.1
Maline Creek, Mo.	57.4	1.2
Robinson's Branch, Rahway, N.J.	18.0	1.1
Mamaroneck and Sheldrake Rivers Basin, New York and Conn.	58.8	1.0
Little Miami River, Ohio	8.5	1.2
Muddy Boggy Creek, Okla.	43.8	1.2
Lock Haven, Pa.	73.4	1.2
Saw Mill Run, Pa.	7.3	1.1
Big River Reservoir, R.I.	78.6	1.2
Boggy Creek, Austin, Texas	19.4	1.2
James River Basin, Va.	93.8	1.1
Chealis River, Wash.	20.4	1.2
Yakima Union Gap, Wash.	8.8	1.2
Scammon Bay, Alaska	1.5	1.2
Blue River Lake, Ore.	28.6	1.2
St. Johns County, Fla.	9.0	1.1
Atlantic Coast of NYC, New York	6.6	1.0
Bethel, Alaska	14.7	1.2
Grand Haven Harbor, Mich.	16.5	1.2
Gulfport Harbor, Mich.	73.8	1.1
Portsmouth Harbor, N.H. and Maine	21.2	1.2
White River, Batesville, Ark.	26.5	1.1
	$1,015.9	

SOURCE: U.S. Senate Committee on Environment and Public Works.

credit demands will keep interest rates unduly high. New housing construction and business investment will increase more slowly than would otherwise be the case. Thus, economic growth and the rise in living standards will be more modest—unless a comprehensive round of budget cuts is carried out.

An effective budget restraint effort must be comprehensive. It requires a truly bipartisan approach. When the conservatives want to cut the social programs in the budget, they should be supported. The public must understand the realities of the entitlement programs: the beneficiaries are receiving far more than they are "entitled" to under any insurance concept that links benefit payments to contributions (including employer contributions and earnings on both). These programs contain a major component of subsidy—from working people to retirees.

When the liberals want to limit the rapid defense buildup to the generous rate that candidate Reagan campaigned on (5 percent a year in real terms), they should also be supported. But the support of both groups should be discontinued when each tries to use its budget savings to restore the budget cuts made by the other. The budget quandary is no arcane matter. It simply represents the unwillingness of the nation to make hard choices. In order to earn the 1981 tax cuts, these cuts must be matched with spending cuts—or the nation will continue to suffer the consequences.

Recommendations

Not only is the budget unbalanced, but the current public dialogue on the budget is also unbalanced. In congressional hearings as well as in professional publications, a great deal of attention is given to proposals for new taxes and increases in existing taxes. Very little consideration is given to ideas for reducing government spending. The tax committees spend much more time examining suggestions for increases in taxes than the appropriations committees devote to considering proposals for reducing expenditures. It may be an underestimate to say that 99 percent of the time spent at appropriation hearings is devoted to listening to agency representatives defend their requests for higher budgets.

Congress now has a rare opportunity to redress this imbalance. A blue ribbon commission of private citizens (the President's Private Sector Survey on Cost Control, popularly known as the Grace Commission) has completed a detailed analysis of possibilities for reducing Federal spending. The following are ten of the major recommendations that the commission proposed in its January 1984 report:

1. *Bring civil service retirement benefits closer to private-sector retirement norms.* Government pensions are now fully adjusted for increases in inflation, while average private-sector adjustments are 33 percent. The typical retirement age is fifty-five in the civil service, compared with sixty-three to sixty-four in the private sector.

2. *Bring military retirement closer to private sector retirement plan norms.* Military retirement benefits equal 75 percent of base pay after thirty years' service—about double private plans.

3. *Denationalize the Federal power-marketing administrations.* Government subsidized power, sold at one-third market rates, costs industrial users only 2.45 cents per kilowatt-hour (kwh) in the Northwest. This compares to 12.08 cents per kwh paid in San Diego for power generated by the private sector.

4. *Require the military to buy commonly used parts and equipment competitively.* For example, the Pentagon has bought screws, available in any hardware store at 3 cents, for $91 each.

5. *Upgrade Federal computer systems.* Federal government computers average 6.7 years in age, twice the private-sector average. Half are so old that the manufacturers no longer service them.

6. *Improve Department of Defense inventory management.* The commission found one segment of the department's inventory system generating 6 million pounds of computer output annually.

7. *Repeal legislation that requires Government to pay "prevailing wage" on Federal construction projects.* Originally intended to prevent outside contractors from undercutting local builders, these laws now discriminate against smaller, more competitive contractors.

8. *Track earnings of Social Security beneficiaries to eliminate erroneous benefits.* The plan to eliminate waste is three years behind schedule. The delay costs the government $128 million in interest in 1983 alone.

9. *Increase delinquent tax collections.* Despite growing noncompliance, the IRS decreased tax examinations from 2.4 percent of all filings in 1977 to 1.7 percent in 1983. Uncollected taxes presently total more than $100 billion.

10. *Tighten up sick leave policy.* Federal employees use 64 percent more sick time (nine days) than private-sector employees in nonmanufacturing industries (five and a half days).

Congress should, therefore, devote one day of open hearings for each department of government, during which the proponents of budget cuts could advise the Congress — and in the process the American public. It is difficult to say whether each of the Grace Commission's proposals is desirable,[11] but a systematic examination of proposed budget cuts — department by department — is long overdue. Some examples of present government activity border on the absurd. The following are examples of "bureaucratic absurdity" reported by the Grace Commission:

1. *Erroneous government mailing lists.* These lists often repeat the same name and address up to twenty-nine times.

2. *Congressional resistance to closing military bases.* Congress obstructs closing of bases the military wants to eliminate.

3. *Poor management of cash seized from criminals.* Cash taken from criminals is simply held instead of being deposited in interest-bearing accounts.

4. *Inefficient post offices.* A third of the post offices in the nation — a total of 12,469 — serve no more than 100 customers each.

5. *High cost of Veterans Administration nursing homes.* The VA spends $61,250 a bed to construct nursing homes. This is almost four times the $16,000 a bed it costs a major private-sector nursing home operator.

6. *Competitive bidding is prohibited on moving household goods.* Existing legislation prohibits competitive bidding on the movement of household goods to Alaska or Hawaii. Such bidding is estimated to reduce moving costs by as much as 26 percent.

7. *Inefficient management of government property.* In comparison to a private-sector company managing comparable space, the General Services Administration employs seventeen times as many people and spends fourteen times as much on total management costs.

8. *Farmers Home Administration loans to nonfarmers.* Seventy percent of the borrowers lent money by this agency are not farmers. The delinquency rate among

these nonfarm borrowers is 26 percent, more than seven times the private-sector average.

9. *Lax loan collection procedures at the Department of Housing and Urban Development.* The department makes only three attempts to collect loans versus an average of twenty-four to thirty-six tries in the private sector.

10. *Freight traffic mismanagement.* The government spends almost $5 billion annually on freight charges but does not negotiate volume discounts with suppliers.

Congress might wish to expand the hearings to cover other suggestions for budget savings, such as those that have been compiled by the Congressional Budget Office.[12]

Advocates for economy in government often bemoan the lack of public support for specific budget cuts. That should not be surprising. Such support will be forthcoming only if the public gets the opportunity to learn about, to consider, and to debate specific alternatives for achieving budget savings. Congress now has the opportunity to exercise bipartisan leadership in launching this vital educational effort.

NOTES

1. See Congressional Budget Office, *Reducing the Deficit: Spending and Revenue Options* (Washington, D.C.: GPO, 1984), 183–240.

2. General Accounting Office, *The Defense Budget: A Look at Budgetary Resources, Accomplishments and Problems* (Washington, D.C.: GPO, 1983), iii.

3. Ibid., iii, vi, viii.

4. *U.S. News & World Report*, 31 October 1983, 18.

5. Martha N. Ozawa, *Social Security: Towards a More Equitable and Rational System* (St. Louis: Washington University, Center for the Study of American Business, 1982).

6. Brooks Jackson and Jeffrey H. Burnbaum, "Dairy Lobby Obtains U.S. Subsidies," *Wall Street Journal*, 18 Nov. 1983, 33.

7. Missouri Committee for the Humanities, Inc., "A Proposal to Index Local History Files and Prepare Histories of the Fourteen Branches of the St. Louis Public Library" (St. Louis, Mo., 1983).

8. "Rules Panel in House to Take Latin Trip," *St. Louis Post-Dispatch*, 27 Nov. 1983.

9. Nancy Drabble, "Just Before Christmas, Congress Gave to Me . . .," *New York Times*, 28 Dec. 1982.

10. Senate Committee on Environment and Public Works, *Water Resources Development Act of 1983* (Washington, D.C.: GPO, 1983).

11. Congressional Budget Office and General Accounting Office, *Analysis of the Grace Commission's Major Proposals for Cost Control* (Washington, D.C.: GPO, 1984).

12. Congressional Budget Office, *Reducing the Deficit*, 13–182.

Equality, Spending Limits, and the Growth of Government

This essay is *not* about why governments should choose to limit spending. If governments wish to increase spending, that is obviously their prerogative. Moreover, the evidence indicates that they are very good at it. Governments therefore need no advice on doing what comes naturally. There need be no solution when there is no perceived problem.

The problem of expenditure limitation exists only when there is a public will but not yet a public way to hold down spending. For whatever reason, governments may wish to reduce the rate of spending increases or to hold spending to a fixed level (either absolutely or in proportion to national product or national income) and find themselves frustrated.

A desire to limit spending, of course, does not necessarily mean that citizens or governments dislike all or even any individual items of expenditure. They may well like each one considered separately and yet dislike the totals to which their desires add up. The people's preferences on totals may well be at variance with their preferences on individual programs. Indeed, so far as one can judge from opinion polls, this is precisely the state of the public mind: most expenditures are approved but total spending is disapproved. Reconciling these incompatible demands constitutes the contemporary political problem of public spending.

In this context, control over spending signifies that governments are able to set totals and stick to them. Obviously, this "setting and sticking" does not happen very often. Rather, the record is one of unrelieved failure interrupted only occasionally and for brief periods with temporary successes. Both absolutely and relatively to the size of the economy, public spending keeps climbing.

Why does government grow inexorably? Why do all of the efforts in the OECD countries fail to slow spending for other than short periods? Obviously, there must be a lack of correspondence between the causes of growth and the methods heretofore employed to contain them. What measures, we must ask in conclusion, would be efficacious? We must ask this question because, if there are no solutions, there are, in effect, no problems. "Imperfection" can still be "perfect" in the prudential sense that there are no known ways of perfecting performance. But before we reach that dismal conclusion, which I believe is unwarranted, we want to review and reappraise existing theories on the rise of public spending.

Economic Determinism Is a Two-Way Street

The most frequently used and accepted explanation for the growth of government is that it is caused by increasing wealth and industrialization. Whether known as Wagner's Law of Increasing State Activity (government grows faster than the economy)[1] or merely the observation that wealth and growth are related, the implication is teleological, i.e., there is an inherent logic of industrialization that propels such societies toward a greater growth of government.[2] Not so, I say. There is nothing inherent or predetermined about it. Of course, the wealthier a society, the more it has to protect; and the easier it is to spend, the larger the absolute increase in public spending. But why should industrialization, with its concomitant increase in wealth, lead to ever-increasing instead of ever-decreasing proportions of gross national product spent by government? Why, indeed, should a wealthier society be unable to provide both absolutely more and relatively less government spending? Why, to ask an even more pointed question, should people who have prospered from capitalism use that very prosperity to turn against it by diminishing the size of their economy and increasing the size and scope of their bureaucracy? The usual answer, not without its share of truth, is that capitalism not only solves certain problems but also creates others with which government is better suited to deal. But if capitalism creates more problems than it solves and does not produce enough to pay for them, resulting in perennial and growing deficits, that fails to explain why all capitalist countries are better off than their predecessors. More important for this discussion, the finding that capitalism is not worth its cost would eventually (say, within half a century) lead to its demise as the state absorbed the economy.

Viewed from a different perspective, there is nothing inevitable about the government growing faster than the economy. It is said, for instance, that in poor countries only government can raise capital for large projects. Why, then, does government grow in rich ones? It is said that capitalism causes urban growth, which leads to high-density living and the need for government to intervene so as to prevent some people from harming others. One could as easily argue that capitalism leads to urban sprawl or that big cities spawn cultural life or even that the per capita costs of public health and police services are lower in industrial centers. Although education is supposed to be essential to industrialization, to take a final example, Western nations spend from 8 to 40 percent of their budgets on that function—an observation suggesting that there is a lot of discretion left in this supposedly deterministic universe. What is missing is an explanation of why societies would want to expand the size of government.

A glance at the relative growth of public programs offers a clue. Since the end of World War II, in every Western nation, with only the partial exception of the United States since 1980, defense has continuously declined as a proportion of the budget and of GNP. Income transfer to individuals in the form of pensions and unemployment compensation and indirect transfer through medical benefits and, to a lesser extent, education account for most of the increase.[3] Observing what has gone up and down leads to the unremarkable conclusion that growth of government is fueled by a belief in greater equality of condition. When we also observe that movements to decrease social distinctions — between men and women, black and white, endangered species and underprivileged minorities, experts and laymen, authority and citizens — aim to achieve equality of condition, the growth of public spending is clearly part and parcel of the movement toward equality of condition. As long as this value increases in importance, and as long as government is viewed as an agent of redistribution of resources, government spending will continue to grow.

Where Is the Institutional Breakdown?

Perhaps the explanation of institutional breakdown is simpler than anyone has suggested: working their will through democratic procedures, people are doing and getting what they want. Otherwise, as Brian Barry has stated, it is "important to know if the forces of electoral competition can be expected to operate in some systematic way to give people what they don't want, or more specifically to give them something that would be defeated by some alternative in a straight vote. For this would suggest that there is some kind of internal flaw to democracy. . . ."[4] Barry is inclined to believe there is no such flaw, or if there is, not of the kind that would lead to undesired high expenditures. Those who hold opposing views are also troubled by the thought that the political process is right and they are wrong. Their perplexity is worth pursuing. According to James Buchanan and Richard Wagner:

> The question we must ask, and answer, is: Why do citizens support politicians whose decisions yield the results we have described? If citizens are fully informed about the ultimate consequences of alternative policy choices, and if they are rational, they should reject political office seekers or officeholders who are fiscally irresponsible. They should not lend indirect approval to inflation-inducing monetary and fiscal policy; they should not sanction cumulatively increasing budget deficits. . . . Yet we seem to observe precisely such outcomes.[5]
>
> There is a paradox of sorts here. A regime of continuous and mounting deficits, with subsequent inflation, along with a bloated public sector, can scarcely be judged beneficial to anyone. Yet why does the working or ordinary democratic process seemingly produce such a regime? Where is the institutional breakdown?[6]

Where indeed?

I emphatically do not subscribe to theories of bureaucratic conspiracy or manipulation by politicians to explain the growth of public expenditure. "What," Barry asked, "could anyone hope for from a system characterized by a collection of rogues competing for the favors of a larger collection of dupes?"[7] I wish to puncture the preposterous Parkinsonian proposition that bureaucrats expand their programs indefinitely by hoodwinking the population. Were these programs not deeply desired by strong social elements, they would not prosper. It is not the conspiracy theory but the POGO theory (named after the comic strip character) that is applicable: *We has met the enemy, and it is us.*[8]

"They" Are Doing It to Us

The elegant theory of bureaucracy propounded by William Niskanen is far more intuitively appealing and aesthetically pleasing. By what criteria, he asks, are bureaucrats judged and rewarded? The differences between the results they achieve and the resources their agencies consume are not among them. Bureaucrats cannot appropriate savings; neither can their agencies carry over funds. Rather, their opportunities for promotion, for salary, and for influence increase with size irrespective of success. Thus they will want more (much more) for their agencies and programs than citizens would prefer under similar circumstances.[9] So far, so good. But why would voters elect government officials who would go along with this? If citizens think taxes are too high or expenditures too large, what stops them from using the ballot box to enforce these views?

I reject the conspiratorial views of the left known as "false consciousness" and those of the right called "fiscal illusion," not because they are wholly wrong but because a partial truth is often worse than none at all. Bluntly stated, the doctrine of false consciousness alleges that the masses in a capitalist country are indoctrinated to prefer policies that are contrary to their real interests by a biased transmission of culture, from schools to churches to the media. No doubt all of us mistake our interests: no one can jump out of his skin and pretend that he was born anew, untouched by human hands or immune from the presuppositions of his society. None of this, however, signifies that others have a "true consciousness" enabling them to claim authoritatively that they know what is better for us than we do. In any event, in the current context, false consciousness would signify that expenditures are too low rather than too high, led by corporate propaganda to prefer private to public spending, which is not, as social workers say, the presenting problem.

Stripped of its surface of complex calculation, fiscal illusion can be understood by everyone, because no one understands all the ramifications of innumerable taxes and expenditures.[10] And citizens may systematically underestimate what they pay and what the government spends. That they pay a lot directly and indirectly, however, is obvious to most people. Witness Proposition 13 in California. Undoubtedly, in view of the unfathomable billions of dollars involved, citizens also underestimate the costs of various programs. Since it would take only a few minutes for them to find out, however, I am not persuaded this matters much. Illusions exist, no doubt, but I doubt that they result in the euphoric feeling of escape from taxation.

Both false consciousness and fiscal illusion serve the function of explaining to followers why a left- or right-wing movement fails. They are the doctrines of inveterate losers. It cannot be that the people are against us; it must be they are misguided. If they had the right information, would the people decide with full consciousness and without illusion to make the right (or is it the left) choice?

Another view, with which I also disagree, though only in part, is Gordon Tulloch's theory that "the growth of the bureaucracy to a large extent is self-generating."[11] The trouble with bureaucrats is that they vote: the more of them there are, the more votes they have and the larger they grow. In support of this hypothesis, (un)certain evidence may be adduced. Civil servants are more likely to vote than other people. Governments are much more labor intensive than private industry, not only where they perform services, as Baumol's theory of increasing cost of service suggests,[12] but also across-the-board. And the larger the size of government, the higher its proportion of administrative costs. All this is tantalizing but far from conclusive. Bureaucrats are by no means a majority. If I am correct in believing that in their role as citizens they do not like big government much more than the rest of us, they would not vote for expansion in general. It is only their part of the public purse they defend. Indeed, according to poll data, 47 percent of state employees in California said they voted for Proposition 13. The grand queries remain: Why don't the rest of us stop them or, even better, why don't their private selves stop their public selves?

Doing It to Ourselves

The POGO theory, by contrast, is that we the people (including citizens, politicians, and civil servants) are doing it to ourselves. This is a cooperative game. We do not like it—no one said that people necessarily like what they do to themselves—but we do do it. How? Why?

It is not only the bureaucrats and their political protectors but all of us who are at the root of our own problems. Citizens like some of those programs—not all, of course, but enough to want to see them go up. Unfortunately, the only way to do that is to push everything up, partly because that is the price of support from other citizens, partly because that is the necessary exchange with politicians who support our programs but others as well and partly because there is usually no way to express a position on total spending aside from the items that make it up. Citizens want some spending more than others; they want their priorities to prevail; and among these priorities is a preference for lower total expenditure.

Bureaucrats are no better than other people. Because they actively want more, or passively cannot resist, does not mean they want the government to grow, at least not so fast. It is just that everybody is doing the same thing or they cannot get theirs without going along with other programs. Like the citizenry (indeed, they are the citizenry—at least a good part of it) bureaucrats bid up the cost of government without knowing they are doing it. As the hero used to say in those old-fashioned seduction scenes, when he was inexperienced and she was eager, "It's bigger than the both of us."[13]

Legislatures and cabinets also enjoy spending more than saving. Of all those writing on these subjects, William Riker's explanation of legislative expansion of the public sector comes closest, in my view, to the correct spirit. He said:

> I think it is probably the case that, if everyone (or if all rulers in a society) agreed to do so, they could obtain the benefits of reducing the size of the public sector. But no such agreement occurs and our question is to explain why it does not. The explanation I offer is that rulers are trapped in a system of exchange of benefits that leads to disadvantageous . . . results.
>
> The system works in this way:
>
> Step 1: Some legislators (or the leaders of some identifiable group with access to legislators) see an opportunity for gain for some of the legislators' constituents by the transfer of some activity from the private sector to the public sector. Usually such gain involves the transfer of a private cost to the public treasury. . . . Typically, of course, the beneficiaries of the transfer are relatively small groups of citizens and only a minority of legislators have constituents in the benefiting groups. Typically also there exist other groups and other minorities of legislators who see opportunities for private gain in other transfers from private to public sectors. The combination of several minorities of legislators acting to benefit constituents are enough to make a legislative majority and so together they can produce significant expansions of the public sector.
>
> Step 2: Such a coalition would be . . . socially harmless (though perhaps unfair). . . . But, of course, this successful coalition is only one of many. Entirely different coalitions, some overlapping, some not, obtain other kinds of transfers to the public sector: coalitions around public works, around military bases and contracting, around regulatory bodies and the favors they pass out to various small economic interests, etc. Beyond economic interests there are ideological interests around which legislators can ally themselves to win support by satisfying deeply felt values of some constituents: racial, ethnic, linguistic, religious, moral, patriotic, etc.—all of which can be promoted by expansions of public sector activities.
>
> The consequence is that nearly every conceivable interest, economic and political, has some legislators promoting its own fortunes in future elections by promoting governmental service to that interest.
>
> Step 3: Since each citizen with one or several interests served by these (usually minority) coalitions of legislators benefits as the coalitions succeed and since each legislator benefits in some degree from the gratitude thus generated in marginally important voters, nearly everyone benefits from successful actions to expand the public sector. Consequently, every legislator has a driving motive to form more or less ad hoc majority alliances of these minority coalitions in order to obtain some public benefits for every interest represented in the alliance. Were a legislator to refrain either from promoting some minority interests or from joining in larger alliances to obtain benefits, he (and his constituents) would merely suffer the costs of paying for the benefits for others while obtaining no benefits for themselves.

Yet in the end the society has a greatly expanded public sector with very high costs and considerable inefficiencies. It seems very likely to me that these disadvantages are so great that nearly everybody is worse off than if the public sector expansion had never taken place. It might be supposed, therefore, that everybody would have a motive to agree to forego public sector benefits—and indeed they do. But an agreement for a grand coalition for abstinence seems well-nigh unenforceable. Everyone has a motive to desert the grand coalition in the hope of getting some public sector benefit before others do so.[14]

The only difference between us is one of emphasis: Riker sees the governors exploiting the governed, and I see all of us in it together. Why did this not happen in the past and why is it happening now?

Decline of Madisonian Theory

In what he called the theory of a "compound republic," James Madison expressed his belief that the large geographic size of the country, as well as the variety of its peoples, would retard the formation of factions (which we would call pressure groups) acting adversely to the interests of others. It would, he thought, be too difficult for them to organize, confer, and act unless they were numerous and until they had secured widespread agreement. Organized interests would be few in number but large in size, reflecting in the very process of formation a general interest likely to be in accord with a shared view of justice. In his own words:

> The smaller the society, the fewer probably will be the distinct parties and interests composing it; the fewer the distinct parties and interests, the more frequently will a majority be found of the same party; and the smaller the number of individuals composing a majority, and the smaller the compass within which they are placed, the more easily will they concert and execute their plans of oppression. Extend the sphere, and you take in a greater variety of parties and interests; you make it less probable that a majority of the whole will have a common motive to invade the rights of other citizens; or if such a common motive exists, it will be more difficult for all who feel it to discover their own strength, and to act in unison with each other. Besides other impediments, it may be remarked that, where there is a consciousness of unjust or dishonorable purposes, communication is always checked by distrust in proportion to the number whose concurrence is necessary.[15]

Modern technology has undermined these Madisonian premises. It is far easier and cheaper for people to get together than he could have imagined.

If modern means of communication were unanticipated, the reversal of political causality, comparable perhaps to redirecting magnetism, was not even dreamed about. Factions exerted force on government, not the other way round. Government might resist but it could never create factions. These might, as in Madison's famous phrases, be sown in the nature of man but not at the behest of government. Yet this is exactly what happens with big government. The more government does for industry and individuals, the more they have to do for it.

Instead of imagining industry instigating action by government, for instance, we now know that government often acts and industry reacts, its organization being a response to an interest government has, by its behavior, newly created. Other levels of government also organize after they observe incentives created by the central government.[16] Indeed, government now pays citizens to organize, lawyers to sue, and politicians to run for office.

The larger government grows, the more policies become their own causes. The more government does, the more it needs to fix what it does. The larger government becomes, the less it responds to events in society and the more it reacts to the consequences of its past policies. Thus big government exacerbates the spending pressure it has difficulty overcoming.[17]

How is coordination carried out? Since they cannot predict the consequences of their activities, the sectors of policy adopt a cybernetic solution. They tacitly agree to cope with the consequences caused by other agencies, just as the others agree to cope with theirs. The cost of coordination is reduced to a minimum. The center becomes another sector, specialized to macroeconomic management. In return for deference on adjusting the economy, it agrees (again, tacitly) not to interfere in agency operations, which, in any case, are too many and misunderstood to be dealt with in detail. Thus, as government grows more centralized, in the sense that there are superdepartments, the center disappears.

This line of sectors, each with a hand on the shoulder of the one nearest to it, could be described as engaging in a game of reverse musical chairs—when the music stops there are extra chairs to fill. Their golden rule is that each may do unto the other as the other does unto it so long as there is more for both. The litany is well known: doing well deserves more and doing badly deserves mountains of money because these unfortunate conditions must be alleviated. What must never happen to shatter the chain is for one sector to take resources from another. The rule of "fair-shares," dividing increases over the prior year and decreases from requests equally among agencies is characteristic. Funds for extraordinary programs, with special appeal, may go up so long as those for other programs do not go down. There is, in the language of evolution, selection "up" but not "out." Thus defense will not decrease but may be kept constant while welfare grows, or vice versa. How are these happy accommodations possible? Because the public sector has been able to solve its internal problems both by absorbing the growth and by decreasing the share of the private sector.

The system of incentives in central government spending makes addition easier than subtraction. Whenever there is a crunch, administrative agencies will add on the costs of their programmatic proposals; they will not, unless compelled, subtract one from the other. Subtraction suggests competition in which there have to be losers; addition is about cooperation in which (within government) there are only winners. When the economy produces sufficient surplus, spending grows painlessly; when there are shortages, spending grows noiselessly as inflation increases effective taxation or tax expenditures and loan guarantees substitute for amounts that would otherwise appear in the red. The budget grows. A downward dip now and again does not slow its inexorable progress. Budgets used to be balanced. What has happened to throw them out of kilter?

Balancing the Budget versus Balancing the Economy

Following the rule of a balanced budget was an effective mechanism for keeping expenditures down. The dislike of raising taxes exerted restraint on expenditure. Deficits were tolerated during emergencies — wartime and recession. But politicians expected retribution if they disobeyed the rule.

To say that public officials once believed in the doctrine of the desirability of a balanced budget may seem like answering one question with another. What we want to know is why this doctrine was abandoned. All these questions may be answered by focusing on the doctrine that replaced it, the neo-Keynesian idea of balance called the full-employment surplus, a doctrine under which there would almost always be a deficit. The balanced budget was everything the full-employment surplus was not.

The attraction of Keynesianism itself is easy to understand. It involves just two variables — spend more when the economy is too slow and spend less when it is going too fast — that politicians on the run believe they can understand and, what is more important, can manipulate. The full-employment surplus is even more attractive. Don't just balance the budget, balance the economy! Why worry about a purely technical balance when resources and people are underutilized? Spend to save. Old-fashioned ideas about the government being like the family, which must not spend more than it takes in, or inflation being connected to using debt financing and money creation to cover deficits, went by the boards. Eventually, higher levels of economic activity would generate greater revenues to bring the budget into balance. The important thing is that once balancing the economy becomes the norm, expenditure can undergo enormous expansion with the blessing of economic doctrine. The full-employment surplus norm, in a word, was a license (almost a commandment) to spend.

The old-fashioned balanced budget norm meant more than we understand today. On one side, it signified a common understanding among elites on the extent of tolerable taxation. Tax rates might go up or down but not much. Given the belief in a balanced budget in peacetime, revenues limited expenditure. The norm of the balanced budget imposed, in effect, a global limit on expenditures. Hence the maxim of opportunity costs — much more for one large program meant much less for others — actually applied.[18] Working together with the other two classical budgetary norms — annualarity and comprehensiveness — the requirement of balance meant that all major spending interests in and out of government have a common interest in restraining budget-busting behavior. No more.

Is Item-by-Item Sensible?

I have not specifically stated the most obvious and direct mode of expenditure limitation — acting intelligently on major items of expenditure. If you and I believe that expenditures are too high, the argument goes, we should say specifically which ones should be cut and by how much. If you want to cut expenditures, you must cut programs. Simply stated, these words have much to commend them. I have used them myself. I do not regret having gone along with this argument on micro matters, but analyzing individual items is misleading as a general guide to limiting expenditures.

That is what we have always done; there must be something wrong with "item-by-item" or it would have worked by now. Moreover, the lack of a limit, especially since the decline of the balanced-budget ideology, means that items need not compete with one another. Comparison of increments at the margins might indeed be sensible if it ever happened. But what really happens is that each item is not compared with but added to the others; and what we want is to substitute some subtraction for all the addition. How?

Who would take the lead in reducing expenditures? Each sector of policy is concerned with its own internal development. More money makes it easier to settle internal quarrels. Those who believe more is better for their agency or their clientele come to this position naturally. Those who favor radical restructuring of programs soon discover that this is exceedingly difficult to do without sweetening the pie. The price of policy change is program expansion. All internal incentives work to raise expenditures.

Suppose you and I agree to cut our preferred programs in the common interest. What good would that do unless everyone else does the same? And why should we if "our" loss is "their" gain?

The political process is biased against limiting spending item-by-item. Were substantial spending desired by strong and lasting majorities, the rules of the political game permit this preference to be registered in budgetary decisions. Spending is simple. Even in the face of indifference, letting things go on as they are automatically leads to increases. But should there be an opposite opinion, reflecting a desire to slow down spending, it does not have an equal opportunity to manifest itself in the budget. There is now no way for slow spenders to get together to enforce equal sacrifice so that the general rule becomes part and parcel of the calculus involved in individual spending decisions. To increase spending, no coordination is necessary; to decrease it, an enormous amount is required.

It appears that we have reached a dead end. If there were an effective ceiling, every participant would have to accept the prospect of getting less. The very thing that is desired — expenditure limitation itself — appears to be its own requisite. To explain the futility of expenditure limitation, a feeling common among would-be controllers, let us conduct a mental experiment.

Imagine an expenditure limit to which all governmental activities were subject for at least a decade and from which none could escape. Would budgetary behavior be different? What would happen inside the government and in society?

Placed in wide perspective, the purpose of expenditure limitation is to increase cooperation in society and conflict in government. As things stand, the purveyors of public policy within government have every incentive to raise their spending income while reducing their internal differences. How? By increasing their total share of national income at the expense of the private sector. Why fight among their public selves if private persons will pay? They present a bill that, in effect, must be paid by higher taxes or bigger debt. Once there was a limit, however, the direction of incentives would be radically reversed.

Organizations interested in income redistribution will come to understand that the greater the increase in real national product, the more there will be for government to spend on these purposes. Instead of acting as if it did not matter where the money came from, they would have to consider how they might contribute to enhanced productivity. Management and labor would be thinking about common objectives, about how to expand their joint product rather than about how to take more from the other. Government regulations that impose financial burdens would not be viewed as desirable in and of themselves, as if they were free, but would be balanced against the loss to the economy on which the size of social services depend.

The incentive to improve internal efficiency will be immense. Knowing that they are unlikely to get more and may well get less (depending on the state of the economy and disposition of the polity), agencies will try to get the most out of what they have. Efficiency will no longer be a secondary consideration, to be satisfied if nothing else is pressing, or no consideration at all if evidence that they can do with less would reduce their future income: efficiency will be the primary path of the steady state in which they find themselves.

Two things will be happening at once: each agency will be figuring out how to defend what it has and how to steal a march on the others in getting new programs approved. An agency will no longer be able to argue that its proposal in and of itself is desirable (for there are few programs utterly without merit or benefit for someone) and that it deserves a higher priority than others being considered. Agencies will need to demonstrate defects in other agency programs. Naturally, these other agencies will defend themselves. Instead of interested public officials having to ferret out weaknesses in agency programs, they themselves will do that for us.

It would be in the interest of each participant to keep the others in line. Subtraction from someone else would become the necessary handmaiden of addition for oneself. The fiction that central controllers can do it all themselves would be replaced by the reality of spenders saving from one another. Who guards the guardians? They guard one another.

Practicing the Theory

The theory is a pleasing thought (some would say "pipe dream"), but the question of how to get from here to there, from resource entitlements (where we are now) to resource limits (where we would like to be), remains unanswered. Some countries have coalition governments that make it difficult to resist demands by one of the partners. Other countries have minority governments too weak to resist majorities. All countries have parties and politicians and pressure groups that like to preempt the process by making their expenditure preferences mandatory. In all, the politics of indexing proceeds apace: conservatives want to index taxes; progressives want to index spending; the likely result is that everything (and therefore nothing) will be indexed and we are back to square one.

Yet, without appearing to have learned much, we have learned a good deal. Negative knowledge — knowledge of what does not work — is not to be despised. Impossibility theorems make up much of what is valuable in science. So, reasoning backwards, we may begin the long march to limitation by looking at what will not work at all and what might.

There is no method that will tell governments how much to spend on this or that or whether to spend at all.[19] The methods leave much to be desired and are themselves based on value premises that require defense. How much you want, moreover, depends in part on how much you can get. Totals are not merely made out of items; items of expenditure, under any rational scheme, depend on totals. Just as one would do not only more but different things with a billion instead of a million dollars, just as where you go has to depend on what you have to get there with, a decision on totals is part of a rational choice on the parts.

Instead of searching for a magic method that would only evaporate in the mist, budgeters should seek procedures and processes that give spenders an interest in saving. Establishing global expenditure limits is one such incentive.

Are global limits desirable? That depends on what way of life one prefers — competitive individualism (capitalism), hierarchical collectivism (socialism), or equality of condition (egalitarianism). The greater the preference for equality, the larger the growth of government. If the desire for equal results declines, however, global limits to ensure that spending does not exceed economic growth would work. Two things are necessary to curb spending: a decline in egalitarianism and institutional incentives to make good that change in values.

NOTES

1. See Patrick D. Larkey, Chandler Stolp, and Mark Winer, "Theorizing About the Growth of Government: A Research Assessment," *Journal of Public Policy*, vol. 1, pt. 2 (May 1981): 157–220.

2. See Harold L. Wilensky, *The Welfare State and Equality* (Berkeley/Los Angeles/London: University of California Press, 1975); and Frederick Pryor, *Public Expenditures in Communist and Capitalist Nations* (Homewood, Ill.: Irwin, 1968).

3. Richard Rose, "The Programme Approach to the Growth of Government" (Paper prepared for the American Political Science Association Annual Meeting, Chicago, 1–4 Sept. 1983).

4. Brian Barry, *Does Democracy Cause Inflation?*, Brookings Project on the Politics and Sociology of Global Inflation, Sept. 1978, 53.

5. James M. Buchanan and Richard E. Wagner, *Democracy in Deficit: The Political Legacy of Lord Keynes* (New York: Academic Press, 1977), 125.

6. Ibid., 94.

7. Barry, 34–35.

8. See Aaron Wildavsky, *How to Limit Government Spending* (Berkeley: University of California Press, 1980).

9. William A. Niskanen, *Bureaucracy and Representative Government* (Chicago: Aldine-Atherton, 1971).

10. On fiscal illusion, see Richard E. Wagner, "Revenue Structure, Fiscal Illusion and Budgetary Choice," *Public Choice* 24 (Spring 1976): 45–61.

11. Gordon Tulloch, "What Is to Be Done?" in *Budgets and Bureaucrats: The Sources of Government Growth*, Thomas E. Borcherding, ed. (Durham, N.C.: Duke University Press, 1977), 285.

12. William J. Baumol, "Macroeconomics of Unbalanced Growth: The Anatomy of the Urban Crisis," *American Economic Review* 57 (June 1967): 415–26.

13. Two sophisticated studies of the causes of governmental growth are Daniel Tarschys, "The Growth of Public Expenditures: Nine Modes of Explanation," *Scandinavian Political Studies* 10 (1975): 29; and Richard Rose and Guy Peters, *Can Government Go Bankrupt?* (New York: Basic Books, 1978).

14. William H. Ricker, *The Cause of Public Growth* (Rochester: University of Rochester, 1978), 24–28.

15. Alexander Hamilton, John Jay, and James Madison, *The Federalist* (New York: Random House, Modern Library, 1937), 60–61.

16. Samuel H. Beer, "In Search of a New Public Philosophy," in *The New American Political System*, Anthony King, ed. (Washington, D.C.: American Enterprise Institute, 1978).

17. See "Policy as Its Own Cause," in Aaron Wildavsky, *Speaking Truth to Power* (Boston: Little, Brown, 1979), chap. 4.

18. See "The Transformation of Budgetary Norms" in Aaron Wildavsky, *The Politics of the Budgetary Process*, 4th ed. (Boston: Little, Brown, 1983), xv–xxxi.

19. A persuasive essay is by W. Irwin Gillespie, "Fools' Gold: The Quest for a Method of Evaluating Government Spending," in *The Public Evaluation of Government Spending*, ed. G. Bruce Doern and Allan M. Maslove (Toronto: Institute for Research on Public Policy, 1979), 39–60.

Managing Defense Expenditures

FRED THOMPSON

Most of the attention given to the Grace Commission report[1] has focused on the numbers—on the meaning, validity, and accuracy of its savings estimates.[2] So far as the Department of Defense (DOD) is concerned, this focus is regrettable. In the first place, total defense outlays appear to be fairly insensitive to program content. No matter what happens to the Grace Commission's proposals, defense outlays will increase in real terms for the next several years. Even if all of the proposals were adopted and successfully implemented, the savings would amount to less than 5 percent of annual defense outlays. Of course, several of the commission's proposals could lead to increased military effectiveness—more efficient investment in weapons and support systems, increased readiness and sustainability, and perhaps even a better match between the military-force structure and logistical-support capabilities, on the one hand, and foreign-policy objectives and overseas commitments, on the other. Given the current gap between the United States's defense strategy—i.e., raising, equipping, organizing, and using the military forces in support of political objectives—and its foreign-policy commitments, such an outcome would be reassuring indeed. Unfortunately, this happy outcome is largely hostage to the way DOD and Congress do business.

In the second place, because there are no numbers to be found there, most commentators have simply skipped over the sections of the report concerned with the management role of the Office of the Secretary of Defense (OSD) and the DOD management climate. Yet these are likely to be the most valuable portions of the report. On reflection, the reasons for their value are apparent. In many respects the DOD is unique:

1. It is by far the United States's largest and most complex organization. It employs more than 3 million people, over 60 percent of all Federal personnel. It spends about $200 billion a year (in 1984 dollars), over 25 percent of total Federal outlays. And it operates over 5,600 installations around the world.

2. Military leadership and tradition are critical to the capacity of the DOD to protect and defend the United States. Military leadership is not entirely or

even primarily a managerial role (one does not "manage" men into combat; they must be led). Military tradition constrains reorganization and personnel options to a considerable degree.

3. Because of its size and distinctive mission, the DOD is the sole customer of many of its private-sector suppliers. Monopsony implies the elaboration of idiosyncratic transactional arrangements. Because the DOD is unique, lessons learned by managing and operating other organizations do not apply to it. Hence, the Grace Commission's proposals generally make the most sense when they deal with problems common to all organizations (e.g., asset management) and the least when they deal with problems specific to the DOD (e.g., management of uniformed personnel or research and development acquisitions). All organizations must make policy, align their structure with their strategy, design and implement managerial controls, and allocate responsibility and authority. Consequently, the Grace Commission report addresses these issues with special insight, eloquence, and urgency.

The Grace Commission Diagnosis

The commission's criticism of the DOD in general and OSD in particular is quite straightforward: the DOD has not confronted these issues. Because top managers in the OSD have failed to perform the functions of top management—planning, organizing, staffing, and organizational development—they have by default been forced to assume lower-level management functions—operating, controlling, and budgeting. Thus overwhelmed by administrative detail, top managers in the OSD have no time to perform their proper functions. As a result, the DOD has become turgid, sluggish, and burdened with offices, departments, and installations that are no longer vital, and managers have no clear idea of their responsibilities and constantly bicker over who should do what. According to the Grace Commission report:

> Government, and DoD in particular, does not delegate authority well. The impact of holding authority at the top of the organization . . . is to weaken the entire organization. The lower levels do not create or innovate. They respond to the hierarchy rather than propose and initiate; they . . . avoid risks . . . . The upper levels of the organization become overloaded. They respond quite naturally by adding deputies and assistants . . . [and] layers to the organization, and this diffuses authority and responsibility even further.
>
> This is in direct contrast to private sector experience which has clearly demonstrated that the effectiveness of a large, complex organization improves when authority is delegated down into the organization along with responsibility. Decisions then are made by those with either the most pertinent knowledge of the situation or with the highest stake in the outcome of the decisions.[3]

The Grace Commission is also critical of certain excuses given for the failure of OSD's top managers to perform top-management functions:

> If the top managers do not have time to plan ahead, and to set goals and manage

by objectives, how can they possibly expect their subordinate managers to do so? We were told repeatedly that goal setting was more difficult in government because the profit motive was absent. Our conclusion is that, because there is no profit motive and because there is such a high turnover in top management, there is far greater need for long-term goal setting in government than in the private sector.[4]

Nevertheless, while the commission criticized the OSD's excuses for its inattention to strategic planning and organizational structure and its consequent failure to delegate authority, it blamed neither the secretary of defense nor his predecessors for this state of affairs. It is clear that each incumbent and his subordinates have been constrained by equally shortsighted, often externally imposed, piecemeal solutions to earlier organizational problems. Those solutions define current problems and limit the available solutions. The cumulative consequences of these earlier decisions were probably never contemplated and were certainly never sought. As P. D. Larkey observed, no one acquires cirrhosis of the liver by choice; it is acquired one sip at a time over an extended period.

The fact is that responsibility cannot be delegated by fiat. Decentralization requires prior clarification of the purpose, function, or product of each organizational unit, procedures for setting goals and incentives, and an information system that links each of these centers of responsibility to the goals of the organization as a whole. When an organization lacks direction and discipline, decentralization provides an ideal environment for the pursuit of parochial self-interest to the detriment of the organization as a whole. In DOD this propensity is most visible in the behavior of the uniformed services, but parochialism permeates the organization.

Unfortunately, OSD has no authority to redesign DOD into an efficient and effective operation. As the Grace Commission pointed out, where the secretary of defense had the authority to act, he has acted. In both the Defense Logistics Agency and the Defense Mapping Agency, the two largest operating units under the direct authority of the OSD, the commission observed experienced senior managers, clear objectives, effective decentralization, and high performance levels.

Although OSD cannot redesign DOD, it can decide where certain decisions will be made. When subordinates cannot be trusted to make sound decisions or to understand the implications of their decisions, the locus of decision making shifts upward, as it has in OSD. Indeed, this shifting of responsibility is a recurring problem in most organizations. Superiors are more capable of recognizing their own advantages than they are of recognizing their subordinates' advantages. One of the major aims of managerial training is learning how to overcome this bias. In the DOD, structural problems make it almost overwhelming.

Its Prescription

The Grace Commission report proposed a radical redesign of OSD/DOD. Its key recommendations included:

1. Reorganization of the civilian management functions of the OSD, perhaps along the lines of the DOD program budget categories, with separate deputy secretaries for production and R&D acquisitions.

2. Careful delineation of organizational units performing line and staff functions.

3. Further pruning of decision making and review committees.

4. Elimination of the civilian military departments: air force, army, and navy.

5. Reorganization and redefinition of the role of Joint Chiefs of Staff (JCS).

6. OSD assumption of responsibility for the delivery of civilian support services: base support operations, wholesale warehousing, traffic management, contract administration, audit, direct health care, and overseas military sales.

This last recommendation would consolidate many of the functions currently performed by the services under the direct authority of OSD. Consolidation, however, is not inconsistent with the commission's endorsement of decentralization. Rather, the report concludes that, so far as civilian support services are concerned, decentralization along service lines makes no sense — that it would be better to organize them on regional or geographic lines.

This conclusion may also be read as an implicit criticism of the procurement decentralization program adopted by Secretary of Defense Caspar Weinberger as part of the so-called Carlucci Initiatives. This program has trimmed the power of central planning units in the OSD and increased the role of the individual service secretaries in the systems acquisition process. The commission did not challenge the thrust of the program, though it observed that "after more than a year, the Initiatives are still mostly top-level talk and grass roots inaction. What has been said by the Pentagon policy makers is not being done. This is sad. . . . Most managers in industry and government alike believe that [many of] the changes . . . proposed by these initiatives . . . will be helpful in reducing the cost . . . of major weapons systems."[5]

The report also hints at a similar dissatisfaction with military organization by noting that a dominant theme of Eisenhower reorganization (Defense Reorganization Act of 1958) was the reorganization of combat command along regional lines. In theory, the area commands created during the Eisenhower administration were to be the principal instruments of United States defense policy, each using forces supplied by all four services. The services were to recruit, train, and equip forces for combat. Eisenhower believed that area commanders were best situated and motivated to plan operations, to carry out assigned combat missions, and to make trade-offs between force size and elements, readiness, sustainability, and investment levels. Furthermore, under this concept, to the extent that they were free to choose between forces offered by competing services, area commanders would have been able to exploit fully the potential benefits of interservice rivalry. However, these benefits would have been realized only if financial or budgetary resources had been provided to the services through the area commands, and the act did not establish this system. Consequently, area commanders are forced to take whatever forces the services choose to supply, and the services retain full administrative control over those forces. Indeed, most area commands are now identified with a single service even where forces from other services are assigned to them.

The Grace Commission report did not explicity endorse the logic of the Eisenhower reorganization, but it did stress that externally imposed organizational constraints severely burden OSD's efforts to use interservice rivalry to advantage (the Grace Commission recognized the benefits that can be gained from intraorganizational rivalry) and to exacerbate its counterproductive aspects.

Some might conclude that the commission overemphasized these constraints, that the report gives too much importance to organizational issues. Eliminating these constraints will not automatically produce a better alignment between military purpose and organizational structure; nor will a good organization guarantee a sound, effectively implemented defense policy. But DOD labors under bad organization, and bad organization makes both wise policy and effective implementation impossible. S. E. Huntington correctly observed that: "Criticism has been directed at many aspects of Defense department organization, including, for instance, procedures for weapons procurement. Varied as the critcisms have been, however, they have tended to focus on the strategic side of the defense establishment—i.e., how decisions are made on overall policy, on the development of military forces, programs, and weapons, and on the use of military force. Those criticisms tend to articulate in a variety of ways a single underlying theme: that there is a gap between defense organization and strategic purpose. This gap is the result of the failure to achieve the purpose of organizational reforms instituted 25 years ago."[6]

Right Disease, Wrong Patient?

The problem with the Grace Commission's diagnosis is not that it is wrong but that it may be irrelevant. To carry out the prescribed reforms, Congress would have to delegate OSD enough authority to manage its operations and to allocate and deploy its resources. Congress has shown no predisposition to do that. On the contrary, Congress has increasingly used its legislative and fiscal powers to deny operational authority to executive branch managers. Indeed, to say that government does not delegate authority well is largely to say that Congress does not delegate authority at all.

Centralized authority is not principally characterized by policy direction from the top, hierarchically established goals, or even central control procedures—all of these may be characteristics of effectively decentralized organizations. Rather, centralized authority is characterized by *ex ante* controls (i.e., rules and regulations that specify what must be done, where, how, and by whom, and what must not be done) as opposed to *ex post* controls (i.e., incentives). Congress has always been predisposed to rely on *ex ante* controls: the organization of OSD, the structure and functions of the JCS, and the missions of the uniformed services are all written into law, as are policies governing staffing, promotion, termination, and compensation of DOD personnel. Recently, however, Congress has increased the rigor and specificity of these controls, especially concerning the military budget and procurement regulations.

Budgets in the private sector are generally used to decentralize authority and responsibility. While most large firms produce comprehensive operating reports describing most aspects of the performance of responsibility centers and programs, their budgets seldom contain many details. Nor should they. In this context, the purpose of a budget is to establish performance targets that are high enough to elicit the best efforts from an organization's operating managers. Conceivably, such budgets could contain a single number for each responsibility center (e.g., a sales quota, a unit cost standard, or a profit or return on investment target).

In contrast, the legislative budget tends to centralize authority. For the most part, operating managers in DOD can do only what the Defense Appropriations Act says they can do; they cannot do what they are not authorized to do. Furthermore, the legislative budget focuses exclusively on resources to be acquired by individual organizational units and how they are to be used—on objects-of-expenditure or line items, rather than performance targets. Congress could delegate the authority to manage resources to OSD, by reducing the individual line items to a handful and by delegating substantial reprogramming authority (i.e., the authority to transfer funds between programs/line items and time periods) to OSD. Instead, it has done the reverse. In fiscal year 1960, the Defense Appropriations Act contained about 200 individual line items; in 1983 there were more than 1,200. Moreover, about two-thirds of these line-items are now placed in the "special interest" category. In these cases, DOD is denied even the minuscule reprogramming authority ($2 million on R&D programs and $5 million on procurement) elsewhere delegated to it. Furthermore, when Congress fails to pass an appropriations act before the beginning of the fiscal year—as is usually the case—DOD remains locked into the previous year's spending schedule on each line item.

The legislative budget now leaves the DOD little flexibility to manage its resources in a cost-effective fashion. What DOD can do is sacrifice performance, stretch out acquisitions programs, and play games with Congress—which is, of course, what it does. While these behaviors are perhaps evidence of managerial initiative within DOD/OSD, they are not perceived that way by Congress. Consequently, congressional dissatisfaction with what it views as failures, on the part of DOD in particular and the executive branch in general, has led to still greater congressional involvement in the details of administration and the elaboration of ever-stricter and more detailed *ex ante* controls.

Not only does Congress decide what DOD will buy, but it also tells DOD how to buy. More than 60 percent of DOD outlays are for the procurement of goods and services supplied by the private sector. These acquisitions are directly or indirectly governed by at least thirty public laws; the regulations that have been elaborated to implement these laws comprise over 8,000 pages of the *Federal Reg-*

ister. Morever, the relevant portions of the *Code of Federal Regulations* increased by one-third during the 1970s, while the sections of the *Federal Register* relevant to defense acquisitions more than doubled.

These regulations are supposed to protect the Treasury and also to ensure other outcomes deemed worthwhile by Congress—that most constituencies are recipients of defense spending, that small and minority businesses get their "fair share" of contracts and subcontracts, that contractors maintain proper security and comply with the standards of Occupational Safety and Health Administration, Environmental Protection Agency, Federal Employees Pay Council, and other agencies. However, the Grace Commission correctly observed that these regulations frequently prevent the DOD from making timely and efficient acquisitions, deny suppliers prompt payment, and result in substantial compliance costs. The commission also provided an implicit estimate of these costs. Most large firms and other governments and jurisdictions realize savings of 3 to 15 percent by purchasing petroleum products on long-term contracts awarded by competitive bid. However, because of the costs of complying with cumbersome, legislatively mandated procurement regulations, many petroleum-product suppliers refuse to offer discounts to DOD. Consequently, DOD pays market prices for about 80 percent of its petroleum products. This implies that the cost of complying with procurement regulations represents 5 to 10 percent of the cost of supplying services to the DOD, or $8 billion to $15 billion annually. Of course, these regulations frequently make sense, and the costs of complying with them must often be borne to avoid even worse outcomes. The point is not that complex procurement regulations are unnecessary but that Congress denies DOD the discretion to determine where to exercise judgment and where to exercise specific rules.

Finally, Congress has long reserved the right to review all DOD proposals to close domestic military bases or installations. However, during the mid-1970s it increased the burden of proof that DOD must bear if it is to justify closure. The Grace Commission report concludes: "The legislation of the mid-1970s has had the effect of making it extremely difficult to close or realign bases. Little has been done for almost four years, even though previous secretaries and top OSD officials . . . believe the current base structure is underutilized."[7]

If centralization within OSD is regrettable (though bad organization is probably better than disorganization), centralization of managerial authority in the hands of Congress is a disaster. In the first place, Congress's distinctive competence is not management. Its proper function is the aggregation and articulation of interests and values, a function it performs best when it deals with broad national issues that demand the attention and scrutiny of the majority of its members. In the second place, the task is overwhelming. Despite the 600 percent increase in budget line items and in witnesses called to testify in committee hearings on the defense budget between 1960 and 1983, Congress still holds only one hour of hearings for each $100 million it spends on defense.

To cope with this increased workload, Congress has increased its internal division of labor and jurisdiction—in 1960, twenty committees and subcommittees in both houses heard testimony on the military budget; in 1983, defense witnesses testified in hearings before ninety-six committees and subcommittees. Unfortunately, undisciplined decentralization is just as conducive to narrow self-seeking in Congress as it is in any other organization. One of the well-recognized consequences of the progressive devolution of authority in Congress—from the party leadership to committee chairmen, then to subcommittee chairmen, and finally to the individual members—has been an increased responsiveness to special constituency interests and the rise of pork barrel politics. As Congress has immersed itself in ever-greater administrative detail, it has also given less attention to what public money buys for the citizenry at large and more attention to how and where it is spent and who gets it.

Military R&D and Procurement Programs

The effect of the shift in the locus of operational authority—first to OSD, then to Congress, and finally to the subcommittee level of Congress or lower—is perhaps most evident in military R&D and procurement programs, as are the consequences of constituency politics. Decisions to initiate, expand, or terminate programs are now routinely made by Congress rather than by OSD. Most students of the procurement process believe that an optimal R&D/acquisition strategy would feature a high degree of experimentation at the concept exploration and testing phase of the systems-development process, carry at least two competitive systems to prototype development, and ruthlessly select systems for procurement from those available for production, producing a relatively small number of new systems at optimal production rates. This process is called the "acquisition funnel." What Congress chooses to do is almost the complete opposite. It is critical of experimentation at each phase of the R&D process; apparently Congress would prefer each systems-development program to contemplate a distinct military mission. Congress also tends to buy every system available for production, even those OSD has tried to kill. Since it cannot afford to produce every system at optimal volumes or rates, almost all of its purchases involve inefficient production rates and therefore excessive unit costs.

This pattern may be wasteful, but it is perfectly rational from the standpoint of constituency interests. R&D projects generate relatively few jobs in a small number of congressional districts; systems procurement produces a large number of jobs in many districts. Production stretch-outs affect unit costs and annual outlays, but they have minimal effects on direct employment levels. Of course, the same level of procurement spending at efficient rates would generate roughly the same number of jobs in about the same number of districts. But the logic of special interest politics tends to be blind to this fact. People are far more likely to participate in the political process to protect what they have than on behalf of a potential opportunity.

Before 1980, OSD responded to congressional propensities with heroic efforts to defend the acquisition funnel and achieved some notable successes (e.g., the lightweight fighter program or the army's multiple launch rocket systems program). However, OSD's efforts were not generally successful. Typically, OSD would propose a responsible R&D and acquisition budget that featured many experiments and few systems for procurement; Congress would then modify that budget by pruning the number of experiments (particularly those involving the greatest technological risk), by increasing the number of systems procured, and by reducing the procurement rates on most of the systems proposed for acquisition by DOD. Over the long run this pattern of interaction between OSD and Congress substantially eroded the United States's military-capital stock.

Top officials of the Reagan administration have apparently abandoned the largely futile defense of the funnel — although it retains a prominent place in the Carlucci Initiatives. Rather, they appear to be trying to exploit Congress's propensities to rebuild the depleted defense capital stock. Having observed that congressional appropriations are a function of DOD requests (Congress influences what DOD will buy but exercises little control over total outlay levels), OSD has in recent years simply asked for everything, including a substantial number of systems that previous administrations had opposed (e.g., AV-8 Harrier) and several systems that are still in the preproduction phase of development.

The payoff to this strategy is illustrated by the cruise missile program. Previous administrations would have likely tried to develop two systems and recommended procurement of one of them. Congress would then have supported the production of a smaller number of both. OSD actually supported the development of five distinct systems performing five distinct missions and requested funds to deploy all five systems, and that is what Congress approved. While none of these systems is currently being produced at an optimal rate, DOD may get twice as many cruise missiles under its current legislative strategy as it would have under its earlier, more prudent approach.

The payoff to DOD's current strategy is also evident when it operates under the authority of continuing resolution (i.e., when Congress fails to pass a defense appropriation act before the beginning of the fiscal year — something it has failed to do in thirty of the past thirty-three years). Efficient production rates imply a moderately high rate of production startups and shutdowns. Under continuing resolution, existing programs must shut down on schedule, but new procurement programs cannot start up until they have been approved. However, under the current OSD strategy, nearly everything that can be produced is already in production and almost no program is scheduled for termination. Consequently, procurement rates are not substantially affected by Congress's inability to enact a budget on schedule.

Furthermore, DOD has resurrected some of the budget ploys it abandoned during the McNamara era, when they were used primarily by the services against OSD (e.g., the "Washington Monument" game, in which DOD claims that failure to provide the desired budget will mean the sacrifice of its highest priority activities; "foot-in-the-door," often combined with the negotiation of high project termination penalties; "coercive deficiency," in which DOD exhausts outlay authority on high-priority projects early enough in the fiscal year to demand a supplemental appropriation, and "take-it-or-leave-it," in which DOD presents Congress with a single price-quantity production acquisition option). Not surprisingly, the Grace Commission was appalled by the incoherence and waste that have resulted from OSD's attempts to exploit congressional propensities and primly criticized DOD for paying more attention to what Congress will buy than to the cost-effectiveness of its proposals.[8]

The commission concluded that since Congress has refused to kill production programs, DOD should:

- Install self-disciplinary limits on the number of new weapons programs started each year.[9]
- Subject every new program to in-depth affordability review over the projected life cycle of the program.
- Review new-start affordability in relation to all other new starts being proposed and programs already in the system.
- Base affordability on [realistic] estimates of DOD total budget resources and price escalation for the ten-year planning period.[10]

Undoubtedly, OSD would prefer to execute its rebuilding program in a cost-effective fashion; taken as a whole, perhaps Congress would, too. But given actual circumstances, OSD will continue to take what Congress appropriates. DOD could act unilaterally, but it will not; neither will Congress.

Prospects for Cooperation

If one assumes that Congress is as much a victim of its own earlier decisions as OSD and that it never contemplated the indirect or longer-term consequences of its reliance on *ex ante* controls, there may be some hope for improvement. Such an assumption is consistent with claims made by most members of Congress that they would gladly relinquish their involvement with the details of administration, if only DOD would demonstrate the competence and the motivation to manage its own affairs. Furthermore, most legislators (unlike their staffers) appear to have a profound respect for their own limited capabilities to manage DOD and to be fully cognizant of their inability to resist special-interest demands when they are forced to do so by OSD failures.

In any case, if this assumption is valid, the situation is a classic prisoner's dilemma. That is, both OSD and Congress would be better off if they cooperated—if Congress were to delegate to OSD the authority as well as the responsibility it needs to manage its own affairs and if the DOD did not use that flexibility to extract higher appropriations from Congress. Unfortunately, cooperation requires trust and, based on recent experience, Congress has no reason to trust the DOD. Nor, if history is any guide, will DOD trust Congress. DOD has chosen to defend its activities piecemeal, because of the fear that, if

Congress did not have to face the tough realities of cutting specific programs, it would make across-the-board budget cuts, rationalizing its action by the claim that DOD could easily be 5 or 10 percent more efficient. Given this choice on the part of DOD, detailed congressional involvement in the management of DOD resources is hardly surprising.

However, in this case the past may not be the best predictor of the future. Historical analogy overlooks two considerations. First, Congress seems nearly as committed to rebuilding United States defenses as the administration. In the near term, the prospect of an across-the-board cut is an unlikely one. Second, OSD is no longer playing the game to lose. What was a winning game for Congress during the 1970s and a losing game for DOD has become a losing game for both, given Congress's commitment to rebuilding United States defenses. Game theorists say it is easier to convert lose-lose situations to win-win than it is to convert lose-win situations to win-win. This conversion, however, requires a contract or treaty that would address the legitimate concerns of both Congress and OSD. Not coincidentally, within a few months of the publication of the Grace Commission report on DOD, the Committee for Economic Development (CED) presented its recommendations on reform of the Federal budget process, which included the outline of just such a treaty.[11] The CED's key proposal is a multiyear legislative budget oriented primarily to total obligation authority (initially providing real increases of, perhaps, 3 to 4 percent a year) and containing guidelines to the allocation of resources between major programs and budget categories. Under multiyear budgeting, Congress would still engage in an annual review of defense spending. For example, given the three-year legislative budget suggested by the CED, Congress would annually add a fourth year to replace the year expiring. However, as J. S. Gansler observed, "this overlap, unlike the current overlap, would force both the executive and the legislative branch to plan for the longer term — something that neither is able to do today."[12] Furthermore, if Congress denied itself the opportunity to tinker with individual line items (perhaps by requiring a two-thirds majority in both houses to reopen the budget issue for either the current fiscal year or the first out-year and by collapsing the number of individual line items to a manageable number), it would provide itself with the opportunity to do what it was designed to do, to "analyze the correlation between national policy objectives and the budget — something else that is not done today."[13] By tying its own hands, Congress would also preempt strategic gaming on the part of DOD. Additional proposals might include:

1. Full authority to execute the multiyear budget should be delegated to OSD and not to the uniformed services. OSD must have both greater authority and flexibility if it is to manage efficient and effective programs.

2. Congress should require OSD to provide it with far better operational reports — including information on the performance of each major program and program element: capabilities, readiness, and sustainability status of each of the regional commands; and comparative data on the cost-effectiveness with which each of the uniformed services have performed their missions as force suppliers.

Flexibility is a necessary but not a sufficient condition for improved management of DOD. Congress must demand evidence that delegation of authority has resulted in higher military performance. DOD must supply that evidence — otherwise, Congress may reassert the panoply of *ex ante* controls under which OSD currently labors. (Indeed, given the conditions outlined here, the threat that *ex ante* controls will be reasserted if DOD performance is unsatisfactory is very probably Congress's most powerful *ex post* control.)

The multiyear budget provides a framework for the implementation of the Grace Commission's proposals on OSD/DOD management climate and organization. Such a contract would address the legitimate concerns of both Congress and DOD. The real problem is negotiating it. The OMB director might effectively manage the executive branch's side of the issue. However, the military appropriations subcommittee chairs would be the obvious spokespersons for Congress — they would also be almost the only members of Congress who would stand to lose from such a contract. This would not appear to augur well for the prospects of negotiating such a contract, but even subcommittee chairs can act contrary to their own narrow self-interest where matters of national importance are concerned (e.g., former Senator Howard Cannon and trucking deregulation).

Conclusion

Defense spending is both overcontrolled and out of control. It is governed by too many rules and not enough (or the wrong kinds of) policy direction. Obviously, this situation cannot be corrected by the imposition of more rules; further congressional attempts to manage DOD will merely exacerbate an already bad situation. Carried to its logical conclusion, the Grace Commission report may be read as a plea to Congress to base its relationship with DOD on far-sighted, self-denying ordinances that would exempt DOD operations from detailed *prior* scrutiny or control. It is also a plea to OSD to accept the responsibility that goes with the authority to manage its own affairs. These are timely pleas. Cost-effectiveness is the consequence of, not the cause of, effective management. The world in which we live is dangerous, our treasure is finite, and we can ill-afford less than the best from our defense efforts, let alone the instability, waste, and incoherence that we now have.

NOTES

1. President's Private Sector Survey on Cost Control (Grace Commission), *Task Force Report on the Office of the Secretary of Defense* (13 July 1983).

2. See, e.g., General Accounting Office — Congressional Budget Office, *Analysis of the Grace Commission's Recommendations on Cost Control* (March 1984).

3. Grace Commission report, 47–48.

4. Ibid., 49.

5. Ibid., 58.

6. S. E. Huntington, "Defense Organization and Military Strategy," *Public Interest*, no. 75 (Spring 1984): 21.

7. Grace Commission report, 107.

8. Ibid., 182.

9. Ibid., 178.

10. Ibid., 85.

11. Committee for Economic Development, *Strengthening the Federal Budget Process: A Requirement for Effective Fiscal Control* (June 1983).

12. Jacques S. Gansler, "Reforming the Defense Budget Process," *Public Interest*, no. 75 (Spring 1984): 68.

13. Ibid., 69.

Reforming Federal Pension Programs

ROBERT W. SCHLECK

As part of its overall examination of ways to reduce Federal expenditures, the President's Private Sector Survey on Cost Control (PPSS), or the Grace Commission, reviewed the operations of three Federal employee retirement systems: the Civil Service Retirement System (CSRS), the Military Retirement System (MRS) (these two systems cover 98 percent of all Federal employees), and the much smaller Foreign Service Retirement System (FSRS), along with the federally administered private-sector pension plan for railroad workers, the Railroad Retirement Board (RRB). This sample was selected out of a total of more than fifty Federal retirement programs.[1]

The Grace Commission concluded that the CSRS, MRS, and FSRS grant benefits and sustain costs three to six times greater than the most generous private-sector retirement plans. They provide retirement, along with unreduced benefits at earlier ages and, through generous postretirement cost-of-living adjustment (COLA) provisions, have attempted to ensure complete protection for beneficiaries against inflation.

Stating its commitment to the principle that Federal pensions should be fair and equitable, the commission contended that the existing plans are both overly generous and unduly costly and that even after the adoption and implementation of proposed revisions the systems would still be more generous to recipients than retirement provisions covering the great majority of private-sector employees. Pointing out that these private-sector workers are also the taxpayers who finance the public-sector plans, PPSS queried whether they should be asked to support public-employee retirement arrangements three to six times more generous than they themselves can expect to receive.

To illustrate the magnitude of the problem, in the ten-year period 1973–82 the Federal government disbursed more than $200 billion in benefits to civil service and armed services retirees. Over the coming decade, the aggregate of such outlays are projected at $500 billion, two and one-half times as great an outlay. According to PPSS findings, if Federal employees' retirement benefits had been equivalent to typical pension plans for the *Fortune* top 500 companies, the cost to taxpayers over the past decade for the two largest public retirement systems, CSRS and MRS, would have been reduced by $103 billion. Enactment of such arrangements could lower the burden on the public purse by no less than $314 billion during the succeeding ten-year period.

As more or less the "punch-line" of its findings, the commission pointed out that in fiscal year 1983 the Federal government spent at least $39.6 billion in those areas of its public-employee pension plans covered by commission recommendations for revisions, with this spending slated to rise to $227.7 billion by the year 2000, should present arrangements be continued. Implementing the commission recommendations, it is claimed, would lower such expenditures to $150.6 billion by the end of the century, a savings of $77.1 billion, or 33.9 percent.

Present Provisions of Retirement Plans

The particularly generous provisions of the Federal retirement systems were originally enacted in the 1920s to compensate for civil-service and armed-services salaries, which were not considered competitive with the salaries of private-sector workers. Rather than incurring immediate costs for raising salaries, the problem of noncomparability was solved by granting more generous pensions, the burden of which could be postponed until the benefit claims of currently working employees would come due.

Since these retirement arrangements were adopted, however, the Federal Salary Reform Act of 1962 mandated pay comparability between Federal employees and private-sector workers; and since 1970 the uniformed-services remuneration has increased more rapidly than civilian pay. A 1983 General Accounting Office (GAO) report concluded that armed-forces personnel were then paid approximately 10 percent more than Federal civilian workers of equal rank (including bed, board, and health benefits). No compensating alterations were made in public-sector pensions, however, for either civilian or military personnel, so that both — the military in particular — now enjoy the best of both worlds.

Currently, both civil-service and uniformed-services retirement plans provide benefits that in most respects are considerably more generous than those for state and local public workers as well as private-sector employees. It was calculated that a Federal civil-service employee with a final three-year average salary of $30,000 could expect to obtain $670,770 more in pension benefits over a twenty-year retirement period than a similarly situated private-sector worker. A 1980 Congressional Budget Office (CBO) report concluded that while Federal civil-service employees, with their 7 percent contribution rate, pay in more toward their pension programs than they would under a two-part private-sector retirement program (private pension plus social security), they obtain such disproportionately greater benefits that the cost to the government may be considered excessive.[2] For fiscal year 1983, expenditures for the CSRS retirement and disability fund alone ($21 billion) ranked this operation fourth among the "entitlement programs," after social security ($165 billion), Medicare ($56 billion), and unemployment compensation ($31 billion).

While the civil-service pension plan is more liberal than arrangements made for private-sector workers, the Foreign Service Retirement System (FSRS) is more generous than civil-service provisions. The government's estimated budgeted cost of FSRS equaled 87 percent of payroll in fiscal 1983; in contrast, the cost for CSRS was 30 percent of pay.

Uniformed-services benefits are far and away the most liberal of all, except in the area of vesting of benefits (none may be vested before completing twenty years of service). The Grace Commission concluded that such benefits are no less than six times more generous than the best private-sector retirement plans. They are slightly more generous than those for Federal air-traffic controllers and, with some exceptions, state and local police officers and firefighters, and generally exceed the benefits of armed-forces retirees in most other countries.

In keeping with the general provisions of MRS, expenditures for this retirement plan have expanded dramatically in recent years, nearly quadrupling (in real terms) between 1963 and 1984. They are projected to rise further from the present $16.5 billion to $19.4 billion a year by the year 2000 and to $22.4 billion by the year 2043 (again, measured in constant dollars).

Specific Benefit Areas

There are three major factors contributing to higher benefit levels and higher costs of Federal retirement plans: (1) provisions for early retirement ages, (2) postretirement cost-of-living adjustments (COLAs), which have aimed at full inflation protection, and (3) liberal benefit formulas to determine the amounts of annuities. Federal civil-service employees may retire as early as age fifty-five, if they have thirty years in government service, with virtually unreduced benefits. In contrast, private-pension and social-security benefits are usually based on retirement at age sixty-five. While most private plans do permit early retirement, benefits are reduced, typically by 3.5 percent for each year from age sixty-four down to age sixty, and by 4 percent for each year below age sixty. Persons younger than sixty-two are ineligible for social-security benefits, and for those between sixty-two and sixty-four these benefits are reduced by 6.66 percent a year.

The Grace Commission found that 63.6 percent of all male CSRS employees retired before age sixty-three, compared with only one-fifth of private-sector workers. The Office of Personnel Management reported, as of 20 September 1982, that only 10 percent of employees eligible to retire before sixty remained in active service at age sixty.

The seven additional years during which the CSRS provides actuarially unreduced benefits (along with postretirement cost-of-living adjustments) are the major cause of the 1,891 percent increase in civil-service retirement costs over the 1960–81 period, more than nine times the rate of inflation over this time span.

Permitting members of the uniformed services to retire after twenty years of service, with initial annuities equal to half of the retirees' high three-year average salary, is perhaps the factor most singled out in critical appraisals of the military retirement system. Average retirement ages were found to be forty-two for enlisted personnel (after twenty-two years of service) and forty-six for commissioned officers (after twenty-five years), with retirement in some cases occurring as early as age thirty-five, and with many retirees receiving pensions for longer periods than their years of active service.

The Grace Commission report found that 26 percent of military service retirees are still in their late thirties; 87 percent of those collecting pensions are still of working age; and the average retiree, who worked only twenty-three years, collects a pension for thirty-two years. The point has been emphasized that failing to provide adequate incentives to serve beyond twenty years encourages early retirement. In this connection, the comments of Representative Barber B. Conable (R-N.Y.) appear noteworthy: "Any organization which gives its greatest incentives and rewards to those who leave it rather than to those who remain cannot be serious about the quality or morale of its employees or the effectiveness of their performance."[3]

The argument that the military should promote early retirement because it is a profession for the young and vigorous may no longer be entirely valid. Wars, it is claimed, are no longer waged exclusively, or even predominantly, by combat infantry, batteries of artillery, warships, or similar front-line formations. According to Admiral (retired) Hyman Rickover, there are few jobs in the military that cannot be adequately performed by persons over fifty-five, and only 5 percent of navy personnel performed duties requiring "youth and vigor."

A General Accounting Office (GAO) study found that among retiring enlisted personnel, 92 percent of their service had been spent on noncombat duty, while 80 percent of enlisted men had served twenty years without engaging in combat. According to the GAO, granting early retirement to all members of the uniformed services is an inefficient way to compensate for the minority of the armed forces whose duties are exceptionally demanding or hazardous. Moreover, Richard V. L. Cooper of the Rand Corporation argued that, given the complexity of modern military equipment and weapons systems, the use of experienced personnel would effect substantial cost savings,[4] while a 1981 Brookings Institution report concluded that the United States military establishment's emphasis on youth and vigor has yielded armed forces too inexperienced to operate and maintain today's sophisticated matériel.

The particularly generous retirement provisions for foreign-service personnel (unreduced pensions at age fifty with twenty years of service; at age sixty with five years of work time) constitute much less of a financing problem in view of the comparatively small size of both foreign-service staff and payroll. Some also argue that unusual amounts of emotional stress, coupled with danger to health and personal safety involved in overseas assignments, often result in premature "burnout" and make early retirement desirable for personnel and beneficial for the efficient operation of the service. However, the Grace Commission pointed out that it was not aware of any requirement of foreign-service employment rendering employees unable to perform duties at age fifty or even sixty. Moreover, as a general observation, while it may be conceded that the early burnout argument has some merit in the case of personnel posted in Teheran, Beirut, El Salvador, or, earlier, Vietnam, working in environments such as London, Paris, Bonn, Rome, Montreal, and Melbourne hardly involves more stress and danger than in many areas of the United States (and perhaps less in some cases).[5]

Cost-of-Living Adjustments (COLAs)

Generous cost-of-living adjustments (COLAs) to postretirement pension benefits have been an even greater factor than the early-retirement allowances in the spectacular burgeoning of Federal pension costs in recent years and, if left in their present form, would be the prime cause of estimated future increases. According to a 1982 Congressional Research Service (CRS) report, "the most costly feature of the CSRS is the full adjustment of benefits for annual changes in the Consumer Price Index (CPI). Actuaries estimate that every 1 percent increase in the CPI increases the costs of a fully indexed system such as the CSRS by 11 percent."[6]

Initially, adjustments were granted when the CPI increased by 3 percent, and then from 1969 to 1976 an additional sweetener, the "kicker," was authorized, raising payments by 1 percent more than the rise in the CPI. COLAs were given on 1 March and 1 September of each year in amounts equivalent to the CPI increase. Since 1981 the adjustments have been granted only once a year, but the 1982 Budget Reconciliation Act provided that, for the years 1983, 1984, and 1985, annuitants under age sixty-two who are not survivors or recipients of disability benefits would receive less than full COLA benefits. A 1981 report by the Congressional Budget Office, cited above, stated that about 89 percent of an estimated $10.1 billion increase in operating costs of the Civil Service Retirement System between 1981 and 1986 would result from the benefit increases derived from COLAs coming into effect between September 1981 and March 1986.

According to the Grace Commission, since 1968 the cost-of-living adjustments for Federal retirees have exceeded both increases in Federal general-schedule salaries and actual rises in the CPI. Thus, Federal employees who retired in 1968 would by 1982 have received three times their original annual annuity, while general-schedule Federal employees who are still working would have received only 2.3 times their average 1968 remuneration (if still employed in the same grade). This means that active employees obtained only about two-thirds of the increases granted to retired workers during this period. Further, 1982 Federal pensions were 7.2 percent higher than if the cost-of-living adjustments had actually matched the rise in the CPI.

One example of this kind of disproportionate increase in benefits was featured in a press report that documented the case of a Federal civil-service employee who retired in 1967 with a GS-14-level salary of $17,000 a year and who had by 1982, as a result of the numerous cost-of-living adjustments to his annuity, received a yearly pension of $29,000, an amount that the beneficiary himself reportedly indicated was "too much."[7]

As with the overall format of the Federal pension system, the intent of the COLA was to offset the supposedly uncompetitive Federal salary schedules and improve the government's ability to compete with private-sector firms in hiring and retaining qualified personnel. The manner in which the COLA provisions have developed, however, has given Federal retirees a distinct advantage over both Federal and private-sector workers.

Many private-sector retirement plans make no provisions for postretirement cost-of-living adjustments, and most of those systems that do make some arrangements do so only on an unsystematic, and not overly generous, basis. According to a 1982 survey (Hay Huggins, *Noncash Compensation Comparison*), cited in the findings of the Grace Commission, of a sample of 737 private pension plans, 40 percent make no adjustments, 52 percent provide increases only on a legally uncommitted ad hoc basis, and no more than 8 percent have formal COLA provisions, many of which limit the amount of allowable increases. Of the plans that do make some arrangements, the average increase is about one-third of the rise in the CPI. Only the social security portion of private-sector pensions have had the benefit of full CPI-related increases, and the Grace Commission concluded that the average estimated cost-of-living adjustments for private-sector retirees, based on a combination of private pension plans and social security, amount to just about 70 percent of the rise in the CPI.

Benefit Formulas

CSRS, MRS, and FSRS compute benefits on the basis of the high three-years of average salary, compared with a high five-year average usual in the private sector, while credit for years of service was found to be from 40 percent to 60 percent higher than in nongovernment employment. The CSR and MSR benefit formulas (1.5–2.0 percent for the former; 2.5 percent for the latter) compare to the 1.2 percent of pay per service year usually found in generous private-sector plans. As comparatively generous as the present situation may be, it is not as generous as it was in the past. Until 1980, benefit payments for armed-service retirees were based not on an average high three-years salary but on remuneration as of the final day of active service.

Double Dipping

While private-sector retirement usually entails a loss of job and salary, the earlier-age Federal retirement often permits retirees to begin a second career and thus qualify for a second (and at times a third) pension. For civil-service employees, these second-career options, which offer additional benefits from a private pension plan, often encourage early retirement. Moreover, while Federal civilian employees until recently could not qualify for social-security benefits on the basis of government service, some 70 to 80 percent of CSRS retirees qualify for at least some social-security payments because of employment in non-civil-service jobs.

Armed-service retirees can take particular advantage of these "double dipping" possibilities. Because they can, and in many cases do, opt for early retirement in their late thirties or early forties, they can then begin second careers that last twenty years or more. In addition, except for commissioned and warrant officers, military retirees — unlike Federal civilian retirees — can take employment in the Federal civil service without forgoing pension rights. Civil-service pensioners may begin a second Federal government career, but only at the cost of having their second salary reduced dollar-for-dollar by the amount of their first career civil-service pension.

There has been a growing tendency for retired military personnel to commence second careers in Federal civilian employment. Partial reports on retired uniformed-services personnel employed in Federal civilian positions conducted in 1976 found that 142,000 former service personnel were so employed, more than half as civilian employees of the Department of Defense. Moreover, when armed-forces retirees become eligible for social-security benefits at age sixty-two, there is no integration or offset of such benefits with their regular MRS annuity. They can and do receive a full pension and full social-security benefits, placing them in a rather uniquely favorable position vis-à-vis other Federal retirees as well as private-sector employees.

Disability Retirement

Federal civil-service employees have been eligible for disability retirement if they have had at least five years of service, are unable to perform satisfactorily and efficiently a particular function of their current positions, and are not qualified for reassignment to comparable positions in the same employing agency. Any member of the armed forces on active duty, whether regular or reserve, and without regard to length of service, is eligible for an annuity if rated at least 30 percent disabled under the Veterans Administration schedule for rating disabilities in line of duty.

According to the Grace Commission, the probability of Federal employees between ages thirty-one and fifty retiring under CSRS disability provisions was more than 50 percent greater than under private-sector stipulations. While Federal disability provisions have been tightened since the publication of the Grace Commission report, those who retired under the more lenient arrangements are contributing to the high CSRS operating costs. For example, at the end of fiscal year 1982, more than 384,000 civil-service retirees, nearly 27 percent of all CSRS pensioners, were drawing disability pensions.

A 1978 Tax Foundation study showed that the defects in the CSRS disability retirement provisions had made it so easy to qualify for such benefits that 95 percent of disability applications were being approved.[8] Disability retirees, many of whom were able to perform the duties required in other government positions, were free to refuse such reassignment and were given significant incentives to do so.

While all of the above is clearly advantageous to the government employee, particularly to members of the armed services, the Grace Commission concluded that it is certainly not in the best interest of the public employer and general taxpayer and should therefore be curtailed.

Financial Problems

In 1982, aggregate outlays for the more than fifty Federal pension systems reviewed by the Grace Commission amounted to $35 billion. For the two largest plans, the Civil Service Retirement System and the Military Retirement System, the expenditures were $34.4 billion. Costs were not only extremely high, but they were also rapidly increasing. Between 1970 and 1982, the CSRS and MRS outlays increased by an average of 16.3 percent a year, so that by 1982 disbursements amounted to more than six times those made in 1970. At this rate, costs double in less than five years. The 17.6 percent annual spending rise for the largest of the plans, the CSRS, during the 1970–82 period means that for this system costs double in slightly more than four years.

Viewed another way, the costliness of these retirement programs is evidenced by the fact that in 1982 they aggregated 8.7 times the total cost of running the Federal government in 1933. Specifically, financing problems of the Military Retirement System show that whereas in 1964 military pensions cost $1.2 billion, or 2 percent of the Department of Defense budget, by 1985 they were expected to cost $18 billion, or 8 percent of the total Defense budget. Already in 1983 more was spent on armed-forces retirement benefits than on new naval vessels or military aircraft for the air force. Moreover, these enormous expenditures are only part of the picture, because the government does not calculate total costs of the unfunded liability for its pension plans and thus seriously understates the amount of future costs involved in keeping the system solvent (unfunded liability represents monies that will have to be paid out by retirement plans at some future date for pension benefits, over and above future receipts and current assets). In the private sector, firms avert this problem by contributing currently more money than necessary to cover present costs.

Traditional methods employed by the Office of Personnel Management, based on provisions of PL 91–93, stipulate that the costs of the CSRS are to be calculated on a "static" basis, which fails to consider future pay raises of currently employed workers and postretirement cost-of-living adjustments to be granted to retirees. Thus, the static approach assumes that the entering employee will receive promotions in the civil service grade schedule but that the wages of these grades will remain the same ("inflation driven" salary raises will not be taken into consideration), while the impact on benefit payments from future COLAs will also be excluded.

Computing the unfunded liability so as to account for all of these additional cost factors, the "dynamic" approach to the calculation of future burdens left, as of 30 September 1982, a total unfunded liability for both CSRS and MRS combined of more than $1 trillion ($514.8 billion for the CSRS; $526.8 billion for the

MRS), at least double the amount arrived at by employing only the static formula. Moreover, this estimated future shortfall of claims against the plans versus plan assets rose by an average of $94 billion a year from 1979 to 1982. These future costs must be made up, in some manner, by current and future generations of taxpayers. To provide some measurement of the burden involved in seeking to resolve this problem, it was estimated that in 1982 the additional costs of amortizing this unfunded liability would have required an additional $41 billion annually, over and above normal operating costs of the CSRS and MRS ($30 billion for the CSRS; $11 billion for the MRS).

Excluding the amortization of unfunded liabilities (i.e., counting just "normal" operating costs), the costs of CSRS and MRS were found to be, respectively, 2.5 times and 3.4 times as great as private-sector pension expenses. Amortizing the unfunded liability in a manner consistent with private-sector practices would make the government's total costs, measured as a proportion of payroll, 85 percent and 115 percent, respectively, for the CSRS and MRS, or six to eight times comparable private-sector costs.

Income for the CSRS trust fund is derived from five sources: (1) a 7 percent payroll contribution by employees participating in the plan (early in the second decade of operation of the plan, employee contributions ceased to cover costs of benefit payments); (2) a matching 7 percent contribution from employing agencies; (3) interest on investment of fund balances; (4) contributions by off-budget agencies, such as the U.S. Postal Service; and (5) annual appropriations from the general fund of the U.S. Treasury, as authorized by the Civil Service Retirement Amendments of 1969. By far the largest proportion of receipts to the fund is obtained from Treasury appropriations (46.5 percent), followed by 26.5 percent for contributions by employees and employers, while interest on balances accounts for 20.7 percent and off-budget agency payments make up the remaining 6.2 percent of fund income.

Judged by the measurement standards used by private-sector pension plans, the Civil Service Retirement System, for example, is not actuarially sound. However, according to projections worked out by the Office of Personnel Management, which administers the plan, concerns about the future solvency of the system are unwarranted, because present financing arrangements, which of course include the right to tap the taxing authority of the United States government, will continue to keep the plan on a sound footing. A similar approach to the problem must have served as the basis for the statement, reported in September 1981, of OPM Director Donald J. Devine: "We [Federal pensions systems] are in sound shape. Unlike Social Security, we don't have serious problems of a rapid increase in costs and a decrease in income."[9]

Such optimistic comments, however, show that the plan is sound only because the Treasury appropriates funds to offset shortfalls in its receipts. In 1982 such payments to the CSRS already amounted to nearly half of the receipts of its trust fund. According to CBO estimates, by the year 2030 general-fund payments will amount to two-thirds of the annual outlays of the Civil Service Retirement plan alone. Thus, only the system's unique funding arrangements give the illusion of a retirement plan in good shape.

Proposed Changes

The Grace Commission proposed a far-reaching package of revisions in Federal retirement systems that would involve: (1) raising the normal retirement age to sixty-two (from the present CSRS fifty-five and MRS forty) with immediate, actuarially unreduced annuities to be paid to retirees only on reaching sixty-two; (2) an immediate phasing-in of a high five-year average pay formula in place of the existing high three-year base; (3) less generous postretirement cost-of-living adjustments for civil service, armed forces, and smaller plan retirees; (4) increasing the service requirements for vesting benefits from five years to ten years for CSRS, while permitting armed-forces personnel to vest and qualify for deferred benefits after ten years; (5) integrating CSRS, MRS, and other plan participants with social security (with, of course, complete social-security coverage for all plan participants); and (6) reducing the possibilities of "double dipping" as a result of such integration by reducing pension benefits by amounts equal to social-security payments, as is done in the private sector. The commission also suggested that the smaller pension plans, such as the Foreign Service Retirement System (FSRS), be revised to conform with the CSRS revisions. The Railroad Retirement Board would become a private, multiemployer plan, to be operated without Federal subsidies by the enactment of a payroll tax on railroads, all administered and financed by the industry and labor groups involved.

Retirement Age

The subject of retirement age, specifically retirement at too early an age, has figured prominently in the proposals of various commissions, committees, and other groups that have addressed themselves to the study of Federal pension systems in recent years. The matter of retirement from the armed forces after twenty years' service has received special attention.

All nine of the major studies of the military retirement system conducted over a recent fifteen-year time span, including five carried out by the Department of Defense itself, recommended changes in MRS provisions to increase incentives for longer service careers. A common suggestion was to make the plan more generous by providing some benefits for those who leave with between ten and nineteen years of service while reducing the benefits for those retiring with exactly twenty service years.

A 1978 study by the President's Commission on Military Compensation recommended replacing the twenty-year retirement arrangements with severance pay and a trust fund for deferred compensation, with old-age annuities to commence only at age sixty-five. The Reduced Annuity and Early Withdrawal plan of the Fifth Quadrennial Review advocated granting full annuities only for personnel completing thirty years of active service time.

The Grace Commission recommended that retirees should receive actuarially unreduced benefits only at age sixty-two, while reduced benefits—for both the civil service and military service—would be obtainable only at age fifty-five (with deferred benefits to be available by vesting after ten years for both the CSRS and MRS). This recommendation would apply only to military personnel with less than ten years' service and to all new civil-service workers as well as those presently working who are under forty-five years of age.

Cost-of-Living Adjustments

Reduction in cost-of-living adjustments has been the one area in which Congress has moved to make Federal pension provisions less generous to pensioners in recent years. In 1976, Congress, reacting to widespread criticism of a formula that granted retirees adjustments 1 percent more than the average rise in the CPI (the "kicker"), revoked this provision, replacing it with automatic cost-of-living adjustments scheduled twice a year. More recently, Congress and the Reagan administration, acting together, moved to reduce cost-of-living adjustments from twice a year to once a year. In addition, Congress delayed granting such adjustments for fiscal years 1983, 1984, and 1985 and reduced the amount of the adjustment for retirees under age sixty-two for the same period. These revisions were aimed at reducing outlays by $435 million in 1982 and $387 million in 1983. Most recently, President Reagan, in approving the Democratic version of the Omnibus Reconciliation Act of 1983, delayed until January 1985 the effective date of COLAs otherwise scheduled to take effect in April 1984. This delay was said to reflect a bipartisan effort aimed at saving $1 billion in Federal outlays over a three-year period.

Current reports of the Reagan administration's intentions to revise government retirement provisions list a possible proposal to limit postretirement cost-of-living adjustments to the first $10,000 of annuities, with amounts over $10,000 to be adjusted by COLA increases equal to no more than 55 percent of the actual rise in the CPI. Further, the Grace Commission proposed changing the rules for cost-of-living adjustments for both civil-service and armed-forces retirees so they would conform with private-sector provisions, whose fully indexed social-security benefits and private-pension adjustments average 33 percent of the increases in the CPI and provide overall protection against inflation of some 70 percent. Under this plan, when current civil-service annuitants and employees over forty-five eventually receive pensions, their benefits would be adjusted upward at a rate equivalent to one-third of any rise in the cost of living (together with social-security benefits, for which all civil-service employees would qualify under the commission's recommendations, the total COLA would be 70 percent).

For military-service annuitants under age sixty-two (and thus ineligible for social-security payments), any cost-of-living increases would be limited to the lower of the rise in the CPI or increases in military salaries. For MRS annuitants sixty-two and over (and thus eligible for social-security benefits), the MRS cost-of-living increase would be the same as that granted to CSRS retirees—33 percent of the rise in the CPI. (Again, this combined with the fully indexed social-security payments would come to an overall 70 percent upward adjustment.)

Benefit Formulas

The Grace Commission would establish a five-year high average salary period as the basis for determining benefit payments so as to conform Federal pension plan provisions with prevailing private-sector practice. Measured on an overall basis, such a change would slightly reduce future annuities. A more serious disadvantage would result for those government workers who leave government employment and then return, after a period of years in the private sector, to boost retirement benefits on the basis of their earnings during their final employment period.

This suggestion is in line with current reported plans of the Reagan administration to revise Federal pension systems, substituting an average five-year high salary period for the present three-year arrangement. In 1980 Congress reduced the benefit formula for newly recruited armed-services personnel by instituting the present three-year salary period in place of what was then the rule of basing annuities on salary obtained as of the final day of employment.

Vesting

Virtually all of the commissions, committees, and other groups that have examined the vesting provisions of the military retirement system (or lack of the same) have advocated more generous vesting rights for uniformed-services personnel, such as granting deferred pension entitlements after five or ten years of service instead of providing no such benefit until after twenty years of active service. The Grace Commission proposals would liberalize vesting provisions for armed-services personnel in accord with these earlier suggestions by making it possible to qualify for some deferred annuities after ten years of service. It would make the arrangements less generous for CSRS participants, however, by permitting vesting only after ten years instead of at the end of five years as allowed by current provisions.

Contribution Rates

Based on conclusions that taxpayers are presently bearing the burden of between 81 and 87 percent of the civil-service retirement system costs (between 87 and 95 percent of MRS costs), the Grace Commission suggested a financing arrangement that would limit pension payments through a so-called defined contribution plan (in place of the present arrangement, which is, in effect, a defined benefit plan). Under this plan, future expenditures would be limited to the amounts of contributions plus the interest earned on assets of the plan. No specific changes in contribution rates were mentioned, however.

Initially, this change would affect only the civil-service retirement plan, since the MRS is noncontributory. Eventually, however, the new arrangement would apply to both CSRS and MRS, since, in the words of the commission, "the fundamental purpose of these recommendations is to limit the increasing costs of the CSRS and MRS, especially the taxpayer costs of these systems."

Altering the arrangements for employee and employer contributions has been studied before. The 1981 Congressional Budget Office report, cited above, explored the possibilities of increasing contributions or leaving them as they are but with some benefit reductions. Most recently, the Reagan administration has suggested increasing the CSRS employee contribution rate in two steps: from 7 percent to 8 percent in 1985 and then to 9 percent in 1986, which, it is claimed, would bring civil-service financing arrangements more in line with prevailing private-sector practice.

From the inception of the plan in 1920 through fiscal year 1960, employee contributions constituted the largest single source of financing, though government payments have been greater since that time. The most recent employee contribution rate increase was in 1969. From 1970 to 1982, while the amount of employee contributions rose by 140 percent, the costs of operating the pension systems increased by 608 percent.

Social Security Coverage

The Grace Commission recommendations for integrating Federal retirees into the social-security system has had considerable support in policy recommendations and even some policy enactments. Military personnel are already under social-security coverage, though there is no integration of social-security payments with military pensions (military retirees qualify for social-security payments without any accompanying curtailment in military pension benefits). Since the United States government pays out more than $1 billion annually in social-security benefits on behalf of armed-forces personnel, this would recoup part of the government's outlay. Further, if current civil-service employees under age forty-five, as well as all new civil-service workers were included in the social-security system, the government could save an estimated $1.8 billion over a three-year period. Integrating the military retirement system with social security would save an additional $225 million over the same time span, a combined total exceeding $2 billion.

Although many Federal civil-service workers qualify for at least minimum social-security benefits on the basis of the requisite quarters of covered non-civil-service employment,[10] civil-service workers as such, until recently, were completely excluded. Over the vehement protest of civil-service workers and their unions, Congress required all Federal employees hired after 1 January 1984 to be covered by social security (along with current and future members of Congress, the president, the vice president, Federal judges, and top-level civil servants and political appointees). With the present CSRS presumably closed to new entrants, this action will require a new civil-service retirement plan. According to the Grace Commission, such a new system should be comparable to good private-sector plans in benefits and costs. With appropriate protection of present CSRS participants for differences in social-security coverage, the commission recommended that the existing CSRS be modified in accordance with the same standards permitted to transfers from the CSRS to the new post-January 1984 system.

According to recent reports, the Office of Personnel Management (OPM) has retained two outside consulting firms to design a revamped Federal pay and retirement system that would combine the civil-service retirement and social-security coverage for workers hired in 1984 and thereafter. Reportedly, the OPM also wishes to propose options for changing the existing CSRS.

Disability Retirement

The Grace Commission called for no changes in military disability payments, though it did propose altering the definition of *disability* used by the civil service to conform with what are felt to be normal private-sector standards, i.e., inability to perform any substantial gainful employment. This is scheduled to reduce the quantity of valid applications for disability benefits and therefore the number granted and obtained.

Prospects for Change

The Federal pension system arrangements have recently faced many caustic criticisms. Congressional pension expert John W. Erlenborn (R-Ill.) characterized the Federal retirement system as a whole as being a "patchwork of inequitable entitlements that have gotten out of hand."[11] Former President Jimmy Carter, referring to the military retirement plan, commented: "I've been particularly concerned at excessive benefits that are available to those who serve in the military, who then retire and get full time jobs working for the government, itself. This is too expensive. Under present circumstances, by the end of this century, our ability to defend our nation might very well be sapped away by excessive personnel costs."[12]

The 1978 study by the Tax Foundation, *Federal Retirement Systems*, also noted that the continuation of military pension costs could bring about a situation in which, within the bounds of a defense budget that does not comprise unduly large proportions of total Federal outlays, sufficient funds will not be available to provide the weapons procurement necessary for the adequate defense of the nation.

The immediate issue, however, is the creation of a retirement program for those Federal workers hired since 1 January 1984, who must be included in the social-security system. The Reagan administration reportedly had hoped that in devising such a new pension plan, Congress would also revise the existing CSRS plan, raising the retirement age to sixty-five, changing over from an average three-year high salary to an average five-year basis for computing benefits, and increasing employee contributions, in two stages, from 7 percent to 9 percent of payroll. Administration officials privately concede, however, that there is little chance that Congress will do much in 1984 except possibly change over to the five-year high base. The House Committee on Post Office and Civil Service, which is now involved in developing the supplemental retirement plan for new civil-service employees covered by social security, reportedly feels that it would be premature and unwise at this time to consider any of the president's proposed civil-service retirement changes, partly on the grounds that Federal retirees and their survivors have already suffered "substantial reductions in retirement benefits."[13]

Organizations representing Federal employees will strongly oppose changes in the existing retirement plans. Existing CSRS provisions were vigorously defended by Kenneth Blaylock, president of the American Federation of Government Employees (AFGE), the largest union of Federal employees. Blaylock conceded that government workers have more generous pension benefits than their private-sector counterparts but asserted that the pension issue must not be addressed in isolation but in the context of what he claimed were Federal pay cuts, reductions in force, and reductions in health benefits.[14]

The military services also supported the present MRS arrangements. Assistant Defense Secretary for Manpower, Installations, and Logistics Lawrence J. Korb recently stated that "the trouble with most proposed reforms to the military retirement system, such as that offered by the Grace Commission, is that they tend to focus solely on the cost of the plan." According to Korb, enactment of the Grace Commission recommendations would reduce lifetime military pensions by about 75 percent, something that he termed "obviously irresponsible."

Again, according to Mr. Korb, the military retirement system has already experienced a significant overhaul in recent years through amendment legislation. For example: (1) in 1976, cost-of-living adjustments were reduced; (2) in 1980 a high three-year averaging technique became effective for new members; (3) 1980 also saw the conversion from semiannual to annual adjustment procedures; (4) 1983 brought a 50 percent COLA cap for members under age sixty-two and a thirteen-month interval between adjustments; and (5) revisions were also made in creditations of service for military retirement, while new prohibitions were established concerning postservice employment.[15]

Further changes will be made in retirement provisions affecting Federal civil-service personnel in the long term. Congress is mandated to propose a new plan in 1985 for those Federal civil-service employees hired after 1 January 1984. Despite legislative reluctance at this time to revise the pension arrangements for the remainder of civil-service workers (participants in the existing Civil Service Retirement System), there may be a greater willingness to consider at least some of the Reagan administration's proposed changes after the 1984 elections.

Playing the prophet in these matters is always risky; however, it seems that significant changes in the Military Services Retirement System are unlikely unless the administration and the Congress choose to replace the present arrangement of voluntarily recruited armed forces with some form of conscription. Such a fundamental policy reversal would obviously be based on considerations beyond those of simply realizing economies in the armed-services pension costs.

So long as the United States retains volunteer forces, the argument will always be made that general pension arrangements are indispensable to offset the less attractive aspects of military life and to recruit the requisite number of volunteer participants. Congressional committees dealing with military affairs are unlikely to be persuaded that the present provisions are not only unduly generous but also fail to retain the experienced personnel needed by today's armed forces. Administration leaders, members of Congress, and the public will probably remain susceptible to the sort of Kiplingesque argument that one ought not "mock the uniform that guards you while you sleep."[16]

Notes

1. Findings and recommendations of the Grace Commission in the Federal pension area are contained in the President's Private Sector Survey on Cost Control, *Management Office Selected Issues, Volume VI, Federal Retirement Systems* (Washington, D.C.: GPO, 1983).

2. Congressional Budget Office, *Civil Service Retirement Financing and Costs* (Washington, D.C., GPO, 1980).

3. "Is the Federal Service Dying of Pensionitis?" *U.S. News & World Report,* 1 September 1981.

4. Comments of Admiral Hyman Rickover and Richard V. L. Cooper in American Enterprise Institute for Public Policy Research, *Military Retirement: The Administration's Plan and Related Proposals* (Washington, D.C., 1980), 19–21.

5. This author was at one time a member of the Foreign Service.

6. Congressional Research Service, *Restructuring the Civil Service Retirement System* (Washington, D.C.: GPO, 1982).

7. Karlyn Barker, "A Retiree with Too Much Money Issues a Plea for Restraint," *Washington Post,* 18 November 1982.

8. Tax Foundation, Incorporated, *Federal Employee Retirement Systems,* Research Publication No. 34 (New York, November 1977).

9. *U.S. News & World Report.*

10. According to figures developed by the American Council of Life Insurance Pension Facts, in one recent year, 60 percent of all Federal civil-service annuitants age sixty-five and over were receiving social security benefits.

11. House Committee on the Budget, *Hearing before the Task Force on Entitlements, Uncontrollables, and Indexing,* 98th Cong., 1st sess., 1983, 2.

12. *Weekly Compilation of Presidential Documents,* 7 March 1977, vol. 13, no. 10, p. 275, cited in Tax Foundation, 21.

13. House Committee on the Budget, *Views and Estimates of the House (Together with Supplemental and Minority Views) on the Congressional Budget for Fiscal Year 1985* (Washington, D.C.: GPO, 1984), 850.

14. Karlyn Barker, "Panel Split on Whether U.S. Retirement System is Too Generous," *Washington Post,* 30 April 1983.

15. Letter to the editor, *Washington Times,* 30 May 1984.

16. See, e.g., letter by Secretary of Defense Caspar Weinberger to William F. Donnelly, president, Army Times Publishing Co., reprinted in House of Representatives, *Hearing before the Task Force on Entitlements, Uncontrollables, and Indexing of the Committee on the Budget,* 98th Cong., 1st Sess., 1983, 97–98. For response of armed forces personnel and retirees to Grace Commission proposals for revision of military pensions, see letters to the editor, *Wall Street Journal,* 11 May 1984, written in response to guest editorial, James Bovard, "Slow the Military-Retirement Gravy Train," 20 April 1984.

Privatization: Theory, Evidence, and Implementation

STEVE H. HANKE

Privatization—the transfer of public assets, infrastructure, and service functions to the private sector—is a new area of public policy and finance. In fact, it is so new that the word *privatize* appeared in *Webster's New Collegiate Dictionary* for the first time in 1983.

Although privatization has become the centerpiece of national policy in some countries—most notably the United Kingdom, where Prime Minister Margaret Thatcher has denationalized several hundred public enterprises—it has made a rather inconspicuous appearance on the policy agenda of governmental entities in the United States.

At the Federal level, privatization has been adopted by the Reagan administration. For example, President Reagan signed Executive Order 12348 on 25 February 1982. This order established a Federal Property Review Board as part of the Executive Office of the President. The purpose of this board is to identify surplus real assets and assist in their privatization. To date, however, the administration has moved slowly to implement its privatization policy.

In addition to the Reagan administration's interest in privatization, the President's Private Sector Survey on Cost Control (PPSS) has produced a privatization report and made recommendations that could save the Federal government $28.4 billion over the next three years.[1] Federal legislators have also expressed an interest in privatization. For example, a bill (S. 1746) is currently being debated in the Senate that would outlaw most Federal commercial enterprises, when the goods and services they produce are also supplied by private firms. Senators and congressmen are also debating the merits of a wide variety of Federal privatization projects in the Joint Economic Committee, where Senator Steven D. Symms is holding a series of hearings on "Privatizing the Federal Government."

Unlike the Federal government, state and local governments have made considerable progress in privatizing public assets and service functions. Many politicians at the lower levels of government have realized that privatization provides an opportunity to deliver the same goods and services at lower costs, raise revenues for current operating budgets, reduce and control future budgets, put unused and underused public assets in private hands and also on the tax rolls, and loosen the grip that public unions have on budgets and ultimately on taxpayers. Other state and local politicians, however, have adopted privatization, not out of a sense of opportunity but rather out of desperation. For example — faced with reduced grant monies from the Federal government, voter disapproval of new bond issues, high debt costs, growing hostility toward increased taxes, and demands to improve public infrastructure and services — many politicians have simply been forced to turn away from public enterprise and toward private alternatives.

Although each privatization proposal has been accompanied by a great deal of emotional debate, theoretical arguments and empirical evidence that address the economics of privatization have been conspicuously absent. The purpose of this essay is to present these arguments and evidence.

Theory

Property-rights arrangements provide the key to understanding the behavior of private and public employees and the performance of private and public enterprises. Private enterprises (assets) are owned by individuals who are free to use and transfer, within the confines of the law, their private property (assets). Consequently, those who own private property have residual claims on private enterprises' assets.

When private enterprises produce goods and services that consumers demand, at costs that are lower than market prices, profits are generated. As a result, property owners' wealth is increased. Alternatively, if losses are realized, the value of private assets declines and their owners' wealth is diminished. Hence, the owners of private firms not only appropriate the gains but also bear the costs that result from the way in which private property is used. In short, private-property owners must ultimately face the "bottom line."

The incentives created by private property rights — by the linkage between the consequences of the use of private assets and their owners' wealth — have profound consequences. Private owners face significant incentives that make it desirable to monitor the behavior of private-enterprise managers and employees, so that they will supply what consumers demand and do so in a cost-effective way. Consequently, private managers and employees find it difficult to engage in shirking behavior or behavior that is inconsistent with maximizing the present value of the private enterprise (the owners' wealth). Hence, private property puts in place incentives that tend to generate efficient performances by private firms.

By way of contrast, public enterprises are not "owned" by individuals who have a residual claim on the assets of these organizations. The nominal owners of public enterprises, the "taxpayer-owners," cannot buy and sell public enterprise assets. Consequently, "taxpayer-owners" do not have strong incentives to monitor the behavior of public managers and employees.

"Taypayer-owners" could capture some benefits from increased efficiency of public enterprises through tax reductions. However, if realized, incremental benefits from improved efficiency would be spread over many taxpayers, so that individuals' benefits would be rather small. In addition, individuals' cost of obtaining these benefits—acquiring information, monitoring bureaucrats, and organizing an effective political force to modify the behavior of public managers and employees—would be very high.

The consequences of public ownership are predictable. Public managers and employees allocate resources (assets) that do not belong to them. They do not bear the costs of their decisions, nor do they appropriate the gains from efficient behavior. Since the nominal owners of public enterprises (the taxpayers) have little incentive to monitor public managers and employees, the cost of shirking to a public bureaucrat is low. Consequently, public managers and employees would probably engage in shirking activity and the acquisition of various perquisites that increase production costs. After all, the costs of shirking and perquisites are borne by taxpayers who have little incentive to police these activities, while the gains from them (more leisure and an easy life) all accrue to the public bureaucrats.

Private enterprises make plans based on what they expect consumers to demand and what they anticipate costs to be. Private owners bear the costs and capture the benefits associated with implementing their plans. While public enterprises also plan, their plans are fundamentally different from private plans, because they are developed by bureaucrats who neither bear the costs of their mistakes nor legally capture the benefits generated by foresight. Hence, from a theoretical point of view, private and public managers and employees can be expected to behave in different ways and, as a result, private firms will be more efficient than public firms.

Empirical Evidence

Although economic theory, as well as common sense, strongly supports the notion that private enterprises should be more efficient and productive than public enterprises, one question remains unanswered: Does the evidence support the theory? We now address this question.

Europe's nationalized industries. Europe's nationalized industries provide an interesting perspective on the performance of private and public enterprises. Public enterprises in Europe produce everything from pots and pans to cars and trucks. They even run hotel chains. In doing so, these public enterprises perform quite differently from their private counterparts.

Sales, adjusted profits, and physical production per employee are lower for nationalized firms. Taxes paid per employee are lower. Sales per dollar investment are lower. Profits per dollar of total assets are lower. Profits per dollar of sales are lower. Per dollar of sales, operating expenses plus wages are higher. Sales per employee grow at a slower rate. And, with the exception of nationalized oil companies, virtually all nationalized companies generate accounting losses.

Evidence from Europe's public enterprises is consistent with the notion that property-rights arrangements are not neutral and that private enterprises are more efficient than public enterprises.

Public-sector wages and productivity. Turning to general evidence about private versus public efficiency in the United States, we examine unit labor cost. Federal employees' pay levels have been found, for comparable skill levels, to be substantially higher than in the private sector.

These wage differentials between the public and private sectors are consistent with property-rights theory. Public bureaucrats do not have strong incentives to drive tough bargains, because they are not bargaining with their own wealth. When negotiating wages, owners of private firms, however, have a significant stake in the outcome of wage negotiations because their own private wealth is at stake.

It has also been found that Federal productivity is lower than productivity in the private sector. Consequently, the unit labor cost levels, for similar types of output, are typically higher in the Federal sector than in the private sector.

Administration. We now focus on more specific data about comparative costs. First, findings about several administrative functions are reviewed:

• Debt owed the Federal government is considerable, about $220 billion, and a substantial amount of this debt is represented by uncollectible accounts. Moreover, as the Grace Commission indicated, the volume of these bad debts has been increasing. Part of the reason for the increasing uncollectibles is due to the relative inefficiency of public debt collection operations. Bennett and Johnson found that, in 1976, one Federal agency spent $8.72 per account to maintain and pursue debt collection, while one of the largest private collection agencies performed the same function for $3.50 in the same year.[2] In addition, private firms reported that it was profitable to pursue collection on debts as small as $25, while the Federal government typically wrote off debts for less than $600. In addition, the Federal government requires a minimum of one year, and frequently much longer, to obtain a judgment against a debtor. Private firms, on the other hand, obtain judgments in about five months.

• In testimony before the Joint Economic Committee, J. Peter Grace, chairman of the President's Private Sector Survey on Cost Control, indicated that it cost the U.S. Army $4.20 to process a payroll check.[3] He stated that the same function is performed by private firms for $1.00 per check.

• Hsiao found that the public cost of processing a Medicare claim in 1971 and 1972 was 35 and 18 percent higher, respectively, than a claim for a comparable private firm.[4] Also, private firms process claims at a faster rate and with a lower error rate than the public sector.

Air traffic control. Air traffic control in the United States has been dominated by the Federal Aviation Administration (FAA). However, private firms have operated smaller airports, where traffic levels did not qualify for an FAA tower. All this changed in 1981, when the Professional Air Traffic Controllers' Organization, a public union, called a strike of public controllers. This gave the private controllers an opportunity to expand their business, and it also presented an opportunity for cost comparisons.

Robert Poole reviewed this experience and concluded that the public air traffic control system was plagued with outdated technology, a lack of cost-effectiveness, unresponsiveness to users' needs, an absence of long-range planning, political interference, and labor problems.[5] Poole indicated that, for the smallest FAA tower authorization, the FAA spends about $1 million to install and about $275,000 a year to operate and maintain a tower. Private firms provide the same services for about $120,000 a year, including amortization of their original capital investments. Poole also reported that, when a private provider assumed the responsibility for operating the Farmington, New Mexico, tower in 1981, its contract was for $99,000 per year. Before that time, the FAA had operated the tower for $287,000.

Custodial services and building maintenance. The Grace Commission's evaluation of the Federal government's custodial services revealed that the General Services Administration employs about seventeen times as many people, and spends about fourteen times as much as private firms, to deliver comparable building maintenance. Bennett and DiLorenzo reported that facilities maintenance at selected military facilities was reduced by 35 percent, when these functions were transferred to private contractors.[6] In Germany, Blankart's analysis revealed similar results.[7] He reported that private custodial services for government offices in Hamburg were between 30 and 80 percent less costly than public custodians. And for the Federal post office system, private custodians were between 30 and 40 percent less costly than public ones.

Day care centers. Public day care centers (federally funded nonprofit organizations) are reported to be more costly than those operated by private self-financed organizations. Bennett and DiLorenzo reported that the monthly public day care center costs per child were $188, compared with $102 for the private centers.[8] They also reported that the primary reason for this cost differential was higher staff-to-child ratios and higher wages in the public centers. Of particular interest is the fact that the quality of service in both public and private centers was deemed to be comparable.

Electricity. There has been a great deal of comparative cost analysis of electric utilities in the United States. These studies support the notion that private firms are more productive than public firms. Typical of the findings is a comparison of Federal and private hydroelectric plants, which was reported by Bennett and DiLorenzo.[9] They found that, for the period 1973–75, the cost per kilowatt hour for Federal hydropower was $3.29, while private hydropower was $2.79.

Fire protection service. The private provision of fire protection service in the United States is a growing industry. According to the Private Sector Fire Association, a private trade organization, seventeen private companies operate in fourteen states. Poole and Smith reported that cost savings that accompany switching from public to private fire companies have typically been 20 to 50 percent.[10]

It is interesting to note that, while the cost of private operations is lower than the cost of public operations, the quantity and quality of private service, as measured by fire-insurance ratings, are superior to public systems. One reason for this is that private companies have incentives to prevent, not fight, fires. If there are no fires, private companies save operating costs and increase their profits.

Forestry. There are over 90 million acres of federally owned commercial forest lands in the United States that are managed by the U.S. Forest Service. Hanke found that these lands generate negative cash flows of about $1 billion a year.[11] Private timber firms, on the other hand, typically generate positive cash flows.

Blankart's analysis of forest lands in West Germany reveals the same picture. He reported that public forests had negative cash flows of 30 DM per hectare, while private forests registered positive cash flows of 15 DM per hectare.[12]

Grazing lands. The Bureau of Land Management manages and leases about 155 million acres of commercial public grazing land in the United States. Hanke found that this land generates negative cash flows of about $100 million annually, while a comparable private range typically generates positive cash flows.[13] In addition, the physical condition of public grazing land is worse than comparable private land.

Hospitals and health care. The Veterans Administration (VA) operates the largest health-care system in the United States. The VA operates 172 hospitals, 93 nursing homes, 227 outpatient clinics, 16 domiciliary units, 73 extended-care wards in hospitals, and 50 satellite clinics.

The VA system has been extensively studied. The PPSS found that the VA system was highly inefficient, when compared with either not-for-profit or for-profit private hospital systems.[14] For example, five university hospitals built between 1980 and 1983 had an average cost per bed that ranged from $97,400 to $140,000, while comparable VA costs for four hospitals ranged from $153,000 to $320,000. The construction costs for VA nursing homes were also found to be much higher than for comparable private not-for-profit and profit nursing homes. In the PPSS sample, the average construction cost per bed for the VA was $61,500, while the private cost was $15,900.

Overadministration, a factor that could be predicted by using the property-rights theory, plagues the VA construction program. The PPSS found that—when compared with the Hospital Corporation of America, the largest private hospital system in the United States—the VA construction administration staff is about sixteen times larger, while the construction programs that they administer are roughly the same.

The PPSS also evaluated operating costs. And, as was the case with construction costs, the VA's operating costs were much higher than either private not-for-profit or private for-profit hospitals and nursing homes. For example, the average costs for an episode of acute inpatient care at VA hospitals were 69.8 percent higher for medical and 48.0 percent higher for surgical care than private not-for-profit hospitals affiliated with medical schools.

The VA has claimed that the reason for its higher costs is the nature of its case-mix. For example, the VA treats more psychiatric and other chronic conditions, which require long hospital stays. After adjusting a 1982 VA comparative cost study for deficiencies uncovered by the General Accounting Office, the PPSS found that the VA's own analysis (which allegedly normalized the VA costs and private not-for-profit hospitals for case-mix) shows that the VA's operating costs were higher than the private not-for-profits'. For example, the private not-for-profits had a 24.3 percent advantage for a medical episode, a 5.9 percent advantage for a surgical episode, and overall a 15.5 percent advantage.

One reason for the comparatively high operating cost in the VA system is the relatively long lengths-of-stay (LOS) in the system. The average LOS for the VA system was 27.3 days in fiscal year 1981, while the average in the private hospital system was 7.2 days. The use of a long LOS by public bureaucrats is, of course, something that could be predicted by using the property-rights theory. The long LOS is an inviting technique for a bureaucrat to use to increase his total budget, employees under his command, and consequently his salary.

Another factor contributing to public-hospital inefficiency is the high level of medical supply inventories. The VA system's inventory levels are forty-five to sixty days. This is 33 to 50 percent higher than typical inventory levels for private hospitals. One reason for the lower private inventory levels is the fact that private owners must pay, either directly or indirectly, for the capital carrying charges on medical supply inventories. Therefore, if inventories are excessive in a private hospital, the asset value of the hospital declines and the private owners' wealth is reduced. Hence, private owners have an incentive to monitor employees, so that inventories are properly managed.

Public-hospital supply procurement is not cost-effective, when compared with private purchases of supplies. The VA, in 1981, purchased 41.9 percent of its supplies at the local level through open-market purchases. The remaining 58.1 percent were purchased through national contracts. By comparison, private systems purchase 75 to 85 percent of their supplies through national contracts. For the same products, this saves the private system 20 percent, relative to what they would pay if they purchased locally in the same proportion as the VA system.

Housing. Public housing projects are typically run-down and epitomize urban blight in the United States and in Europe. In addition, they are costly to construct and operate. For example, Weicher found that the cost of new public housing units is about 25 percent higher than comparable private housing.[15] The American Enterprise Institute's research also indicates that private management can lead to significant cost savings, when compared with public management. A switch to private management leads to reduced administrative costs, maintenance costs, and higher rental income through improved rent collection and reduced vacancy rates.[16]

Military support and maintenance. The U.S. Defense Department contracts with private providers for many base support and maintenance services. Bennett and DiLorenzo reported the results of a sample of these activities, and found that private firms provided services at an average cost savings of 15.1 percent, with savings that ranged from 0.1 percent to 35 percent.[17]

The Grace Commission reported findings that are consistent with those reported by Bennett and DiLorenzo. One of the commission's detailed analyses is particularly revealing. Since 1960 the Air Training Command (ATC) has contracted with a private firm to perform base support services for Vance Air Force Base in Enid, Oklahoma. Contract performance standards have specified what the private contractor was to do but not how it was to do it. The private contractor by using less manpower, more specialized personnel, flexible procurement policies, and a stable work force has been performing its contract at 22 percent lower cost than Federal employees. The private firm at Vance, for example, uses 40 percent and 27 percent, respectively, less manpower to maintain T-38 and T-37 training aircraft than does the public ATC. Using fewer personnel, the private firm also provides a higher quality service than does the public sector. The private firm has only 18.8 percent of the T-38s and 14.3 percent of the T-37s out of operation for maintenance on the average, compared with 21.5 percent and 15.4 percent, respectively, for the ATC public system. The private firm has 87.3 percent of its T-38s and 95.4 percent of the T-37s that it maintains fully mission capable, compared with 84 percent of the T-38s and 92.5 percent of the ATC publicly maintained planes.

Postal services. Even though private, first-class mail statutes prohibit firms from competing with the U.S. Postal Service for first-class service, many private firms do compete for other classes. These private providers have adopted innovative postal technology and have also been able to deliver a higher quality service at a lower cost than the U.S. Postal Service. For example, the United Parcel Service handles twice as many parcels as the U.S. Postal Service, charges lower rates, makes faster deliveries, and has a damage rate that is 80 percent lower than that of the public post office. In addition, the United Parcel Service makes a profit, whereas the U.S. Postal Service has typically generated losses.

Further evidence of private enterprise's relative efficiency in the field of postal service has been provided by the Grace Commission. The commission reported that it cost the U.S. Postal Service, on the average, $0.24 per dollar of revenue generated to operate a postal window at a public post office. Alternatively, the U.S. Postal Service contracts out with private enterprise to operate postal windows at a much lower cost. For example, in 1981, the U.S. Postal Service in Tucson, Arizona, had twenty-three private contract stations, and the cost per dollar of revenue generated at these stations was only $0.028.

Prisons and correctional facilities. At present, there are about 150 counties and 39 states that are in litigation or under court order to improve their public prisons or correctional facilities. And between 60 and 80 percent of all the nation's public prison cells are designated as being "overcrowded."

Faced with the need to expand capacity, on the one hand, and the taxpayers' reluctance to finance new prisons, on the other, public officials have begun to turn to the private sector. Since 1979, the Federal Bureau of Prisons has contracted out all of its halfway-house operations. Some states have done the same. The Immigration and Naturalization Service has contracted out for some of its lock-up facilities. In all, there are some 30,000 juvenile offenders housed in about 1,500 facilities owned and operated by private firms. In addition, Bucking Security will begin to design, build, and operate the first high-security penitentiary for adult offenders in the near future.

The reported evidence indicates that private firms have been able to build and operate low-security facilities at costs that are 10 to 25 percent lower than those of public facilities. Moreover, they can complete the design and construction of these facilities in six to twelve months, as opposed to an average of five years for the public sector.

The reality of these private-prison cost savings has recently been recorded in Houston, Texas, where a private firm built and now operates a 350-bed holding facility for the Immigration and Naturalization Service, for $24 a day per prisoner. This is about 35 percent lower than the public cost.

Property assessment. Robert Poole reported that about 10 percent of all property tax assessment work at the state and local levels was conducted by private firms.[18] Although some jurisdictions forbid private assessment work, Ohio requires private provision. The quality of assessment work in Ohio, measured by the relationship between assessments and actual sales prices, is the best in the nation. Also, the average cost per assessment is 50 percent lower in Ohio than the United States average.

Railroads. Public railroads have remarkably low productivity, when compared with similar private lines. Bennett and DiLorenzo reported, for example, that in 1979 a comparison of Amtrak with four private firms showed that Amtrak repaired 182,955 ties with an average work crew of 69, while the private firms repaired 684,338 ties with an average crew of only 26. Amtrak removed 71.8 miles of rail with an average crew of 129, while the average removed by the private firms was 344 miles with an average crew of 77. The average private firm surfaced 864 miles of track with an 18-man crew, compared to Amtrak's 141.4 miles with a 16-man crew.[19]

Refuse collection. Savas reported results of an extensive study of refuse collection costs.[20] His study included a national sample of about 1,400 communities. Savas used 1975 data, and his analysis revealed that, for cities over 50,000 population, private collectors were about 30 percent less costly than public ones.

Less ambitious studies than Savas's confirm his findings. For example, Bennett and Johnson compared the prices charged by twenty-nine competing private refuse collectors operating in Fairfax County, Virginia, with the prices charged by the county, which serves about one-third of the single-family residences within the county.[21] The average annual county fee was $126.80, while the private firms charged between $48 and $148 annually for an average of $85.76, with only one firm charging more than the county.

Security services. The private security industry in the United States has a long history. All of the original local police functions were private. And, of course, Pinkerton and Wells Fargo were originally known for their security forces that handled stagecoach runs. In fact, 1829 marked the establishment of the first public police force in the Anglo-American world. It was then that the London Metropolitan Police was established. Today, private security forces outnumber public ones in the United States by at least two to one.

The efficiency of private over public security is attested to by a 1976 study of New York. New York was able to contract out security for a total cost of $4 to

$7 an hour per guard. The public cost per hour for a guard was $15, and this did not include any overhead or amortization costs.

Ship maintenance. Many of the navy's support ships are similar and perform functions that are identical with the private merchant marine. Bennett and Johnson[22] as well as Bennett and DiLorenzo[23] reviewed comparative performances and cost data about the public and private fleets. They reported that private ships were typically on sea duty between two and three-and-one-half times more than the public fleet. So, the private output per ship was much higher than public output. Given that the output per ship was significantly higher, one might assume that the total maintenance costs per ship would have been higher for the private fleet. However, this was not the case.

The average annual maintenance cost for a navy support ship was $2 million, whereas the average cost for a private ship was $400,000. Further, more disaggregated data for eight specific equipment repair items revealed the public cost for the identical job ranged from three to fifty-two times more expensive than private vessels.

Urban buses. The response of private bus companies to a different set of incentives leads to their relative efficiency, both in the United States and abroad. For example, public buses in New York generated $16,694 in annual revenues per employee, whereas the figure for comparable private lines in the metropolitan area was $26,279. In Australia, private urban bus systems are 50 percent more cost effective than public ones. The pattern is similar in Germany, where the nationwide average cost for public buses was 160 percent more per kilometer than the contract price for comparable private bus service.

Wastewater. Because of construction and operating efficiencies, the costs of private wastewater supply typically run 20 to 50 percent lower than public supply. These cost savings result from the fact that it takes only about two to three years to design and construct a private plant, whereas a public plant requires seven to eight years. In addition, public plants must follow the U.S. Environmental Protection Agency's design criteria, which result in "overdesigned" plants. The public plants must also often pay construction workers wages that are higher than market wages because of the requirements of the Davis-Bacon Act.

One of the most recent examples of how private wastewater plants save money is found in Chandler, Arizona, a community with a population of 45,000, thirty-five miles southeast of Phoenix. Chandler has contracted for a private wastewater plant. The city of Chandler has determined that its private plant will save 37 percent relative to what it would have cost to build and operate a public plant.

Water supply. Crain and Zardkoohi used 1970 data from a sample of twenty-four private and eighty-eight public water enterprises in the United States to construct an econometric cost model for water supply.[24] They established that the private operating costs were about 25 percent lower than for the public operations. Further, they found that this was caused by relatively low labor productivity in the public systems and an underutilization of public enterprises' capital.

Weather forecasting. Bennett and DiLorenzo reported that the weather service was contracted out at National Airport in Washington, D.C.[25] The contract contained incentives for accurate forecasts, with payments being reduced for below-average forecasts. The cost savings from this privatization project were 37 percent, and the quality of the forecasts improved.

Implementation

Two generic approaches can be employed to implement privatization: the technocratic approach and the political one. Although these approaches are not necessarily mutually exclusive, they will be treated here as if they were. The technocratic approach requires public bureaucrats to apply techniques that are used in the private sector to promote efficiency. For example, in choosing whether to privatize the production of goods and services produced in-house within the Federal government, bureaucrats use, or are supposed to use, the Office of Management and Budget's Circular A-76. This document defines policies and procedures for comparing the costs of public versus private provision. In principle, if the results of an A-76 evaluation reveal that public costs are greater than private costs, then the activity in question should be privatized. By employing this technocratic procedure, goods and services used by the government should be supplied in the least-costly way.

Another technocratic approach has recently been suggested for determining whether real assets held by public entities should be retained or privatized. To employ the suggested procedure, the rates of return on real assets should be calculated, and if the rates fall below a predetermined target rate of return, then the assets should be privatized.

Not surprisingly, A-76, which was first introduced in 1955, has been infrequently used. Moreover, when it has been employed, it has been highly biased toward retaining the production of goods and services within the Federal government. Although the technique described for determining whether real assets should be retained or privatized represents only a proposal, there is little hope that, if implemented, it would be more successful than A-76.

The reason why the technocratic approach is bound to fail and why the public sector cannot mimic the private sector centers on the differing incentives created by public and private property. In the private sector, the owners of private property can augment their wealth only by continually applying techniques that will ensure that the least-costly production techniques for supply are employed. In addition, private owners must determine the rates of return on assets that they hold in their portfolios, so that they can determine which ones to retain or sell. The public bureaucrats do not face these incentives, when they apply private-sector techniques for improving efficiency. This does not imply that the public bureaucrats are neutral with respect to the application of private-sector efficiency techniques and to the retention versus privatization options. Public bureaucrats are biased toward retention, since their job security and personal incomes are tied to retaining public assets and public production of goods and services. In short, it is in bureaucrats' personal interests not to apply the private-sector efficiency techniques in an even-handed way.

Given the bureaucratic biases and past failures of the technocratic approaches to public-sector effciency, the most promising method for implementing privatization is the political approach. The political solution amounts to nothing less than passing legislation that mandates privatization. For example, a bill currently being debated in the U.S. Senate (S. 1746) would do just that. It would simply prohibit the Federal government from engaging in most of the 11,000 commercial activities that it is now engaged in. Although this type of political solution might be initially more difficult to gain support for than a technocratic solution, the results from adopting a political solution appear to be much more assured than the application of the technocratic approach.

In gaining political support for privatization policies, advocates should be clear as to what the real issues are, and they should also avoid false arguments. For example, those who oppose privatization often argue that private supply of public goods and services is unacceptable because the poor cannot afford to purchase from private suppliers. This argument about the poor should have nothing to do with the choice between private and public supply. The issue about the poor concerns the choice between private and public finance. The point here is simply that decisions about supply and finance are separable issues and should not be aggregated. If private supply is most cost-effective, it should be advocated. To the extent that the poor require assistance in purchasing privately supplied goods and services, public finance, through vouchers, can be employed to deal with this issue.

Before concluding this discussion of privatization implementation, it is important to mention that the propensity of politicians to impose price controls on goods and services, once they are supplied by private enterprise, can create serious problems and dramatically hinder the ability of private firms to perform. In the United States, for example, price controls are one of the major reasons why so many activities that were originally supplied by private firms are now supplied by public entities. The problems occur in the following way: private firms raise nominal prices, either because service improvements are mandated or because of inflation; this brings forth demands for politicians to control prices; after price controls, the private firms find that the only way they can maintain profit margins is to reduce the quality of services; as service declines, the public becomes anxious and demands that the private firms be taken over by a public entity because the private firms are not capable of providing reliable service.

Deregulation, therefore, is an important element that must accompany any privatization projects. Market demand and supply should be allowed to control prices for successful private provision of public goods and services. If, for political reasons, it is determined that market-determined prices are too high and certain groups of individuals within the service area cannot afford to pay for privately supplied services, price controls should be avoided. In these cases, public finance, through the use of vouchers given to needy individuals, should be considered as a mechanism to assist needy individuals in their purchase of "necessary" goods and services whose prices are determined in deregulated, open markets.

For those who wish to advocate privatization, the rules for success should be rather clear: (1) present the theoretical arguments and empirical evidence that demonstrate the superiority of private supply; (2) keep all debate concerning the choice between public and private finance separate from the choice between public and private supply; (3) keep all decisions concerning private versus public supply out of the hands of public bureaucrats; and (4) make certain that deregulation accompanies privatization.

NOTES

1. President's Private Sector Survey on Cost Control (PPSS), *Report on Privatization* (Washington, D.C., 1983).

2. J. T. Bennett and M. H. Johnson, *Better Government at Half the Price: Private Production of Public Services* (Ottawa, Ill.: Caroline House Publishers, 1981), 52.

3. Joint Economic Committee, Subcommittee on Monetary and Fiscal Policy, *Testimony of J. P. Grace*, 98th Cong., 2d sess., 1984.

4. W. Hsiao, "Public Versus Private Administration of Health Insurance: A Study in Relative Economic Efficiency," *Inquiry* 15 (December 1978): 379–87.

5. R. W. Poole, Jr., "Air Traffic Control: The Private Sector Option," *Heritage Foundation Backgrounder*, no. 216, 5 October 1982.

6. J. T. Bennett and T. J. DiLorenzo, "Public Employee Unions and the Privatization of 'Public' Services," *Journal of Labor Research* 4 (Winter 1983): 43.

7. C. B. Blankart, "Bureaucratic Problems in Public Choice: Why Do Public Goods Still Remain Public?" in *Public Choice and Public Finance*, ed. R. W. Roskamp (Paris: Cujas Publishers, 1979), 155–67.

8. Bennett and DiLorenzo, 41.

9. Ibid.

10. R. W. Poole, Jr., "Fighting Fires for Profit," *Reason* (May 1976): 6–11; R. G. Smith, "Feet to the Fire," *Reason* (March 1983), 23–29.

11. S. H. Hanke, "The Privatization Debate: An Insider's View," *Cato Journal* 2 (Winter 1982): 656.

12. Blankart, 158.

13. S. H. Hanke, "Land Policy," in *Agenda 83*, ed. R. Holwill (Washington, D.C.: Heritage Foundation, 1983), 656.

14. *Report on Privatization*, 94–108.

15. J. C. Weicher, *Housing* (Washington, D.C.: American Enterprise Institute, 1980), 59.

16. S. Butler, "Public Housing: From Tenants to Homeowners," *Heritage Foundation Backgrounder*, no. 359, 12 June 1984.

17. Bennett and DiLorenzo, 43.

18. R. W. Poole, Jr., *Cutting Back City Hall* (New York: Universe Books, 1980), 164.

19. Bennett and DiLorenzo.

20. E. S. Savas, "Policy Analysis for Local Government: Public vs. Private Refuse Collection," *Policy Analysis* 3 (Winter 1977): 49–74.

21. J. T. Bennett and M. H. Johnson, "Public Versus Private Provision of Collective Goods and Services: Garbage Collection Revisited," *Public Choice*, no. 34 (1979), 55–63.

22. Bennett and Johnson, *Better Government at Half the Price*.

23. Bennett and DiLorenzo.

24. M. W. Crain and A. Zardkoohi, "A Test of the Property Rights Theory of the Firm: Water Utilities in the United States," *Journal of Law and Economics* 14 (October 1978): 149–65.

25. Bennett and DiLorenzo, 39.

Policy Consequences of Government by Congressional Subcommittees

KENNETH A. SHEPSLE
BARRY R. WEINGAST

Dissatisfaction with the performance of government intervention in the economy is widespread. Those who oppose a strong Federal presence denounce overregulation, massive deficits, "out-of-control" bureaucracies, and exploding entitlement expenditures. Those who favor a strong governmental presence find fault with public laws, programs, and regulatory decisions that are typically rigid and bureaucratic, without coordination or rationality. Still others indict the government for serving special interest groups with generous subsidies, tax preferences, and anticompetitive privileges, as well as for its concomitant failure to provide for the more general interest.

Disagreements over what constitutes the problem extend to differences in the diagnosis of the causes as well as to potential cures. This lack of consensus on why the government does what it does — independent of personal value judgments — reflects the serious disagreements over and misunderstandings of how the system works. Regulatory decisions on particular entitlement programs do not just happen. Rather, the pattern of policy decisions follows a profound and subtle logic. Improving policy, no matter what the goal, must be based on an understanding of the logic of public policy.

Critics of governmental effectiveness and efficiency usually focus on the executive branch, occasionally on the judiciary, but seldom on the Congress. Yet most of the nation's present economic difficulties have their roots in Congress, because that is where the dominant force for growth in Federal activity, for bureaucratic provision, and for catering to special interest groups is found. At least since the

Some of the ideas in this essay were discussed in Kenneth A. Shepsle, Barry R. Weingast, and Clifford M. Hardin, "Public Policy Excesses: Government by Congressional Subcommittee," Formal Publication No. 50 (St. Louis: Center for the Study of American Business, 1982). The authors are grateful to Dr. Hardin and the center staff for their encouragement and criticism.

turn of the century, members of Congress have been motivated by two strong desires—to secure reelection by serving their constituents and to develop a personal power base in Washington. Unfortunately, the political maneuvering around these desires has begun to alter the legislative procedures and the institutional structures of Congress.

Accompanying this alteration of legislative structure and procedure are other familiar characteristics of expanded governmental scope and congressional decision making: boom times in Washington's "K Street Corridor," where lobbyists, trade associations, and political law firms are located; tremendous growth in the scale and bureaucracy of the legislative branch (in 1979 its budget passed the $1 billion mark, and more than 31,000 employees were on the payroll); autonomous control of the policy agenda by coteries within the various special interest groups, legislative subcommittee members, and executive-branch offices; and, finally, the remarkable ability of incumbent legislators, especially since the mid-1960s, to get themselves reelected. Though often mistaken for causes, these are the symptoms of congressional dominance over policy. In turn, they have contributed to the deterioration of congressional leadership, the decline of party discipline, and the rise of government by subcommittee.

In the 1950s and 1960s, most of the important congressional business originated in the fifteen standing committees of the Senate and the twenty standing committees of the House. Subcommittees were used but not in controlling the development of legislation. Today there are 240 standing subcommittees (149 in the House, 91 in the Senate), and they have become major forces. In fact, in 1973 the House passed a "Subcommittee Bill of Rights," which enhanced their autonomy and influence. Most of the members of subcommittees are legislators whose districts have a vested interest in the policy issues. The new system, in short, has increased the powers of program advocates who are biased toward protecting and enhancing benefits for their constituencies. The influence of these subcommittees is both subtle and typically overlooked, because their strongest power—the capacity to block proposed changes in programs within their jurisdiction—need not be actively or publicly exercised in order to be effective. In other words, subcommittees are powerful because they can say no and do nothing. The veto power of the subcommittee is the political currency of the realm and is inextricably intertwined with unsatisfactory public performance.

Congress: The Root of the Problem

According to the conventional wisdom,[1] the twentieth century has witnessed the decline of Congress and the strengthening of the presidency. There was something of a resurgence by Congress during the 1970s—the War Powers Resolution of 1973, the Budget Act of 1974, the growth of oversight, the legislative veto, and the "fallout" from Watergate. But Congress has generally been viewed by academics, popular commentators, and even congressmen as a much weakened branch of government. This common view, if not erroneous, is an extreme and unbalanced one.

Outside observers, focusing on important issues, such as inflation, deficits, and "out-of-control" spending, often forget that these are simply labels covering a multitude of problems. They are the names given to the effects of an accumulation of many smaller, seemingly unrelated, policy decisions. In order to address these broad effects and to ameliorate their consequences, it is necessary to appreciate exactly how policies are made.

With this in mind, we argue that the so-called decline of Congress has not meant an ascendant executive branch. Instead, both Congress and the presidency have been eclipsed by the now autonomous committees and subcommittees of Congress, which over the past fifty years have developed a much freer hand in policy making within their jurisdictions. Each is positioned in its own issue bailiwick to protect relevant constituencies from adverse changes. While no single committee or subcommittee can plausibly be blamed for any of the "grand problems," each contributes its own small part.

The consequent problems of the Federal government may appear out of control and unresolvable — but not because of imperial presidents or evil bureaucratic spirits dominating a supposedly powerless legislative branch. Rather, it is because key institutional figures — subcommittee members — are biased against remedies that harm their constituents, and these members have the power to block ameliorative initiatives. Those with the incentive to advocate and pursue remedial courses of action — the president and major party leaders — lack the institutional power to effect these changes. The problem, then, is not one of uncontrollable policies. It is one of mismatched capabilities and incentives — those who can change policies will not; those who want to cannot.[2]

Broadly speaking, this interpretation of events focuses on the evolution of committee and subcommittee autonomy in Congress. Accompanying this evolution — indeed elevating it to decisive status — is the decline of institutional constraints inside the legislature. Congress can no longer check the narrow, provincial impulses of its subunits. Indeed, the major flaw in current reform proposals is their failure to accommodate this central fact.

Table 1 shows some of the major congressional landmarks of the twentieth century. Most of the details trace either shifts in power to the executive branch from the legislative branch or internal trends of decentralization inside the House. This is not meant to imply that the Senate has been immune to these trends, but the developments in the House have been more dramatic. Many of the features of policy making that have come to characterize the House have been part of the Senate's standard operating procedure for most of this century. The House, as a legislative institution, has drifted toward the Senate. Although some of the specifics are tailored to the situation in the House, the general conditions apply to the Senate as well.

While space precludes a detailed discussion, several observations can be made.[3] First, there has been a remarkable trend toward decentralization of control in Congress, involving the transfer of power from strong institutional and party leaders, initially to committees and later to subcommittees. The process began in the second decade of this century with the revolt against the imperious Speaker of the House "Boss" Cannon, whose enormous powers ultimately gravitated to the chairmen of the standing committees. By the mid-1930s, partly in response to Roosevelt's New Deal, cross-party ideological coalitions in both the House and the Senate (the so-called conservative coalition) further weakened central party control. In the 1960s, the power of institutional-regulator committees, such as Rules and Appropriations, was weakened. By the end of the 1970s, several additional events served to consolidate the fifty-year trend toward decentralization. The Legislative Reorganization Act (1970), the Subcommittee Bill of Rights (1973), and the Committee Reform Amendments (1974) constrained full committees and strengthened the hand of and provided independence for the increasingly numerous subcommittees. On the surface, these events appeared to weaken the influence of Congress over policy making because they diminished the capacities of the old power centers (the Speaker, party leaders, and committee chairmen). Below the surface, however, new power centers were developed inside Congress.

A second observation is that there has been a trend toward giving powers to the president, seemingly at the expense of Congress. The Budget and Accounting Act of 1921 made the president responsible for proposing an executive budget each fiscal year. The Reciprocal Trade Act of 1934 gave the executive branch the power to set tariff levels. The Employment Act of 1946 made the government

TABLE 1

Calendar of Some Twentieth Century Legislative Developments

Year	Development
1911	Revolt against the Speaker of the House: independence of committees and committee chairmen; strengthening of minority party.
1911–20	Growth of the seniority system: separation of party and committee leaders.
1921–22	Budget and Accounting Act of 1921: recreation of separate House and Senate Appropriations Committees.
1934	Reciprocal Trade Agreements Act: transfer of responsibility for tariff making from the Congress to the president.
1938	Origins of Republican/Southern Democratic "conservative coalition."
1946	Legislative Reorganization Act creating the "modern" committee system in the House and Senate.
1946	Employment Act.
1961	Attack on the ability of the House Rules Committee to control and restrain legislative flow.
1964–66	Growth of incumbency effect: reelection of congressional incumbents becomes more regularized.
1970	Legislative Reorganization Act (greatly accelerating the growth of legislative staff).
1973	Subcommittee Bill of Rights: fixed subcommittee jurisdictions, automatic referral of bills to subcommittees, guaranteed budgets for subcommittees, guaranteed staff for subcommittees, seniority criterion for subcommittee chairs, bidding process for subcommittee assignments.
1974	Committee Reform Amendments in House; the removal of powerful committee chairman.
1974	Congressional Budget and Impoundment Control Act.

responsible for full employment in the economy, and the president has been embroiled in the economy's macroperformance ever since.

An odd feature of this story—the weakening of Congress and the strengthening of the presidency—is the belief that redistribution of power between the two branches of government has been conducted only in one direction. This belief leaves an erroneous impression, because it places little weight on the congressional adaptations and adjustments that followed these major develoments. Reforms of the last half-century have indeed weakened the institution of Congress. But the institutionalized presidency has not been the only, or even the most important, beneficiary. These reforms, especially those of the early 1970s, have produced significant effects and adaptations inside the legislature. First, they have emancipated individual representatives and senators from the restraints of their parties; and, second, they have liberated congressional committees and subcommittees from the preferences of chamber majorities.

Senators and representatives are now free to serve their geographic constituencies and, consequently, their own electoral ambitions. They sit on committees and subcommittees that are capable of operating with relative independence in well-defined policy jurisdictions. Thus the destruction of institutional and party power centers during the last half-century of reform and decentralization in Congress must be seen alongside the creation of new power centers (committees and subcommitees). In the same light, the nominal shift in policy-making initiative to the president must be interpreted alongside (and qualified by) the veto power and "continuous watchfulness" (in the words of the Legislative Reorganization Act of 1946) of decentralized committees and subcommittees. Even if policy making appears to come at the initiative and insistence of the executive branch, even if implementation and administration appear to be at the behest of an enormous executive bureaucracy, and even if Congress appears unable to respond decisively or expeditiously, the jurisdictional subunits of the legislature—the committees and subcommittees—are increasingly vital to the policy-making process. Members of these subunits, because they have been freed from party control and the oppressive tactics of institutional leaders, are at liberty to pursue their own narrow interests. Even majorities in the full chambers are placed at a disadvantage, since their initiatives may be vetoed or blocked by committees and subcommittees if those actions would jeopardize the benefits currently being enjoyed by committee and subcommittee constituents. Policies, as a consequence, are victimized by two territorial imperatives emanating from the legislative branch—geography and jurisdiction, constituencies and committees.

With the decline of political parties since the end of World War II, the legislator has come to learn that he can serve but one master—his constituency. During the 1950s, Speaker Sam Rayburn could tell freshman Democrats, "To get along, go along," but even then that appeal to party loyalty was quite weak. It was weakened further during the 1960s and 1970s as legislators began amassing the taxpayer-supported private perks—franking privileges, personal staff, district offices, and trips to the home district—that enabled them to forge independent electoral support in their districts, bypassing legislative party leaders altogether.

In sum, legislators are bound to the tugs of geography, since it is the geographic constituency that looms largest in the legislator's career calculations.[4] Occasionally this link is weakened by a partisan or presidential appeal. Party leaders do, in principle, have some leverage with the rank and file through their influence on committee assignments, scheduling of legislation, and other institutional controls. But, in practice, they hesitate to use these levers and typically defer to the interests of members and committees. Somewhat more frequently, the legislator-constituency link is weakened as members seek broader support (especially campaign contributions) from political action committees serving trade, labor, and single-issue interests. Ultimately, however, most legislators are preoccupied with reelection.

There is a second important consequence of the electoral connection. Committees and subcommittees are instrumental to legislators grappling with the pressures of geography.[5] When a legislator arrives in Congress he finds a complex division-of-labor system consisting of over 20 standing committees and nearly 150 subcommittees. Each of these units has a well-defined policy jurisdiction in which it occupies a commanding position in originating new legislation and in monitoring and overseeing existing statutes implemented by executive-branch agencies. If a legislator expects to have some impact on new and existing policies that are especially important to his constituents, he must seek an appropriate niche in the division of labor. And the evidence on committee assignments is quite conclusive: he does! Most legislators gravitate to the committees and subcommittees whose jurisdictions are most relevant to their geographic constituencies.[6]

As a consequence, committees and subcommittees are not collections of legislators representing diverse views from across the nation. Nor are they collections of disinterested members who develop objective policy expertise. Rather, they are populated by those with the highest stake in a given policy jurisdiction. Hence, farm-state congressmen dominate the agriculture committees; urban legislators predominate on the banking, housing, and social welfare committees; members with military bases and defense industries in their districts are found on the armed services committees; and westerners are disproportionately represented on the public works, natural resources, and environmental committees. In short, the geographic link, forged in the electoral arena, is institutionalized in the committee system of the legislature.

Committee and Subcommittee Jurisdictions

Particular committees and subcommittees are sought by legislators because they occupy key locations in policy making. Three distinct reasons underpin their importance. First, committees and their subcommittees originate legislation. Although there is some built-in overlap in committee and subcommittee jurisdictions, these units typically have a jurisdictional monopoly over specific pieces of public policy. Changes in statutory policy will therefore require the assent of relevant committee and subcommittee majorities. Put differently, changes in policy may be vetoed by committees and subcommittees if their preferences are not reflected in the new policy.

Second, committees and subcommittees are oversight agents. The conventional wisdom on the ascendancy of the executive branch often cites the infrequency of official, public, oversight hearings, and investigations as evidence that Congress has abdicated its job of overseeing executive activities. Oversight, however, neither implies nor requires legislative intervention in executive administration. With the growth of congressional committee staffs, a good deal more oversight goes on, often surreptitiously, than is acknowledged by those who see only an unchecked executive branch. The traditional interpretation is also based on the premise that, in order to know whether an agency is pursuing the right course, intensive study, in-depth hearings, and investigations are necessary. This underlying premise is false. Rather, congressmen on a particular subcommittee know whether an agency is making "appropriate" decisions by the level of argument. Something is amiss when they hear their constituents clamoring. Finally, a subcommittee wields a "club behind the door." It possesses a variety of sanctions that it may impose on errant agencies. In 1980, for example, the Federal Trade Commission (FTC) was forced to close its doors for a day when Congress failed to approve its budget for the fiscal year. Like a warning shot, that action was intended to have a sobering effect.

These mechanisms restrain executive agencies in their implementation of current policies. The wise bureau chief appreciates that, in exercising whatever policy discretion he has, he must attend to the concerns of relevant committee and subcommittee members who can embarrass or otherwise complicate his life through the adverse publicity of oversight and who can directly affect his bureau's authority and budget through the annual authorization and appropriations process.

The recent events at the FTC illustrate this view.[7] From 1979 through early 1982, the FTC was vigorously criticized by its oversight subcommittee for "regulating all kinds of business activities that should not be the concern of the government." The congressmen participating in this assault, as well as much of the popular press, viewed the furor over the FTC as an instance of Congress finally catching a "runaway, uncontrollable bureaucracy." Indeed, in this three-year period, nearly every program initiated by the commission during the 1970s was substantially altered or eliminated. But this rendering of the conventional wisdom had little to do with the realities of recent policy reversals and sanctions at the FTC. The major FTC initiatives of the 1970s are more accurately interpreted as a partnership between an activist commission and an activist Senate subcommittee. Members of the Senate Commerce Committee's oversight subcommittee sought to establish themselves as advocates of the new consumerism (the most visible were Senators Warren G. Magnuson, John Moss, and Philip Hart). In 1977 these activist members all left the subcommittee.[8] Their places were taken by opponents of the consumerism they had fostered. Prior to 1977, activists in the FTC worked hand in hand with activists on the subcommittee. The sanctions that followed in 1979 were the result of a newly composed subcommittee reversing the policies of its predecessor, rather than the harnessing of a runaway, uncontrollable bureaucracy. The point here is that ties between agencies and subcommittees are subtle, behind the scenes, and easily missed by outsiders.

The origin of legislation and the monitoring of its implementation explain not only why committees and subcommittees are important in policy making but also how such policies will be tailored. Given the unrepresentativeness of committee composition, agencies in the executive branch respond to biased interests. Thus, it is not surprising that observers have reflected on the decline of Congress; from all outward appearances, any given executive-branch agency is not responding to legislative majorities. In reality, these agencies are responding to the dominant coalition on the subcommittee overseeing it, whose members are rarely representative of the larger legislature.

There is a third piece of evidence in the case for the decisiveness of legislative committees. For committees and subcommittees to prevail, legislative majorities or other power centers in the legislature must not frustrate their designs. This circumstance is achieved by the honoring of subcommittee veto power. Each subcommittee has its own turf to protect. The current arrangement among the committees embodies the bargain, "You can retain veto power in your area, if I can retain it in mine."[9] The important consequence of subcommittee veto power is that those on the relevant subcommittees hold the power to protect the flow of public benefits to their constituents.

To summarize the foregoing argument, subcommittee jurisdiction and veto power have an enormous but largely unappreciated impact on policy making. While committees and subcommittees may not have free rein in formulating new policy, once a program or agency is in place, subcommittees can protect it against policy change they deem undesirable. The obvious consequence of this power is what others call the uncontrollability of government operations. Reform proposals and policy initiatives to alter bad programs regularly fall on deaf ears or have little effect when put in operation. The reason is that subcommittees veto all proposals that make their constituents worse off. And they may do so in an innocuous manner — simply by taking no action. Their monopoly jurisdiction — protected by congressional majorities composed of representatives who have something to protect — ensures that there are rarely penalties for inaction. Attempts to improve even some of the most egregious features of programs are rejected, because such reforms typically make current beneficiaries worse off. The result is that programs are difficult to reform, not because the executive branch is too powerful but because the programs are protected by subcommittees composed of the programs' most (and perhaps only) enthusiastic supporters. Members find this arrangement electorally rewarding since it gives them a decisive voice in policy areas that concern their constituents.

Having examined the dominant factors of geography and jurisdiction in Congress, the only remaining possibility for moderating committee and subcommittee decisiveness is the existence of other institutional power sources. Congress once had powerful Speakers, strong party leaders, and dominant appropriations and rules committees that, to some extent, thwarted overly ambitious schemes hatched by authorizing committees. These "institutional regulators" have been constrained and compromised (often in the name of reform). By the mid-1970s, Congress had dramatically modified its two most important institutional regulators — the House Committee on Rules and the Committee on Appropriations. It had also restructured itself — through the Legislative Reorganization Act of 1970, the Subcommittee Bill of Rights of 1973, and the Committee Reform Amendments of 1974 — into an organization dominated, in each chamber, by its subcommittees. Even the full committees and their chairmen were generally reduced to "holding companies" and "traffic cops," respectively. The destruction of internal regulators for short-term advantage has left Congress vulnerable to the serious long-term problem identified by the cartoon character Pogo —"We has met the enemy, and it is us." Congress has been eclipsed not by the executive branch but by its own subunits. The decline of Congress is, in fact, the rise of government by (sub)committee.

The 1970s were a high-watermark for institutional reform. Predating this spate of reform activity, however, some important early developments set the stage for current problems. In the 1960s there were two legislative obstacles to a program of policies supported by the Kennedy and Johnson administrations as well as majorities in the House and Senate. In the process of eliminating these obstacles, changes were made in the House that ultimately aided and abetted the rise of subcommittee power.

The first obstacle to the Democratic agenda of social programs in 1961 was a coalition of Republicans and southern Democrats who dominated the House Rules Committee, claiming its chairman, "Judge" Howard Smith, as one of their own.[10] This coalition could block the new legislative initiatives of the administration by denying it access to the House floor (one of the central "regulatory" roles played by the Rules Committee in the House is the scheduling of legislative debate and the establishment of the terms of debate and procedure). This had been the experience of the previous two years. Despite large liberal majorities in both houses following the 1958 elections, Democrats were a frustrated lot during the Eighty-sixth Congress (1959–61). Fearing his new president's program would suffer the same fate, Speaker Rayburn commenced the Eighty-seventh Congress by breaking the conservatives' control of the Rules Committee. He enlarged the committee from twelve to fifteen members. The newly constituted Rules Committee, with an 8–7 liberal majority, was more permissive in its dealings with the legislative committees.

During the remainder of the decade and into the 1970s, the Rules Committee's independence was further compromised. By the end of the 1970s, all members of the Rules Committee were being appointed each Congress by the Speaker; and, on a vote by the Democratic Caucus, its committee members could be instructed on how to vote in committee deliberations. Short-term objectives, which governed the reform of the Rules Committee, had unanticipated long-term consequences. A strong and independent Rules Committee capable of restraining the excesses of either an ambitious executive or overindulgent legislative committees ceased to exist. No longer constituting an obstacle to legislative permissiveness, the Rules Committee took on the role of expediting legislative procedure. It generally worked in tandem with, not as a restraint upon, committees and subcommittees, thereby paving the way for the spurt of legislation in the mid-1960s that came to be known as the Great Society. The current difficulty with Great Society entitlement and credit programs can be traced, in part, to this institutional reform.

In order to implement a program, an executive agency requires both statutory authority and the appropriation of monies. The second legislative obstacle to the social programs of the 1960s was the House Appropriations Committee. During that decade, especially during the Great Society period, legislative committees eagerly provided new authority. The stumbling block was the House Appropriations Committee, dominated by fiscally conservative legislators. These legislators operated on the assumption that every budget was padded and should be cut. The members of the Appropriations Committee saw themselves as the "guardians of the Treasury," the last bulwark against assaults on the Treasury by legislative committees, executive agencies, and the Senate.[11]

The Appropriations Committee, consisting of fifty members, was too large and fiscal conservatives were too entrenched to break their hold on appropriations decisions. The strategy used against the Rules Committee (stacking the committee with additional liberal legislators) could not be made to work here. Instead, legislative committees and their supporting chamber majorities, in cooperation with executive agencies and with the blessing of majority party leaders, began making "end-runs" on the Appropriations Committee. Several devices were employed.

Entitlements, obligating Federal payment to "entitled" categories of citizens, began to grow in popularity. This technique allowed legislative committees to mandate payments from the Federal Treasury without prior consent from Appropriations. These committees devised criteria of eligibility and payment schedules linked to these criteria, so that any citizen who qualified held a claim against the government for payment. The Appropriations Committee was obligated to provide the necessary monies; it was faced with a fait accompli.

Entitlements are not simply the product of authorizing-committee ingenuity. It is no accident that the two largest and fiscally problematic entitlement programs, social security and Medicare, apparently required an activist president in cooperation with an unprecedented majority in Congress. In each case, a means around Appropriations was found — through Ways and Means — that insulated these programs. The mechanism put in place to protect the programs are *congressional* mechanisms.

In what would seem a significant move, the Budget Act of 1974 put an end to any new entitlement programs unless consented to by Appropriations. But much of the damage had already been done. Pre-1974 entitlement programs were given protection by way of a grandfather clause in the 1974 Budget Act — a strong indication of the ability of subcommittees to protect and entrench previous programs from efforts to contain or gut them.

Although the Budget Act controls the creation of additional entitlement programs, new policy instruments and practices were honed to neutralize the Appropriations Committee in the post-Budget Act environment. Two of special significance are regulatory controls and credit programs. The former bypass Appropriations in large part by shifting financial responsibility to the private sector or other levels of government. The latter are "off-budget" and, much like the entitlement programs of the 1960s, present Appropriations with spending obligations that are faits accomplis. This little known but potent process works as follows. The Federal Financing Bank (FFB) handles loans granted by Federal agencies. When an agency reaches its appropriated limit on direct loans, it turns its notes over to the FFB for cash. The FFB has almost no discretion over whether to purchase the notes. Since an agency may repeat this process, the limits imposed by Appropriations on an agency's ability to lend money are virtually without effect. Moreover, the FFB's budgetary authority and outlays are by law excluded from the unified budget totals of the government. FFB activity had reached nearly $30 billion by 1981.

With this series of developments, committees, subcommittees, and the forces of geography and jurisdiction they represent have been unleashed. The destruction of prime institutional regulators—parties, rules, and the appropriations process—removed constraints on producing new programs and agencies. Once in place, subcommittee veto power insulated these programs from outside influence. Congress may thus appear rudderless and ineffectual; governmental programs may appear uncontrollable. But both effects are underpinned by the rise of committees and especially subcommittees as the dominant institutional forces within the government.

Shortcomings of Current Proposals

Proposals that have been promoted as solutions to policy problems misconstrue the sources of current policy and consequently fail to appreciate and restrain the decisive influence of committees and subcommittees. They attempt to treat the symptoms instead of the disease and thus are unlikely to have any beneficial effect; indeed, they may make problems worse.

The congressional budget process represented Congress's early attempt to regain the power of the purse and to systematize its procedures in the realm of tax and expenditure policies. But, while having an important impact, this process has failed as an effective vehicle for confronting national fiscal problems. In our opinion, this result follows from the failure of the process to constrain effectively the underlying causes of fiscal problems—namely, the power afforded committees and subcommittees.

The congressional budget process is the product of the Congressional Budget and Impoundment Control Act of 1974. The centerpiece of this act is a process in which two budget committees (newly created at the time of the act) are responsible for obtaining House and Senate approval of two concurrent resolutions—

the First and Second Budget Resolutions. The first resolution sets nonbinding targets for total spending ceilings (disaggregated into nineteen functional categories), revenue floors, and deficits. After both houses pass a first budget resolution, ideally no later than mid-May preceding a new fiscal year, the normal business of authorization and appropriation for the ensuing fiscal year proceeds. The Congressional Budget Office (also newly created at the time of the act) keeps track of how well Congress is doing in comparison to the targets.

By 15 September of each year, approximately two weeks before the beginning of the new fiscal year on 1 October, the House and Senate must pass the second budget resolution — a *binding* ceiling on total outlays and a *binding* floor on total revenues. If the taxing and spending decisions made in the authorization-appropriation phase are inconsistent with these binding restraints, then either a new second budget resolution that restores consistency (by raising the spending ceiling or lowering the revenue floor) must be approved, or a reconciliation procedure must be enacted. The latter is a set of instructions to relevant committees commanding them to find ways to reduce outlays or increase revenues by specific amounts in order to bring the totals into compliance with the second resolution.

There is little doubt that eight years of the Budget Act regimen have sensitized legislators to the economic consequences of their collective fiscal behavior. It is one thing, however, to affect legislative attitudes and information; it is quite another to affect legislative behavior. At the time of the first budget resolution, many legislators are prepared to support the appearance of fiscal prudence. But in the legislative trenches — in the committee and subcommittee hearing rooms and markup sessions where statutory authority is provided and monies appropriated — they revert to previous form. When all is said and done, each legislator is protective of his constituency and his committee (geography and jurisdiction, again). Congress has found it very difficult to translate fiscal prudence at the level of budget totals into a workable procedure for compliance by committees and subcommittees. Part of the difficulty may be traced to the fact that, while the fiscal constraints of the budget process apply to *totals*, committee and subcommittee decision making occurs at the much narrower level of separate policy jurisdictions. Congress has been unable or unwilling to translate these constraints into binding instructions. The effect is that the second budget resolution becomes an "adding machine": in most years prior committee-sponsored outlay decisions are simply totaled and declared the spending ceiling in the second resolution.

Two important ironies are associated with the budget process. The first, which has seriously jeopardized the process, is the role played by those indexed entitlement programs "grandfathered" in by the Budget Act. Grandfathering has extended the protection of committee veto to these programs and is the major reason they are "uncontrollable" today. As outlays for these purposes have grown, the only way to control spending (without statutory changes in entitlement programs) is to reduce outlays in the nonentitlement, "controllable," programs. Committees, naturally enough, have resisted this meddling as much as possible, with mounting outlays and deficits the immediate consequence.[12]

A second irony involves adaptive behavior. Fiscal constraints invite political ingenuity. Congress has moved massively into the credit area precisely because government loans and other forms of credit subsidy and regulation are not counted in the outlay totals governed by the Budget Act. Most of the credit expenditures are "off-budget" and therefore provide a convenient device by which to subsidize privileged sectors of the economy while remaining nominally in compliance with the strictures of the Budget Act.[13]

The same may be said for the spate of regulatory activity of the last decade. By imposing costly requirements on private economic actors, policy objectives may be accomplished with only a fraction of their total expense borne by the Treasury.[14] It is no accident that surges in both regulatory activity and government credit manipulation have been the twin companions of the budget process.

The final word on the budget process is that unless and until Congress deals directly with its subunits, it will ultimately be compelled to depend on events and personalities beyond its control in order to reduce fiscal excesses.

Frustration with Congress and the failures of its budget process has led some to promote the more drastic constitutional approach to restrict expenditures, limit taxes, and reduce deficits. Of the several proposals currently circulating, only Senate Joint Resolution 58 has received the endorsement of President Reagan and the necessary two-thirds support of the full Senate. Though it recently failed in the House, its strong showing there suggests it will reappear next year.

S.J. 58 requires Congress, before each fiscal year, to "adopt a statement of receipts and outlays for that year in which total outlays are no greater than total receipts." Congress may provide for a deficit only if three-fifths of each body explicitly votes for it. "Outlays" are broadly defined so as to cover what are currently categorized as "off-budget." Moreover, the capacity to "balance the budget on the backs of the taxpayers" is circumscribed by a section of the amendment that prohibits tax receipts to grow faster than national income (unless majorities in each house vote to the contrary). Thus, by restricting the growth in receipts and requiring budgetary balance, S.J. 58 also acts to limit expenditures.

There are numerous difficulties with this amendment, especially in the area of implementation, where it is ambiguous. Most disturbing is its failure to detail how constraints on aggregate congressional behavior will restrain the currently excessive spending behavior of decentralized congressional subunits. Like the budget process, S.J. 58 reflects a strategy that aims not at the source of the problem but at its symptoms. Federal spending, taxing, and budgetary imbalance do not just happen; they are the consequence of many smaller events. Once again, committees and subcommittees in Congress are not seen as the root of the problem. It is wishful thinking to believe that constraints at the top will trickle down to the guilty parties.

S.J. 58 also fails to anticipate adaptive behavior mitigating the amendment's intended effect. Legislators turned to regulation and credit manipulation in response to the fiscal constraints of the congressional budget process a decade ago. We anticipate similar adaptations to a balanced budget amendment. Political incentives to provide public benefits to constituents remain securely in place despite the constitutional amendment. Fiscal constraints invite political ingenuity. If the amendment is approved, therefore, legislators will probably find a way to provide benefits that comply with the new constitutional order. Only the most benign view suggests that these new means will have less onerous consequences than the current ones. Senator Pete Domenici, chairman of the Senate Budget Committee, has acknowledged the following possibilities: more Federal loan guarantees, capital budgeting outside the unified budget, and especially mandated private-sector spending through regulation. Moreover, the evidence from the experiences of states' grappling with their own balanced budget requirements reveals the invention of a host of "off-budget enterprises" that often escape the attention of even duly constituted legislative authorities.[15] From this perspective, perhaps the most serious consequence of passage of a constitutional amendment is that many people will be lulled into thinking that the problem has been solved.

We have argued that reforms that fail to deal with the motives of legislators in their capacities as members of committees and subcommittees cannot achieve their objectives. Increasingly, over several years, a set of legislative actions gave these units additional powers — the legislative veto — for dealing with programs under their jurisdiction. In this light, the legislative veto would worsen the situation, because it is founded on the belief that the problem lies not in the legislative branch at all but rather in the executive agencies' misuse of legislative delegations of power. Proponents of the legislative veto assume that the requirements of administration are such that Congress must make broad grants of authority to the executive branch. Congress, it is argued, cannot always write into statute a specific formula or detail for every contingency. Thus, in order to preserve legislative authority, the legislative veto gives Congress an opportunity for an "official look." It is a device that enables a prior delegation of authority to the executive branch under the condition that Congress has an ex post opportunity to negate actions it judges in violation of legislative intent.

Approximately two hundred statutes contained such provisions when the Supreme Court declared them unconstitutional. Enough experience had shown that the legislative veto, intended to operate as an after-the-fact device by which the legislature may correct agency misuses of legislative delegations of power, acted on agency heads and bureau chiefs as an incentive to avoid doing anything in the first instance that might trigger the veto. But jurisdiction over a veto resolution fell to the committee or subcommittee that originated the statute granting the initial legislative delegation. So long as the agency head or bureau chief attends to the desires of the committee and subcommittee holding jurisdiction, he can preempt the veto option. The legislative veto is therefore counterproductive, because it strengthens the link between government agencies and congressional committees and subcommittees.

Given the self-selection that characterizes committee and subcommittee membership, the legislative veto strengthens the hands of precisely those legislators whose policy interests are the most extreme. Yet this is the source of the problem, not a solution to it. Farm-state representatives, sitting on the Agriculture Committee, seek the most generous terms and eligibility requirements in agricultural credit programs; Armed Services Committee legislators are the most adamantly opposed to closing defense facilities (often located in their own districts); Commerce Committee members take a keen interest in industry regulations written by the Federal Trade Commission; members of the Education and Labor Committee are supportive of the most liberal terms for student grants; and so on. The committee/subcommittee capacity to veto, or at least to initiate that process, encourages agency personnel to take certain actions (and to avoid others) in order to short-circuit the veto process. The legislative veto simply exacerbates the government-by-subcommittee syndrome.

Sunset legislation also strengthens the hold of oversight subcommittees, though in a more indirect way. The support for sunset legislation is stimulated by the belief that old agencies never die. By writing into their charter an automatic expiration date that takes effect unless the charter is renewed by an act of Congress, the sunset provision gives Congress some control over the actions of agencies, as well as the capacity to weed out inefficient or redundant executive-branch entities.

But who gets this control? Congress may always turn to the appropriations process to effect economies and to eliminate wasteful activities. Hence, these nominal objectives of sunset provisions surely cannot be their driving force. Rather, sunset legislation strengthens the hold of authorizing committees because it is a powerful (though perhaps clumsy) instrument by which an authorizing committee may discipline "runaway bureaucracies." Its mere existence is intended to have a sobering effect. Although, as noted, it is a clumsy instrument, agency heads and interested others are not, by nature, risk-takers. The threat, therefore, has some value for the committee of jurisdiction in further enhancing its hold on agencies.

Implications for Reform: Designing Solutions to Fit the Problems

Current proposals have failed to check the excesses of subcommittee government. As described in the preceding sections, the transmission of authority to committees and subcommittees in Congress and the restriction or destruction of legislative institutions of self-regulation have given a relatively free-hand, in each policy jurisdiction, to self-interested collections of legislators. Animated by the electoral connection, these legislators gravitate to, and then dominate, relevant committees and subcommittees. What emerges is a policy-making subsystem in which the chief legislative actions come from those legislators with the greatest stake in each policy jurisdiction.

The central theme of this essay has been the active and pivotal role of congressional committees and subcommittees in the growth of the Federal government and the intrusiveness of Federal policies. The source of overly bureaucratic agencies, of service to special interest groups, and indeed of the growth of government lies with Congress and not with "runaway agencies" or "uncontrollable" spending. Congress is always present at the creation, so to speak, and must therefore be assigned the responsibilities of paternity. Bureaucracies are "runaways" and spending programs are "uncontrollable" because Congress made them that way.

Even to speak of *Congress* as the problem is to misstate the fact of the matter, for legislative majorities are often as frustrated as ordinary citizens with current conditions. It is the decentralized condition of the Congress today, reflected in legislator independence and committee/subcommittee autonomy, that makes it impossible to rein in the twin forces of geography and jurisdiction. Congress has lost the capacity for self-discipline. It has destroyed its institutions of self-regulation.

Solutions to policy problems must therefore concentrate on mechanisms that constrain the autonomy of legislative committees. Problems like regulation, credit, and indexed entitlements (to name the most apparent) have proved impenetrable and uncontrollable by either Congress or the executive branch. The particular pattern of public policy decisions is not the result of evil spirits, and the impenetrability is not the product of entrenched, insidious bureaucrats who have the upper hand against Congress and the president. These difficulties derive from subcommittee autonomy, subcommittee veto power, and subcommittee self-interest (indeed, conflict of interest). Programs with socially undesirable consequences continue because someone benefits from them. Current legislative arrangements are perverse in that the representatives of these beneficiaries, sitting on appropriate subcommittees, have veto power. They are in a position to sabotage, water down, or simply ignore ameliorative changes (i.e., changes that would put those benefits at risk). In short, the fox is guarding the chicken house!

Put more constructively, while still retaining the apparent advantages of a division-of-labor that the committee system offers, Congress must reestablish its previous control over the excesses of committee and subcommittee autonomy. Briefly, then, such checks might take the following form:

• Strengthen the Budget Act: Elevate the Budget Committees to standing committees of full rank; strengthen their hand at the stage of the First Budget Resolution; make it difficult to alter targets in the Second Budget Resolution to accommodate legislative committee desires; incorporate credit and other off-budget activities into a unified budget subject to the Budget Act; and make it more difficult to waive provisions of the Budget Act to suit the wishes of committees and their temporary allies.

• Revitalize the Appropriations Committees: Bring entitlement programs under their jurisdiction by permitting them to incorporate expenditure reductions in annual appropriations bills (the Holman Rule); create a unified budget with all outlay decisions—for example, credit programs—coming under their purview; reestablish the power of the chairman, through strengthened powers to make subcommittee assignments, to control committee staff, and generally to rein in the independence of subcommittees; and encourage joint consideration by the committee of all appropriations bills, rather than the current practice of piecemeal consideration of thirteen distinct measures.

- Revitalize the Rules Committee: Eliminate the power of party caucuses to instruct its members on votes; strengthen the capacity of Rules Committee majorities to block or extract concessions from legislative committees; and protect the rules of procedure laid down by the Rules Committee for consideration of a piece of legislation from amendments.
- Reform the Subcommittee Bill of Rights: Reinvigorate full committee chairmen by giving them more input in subcommittee assignments, more control over the allocation of staff and budgets to subcommittees, and more influence over subcommittee agendas.
- Integrate the president more fully into the legislative process: Short of an item veto (the ability to veto particular sections of bills), which is constitutionally proscribed, enable the president, before signing a bill into law or vetoing it, to attempt to reconcile the legislature's product with his own proposals; remove legislative liaison personnel from executive departments and centralize them, instead, in the Executive Office; and tighten "central clearance" procedures in order to minimize subdepartmental "end runs" to Congress.

Specific solutions will undoubtedly have flaws of their own. Any arrangement that seeks to endow an organization with the capacity to act but to constrain it from acting excessively must make some trade-offs. Where to draw this line is not self-evident. But any institutional arrangement with the line drawn at either extreme will either be immobilized or ravaged by insatiable appetites. To correct for the former, the legislative reforms of the last twenty years have fallen prey to the latter.

Reform of particular programs, efforts to improve overall public performance, and even attempts to limit the growth of government must somehow deal with Congress by reestablishing some of those checks on insatiable appetites. Basically, the problem is one of legislative self-governance. Failure to address it at its source — the Congress — ensures that public policies will continue to be distorted by the intense preferences of self-selected legislative committees and unrepresentative geographic constituencies.

NOTES

1. A comprehensive recent statement is found in James L. Sundquist, *The Decline and Resurgence of Congress* (Washington, D.C.: Brookings Institution, 1981).

2. Morris P. Fiorina, "Control of the Bureaucracy: A Mismatch of Incentives and Capabilities," Formal Publication No. 28, Center for the Study of American Business, Washington University, St. Louis, 1979. See also his masterful study, *Congress: Keystone of the Washington Establishment* (New Haven: Yale University Press, 1977).

3. For a popular historical account, see Alvin H. Josephy, *On the Hill: A History of the American Congress* (New York: Simon and Schuster, 1979). See also Kenneth A. Shepsle, "Geography, Jurisdiction, and the Congressional Budget Process," Working Paper No. 73, Center for the Study of American Business, Washington University, St. Louis, 1982.

4. See Shepsle, "Geography and Jurisdiction" and Richard F. Fenno, *Home Style* (Boston: Little, Brown, 1978).

5. See Richard Fenno, *Congressmen in Committees* (Boston: Little, Brown, 1973) and David Mayhew, *Congress: The Electoral Connection* (New Haven: Yale University Press, 1974). Also see Fiorina, *Congress*.

6. The evidence is presented in Kenneth A. Shepsle, *The Giant Jigsaw Puzzle: Democratic Committee Assignments in the Modern House* (Chicago: University of Chicago Press, 1978).

7. The evidence summarized in this section is taken from Barry R. Weingast and Mark J. Moran, "Bureaucratic Discretion or Congressional Control: Regulatory Policymaking by the Federal Trade Commission," Working Paper No. 72, Center for the Study of American Business, Washington University, St. Louis, 1982. See also idem, "The Myth of the Runaway Bureaucracy: The Case of the FTC," *Regulation* 6, no. 3 (1982): 33–38.

8. See Weingast and Moran, "The Myth of the Runaway Bureaucracy."

9. This unappreciated part of the reciprocity system in Congress is described and its implications traced in Donald Matthews, *U.S. Senators and Their World* (Chapel Hill, N.C.: University of North Carolina Press, 1960). Also see Mayhew, *Congress* and Morris P. Fiorina, "Legislative Facilitation of Governmental Growth: Universalism and Reciprocity Practices in Majority Rule Institutions," Social Science Working Paper No. 226, California Institute of Technology, August 1978.

10. See Robert L. Peabody, "The Enlarged Rules Committee," in *New Perspectives on the House of Representatives*, 3d ed., ed. Robert L. Peabody and Nelson Polsby (Chicago: Rand McNally, 1977).

11. The seminal treatment of the House Appropriations Committee is found in Richard F. Fenno, *The Power of the Purse* (Boston: Little, Brown, 1966). An updated statement is Allen Schick, *Congress and Money* (Washington, D.C.: Urban Institute, 1980).

12. See Clifford M. Hardin and Kenneth W. Chilton, "Budget Control and Indexed Entitlements: Are They Compatible?", Formal Publication No. 40, Center for the Study of American Business, Washington University, St. Louis 1981.

13. See Clifford M. Hardin and Arthur T. Denzau, "The Unrestrained Growth of Federal Credit Programs," Formal Publication No. 45, Center for the Study of American Business, Washington University, St. Louis, 1981.

14. See Murray L. Weidenbaum, "Benefit-Cost Analysis of Government Regulation," Formal Publication No. 37, Center for the Study of American Business, Washington University, St. Louis, 1981.

15. See James T. Bennett and Thomas J. DiLorenzo, "Off-Budget Operations and Fiscal Responsibility," *Policy Report*, 4 (April 1982).

Constitutional Amendment to Limit the Growth of Spending

MILTON AND ROSE FRIEDMAN

A Constitutional Amendment requiring the federal government to balance the budget and limit spending has been working its way through the Congress. The requirement to balance the budget will require a legislature that votes for spending also to vote for tax increases. The requirement to limit spending will require one program to be measured against another program.

The Senate passed such an amendment on August 4, 1982, by a vote of 69 to 31—two more than the two-thirds vote required for approval of a Constitutional Amendment. The approval was bipartisan: 47 Republicans, 21 Democrats, and 1 Independent voted for the amendment.

The House Democratic leadership tried to prevent a vote on the amendment in the House before the November 1982 elections. However, a discharge petition forced a vote on it on October 1, the last full day of the regular session. The amendment was approved by a majority (236 to 187), but not by the necessary two thirds. Again, the majority was bipartisan: 167 Republicans, 69 Democrats. In view of its near passage and the widespread public support for it, the amendment has been reintroduced and remains a live issue.

The amendment adopted by the Senate is as follows:

PROPOSED CONSTITUTIONAL AMENDMENT

SECTION 1. Prior to each fiscal year, the Congress shall adopt a statement of receipts and outlays for that year in which total outlays are not greater than total receipts. The Congress may amend such statement provided revised outlays are no greater than revised receipts. Whenever three-fifths of the whole number of both Houses shall deem it necessary, Congress in such statement may provide for a specific excess of outlays over receipts by a vote directed solely to that subject. The Congress and the President shall, pursuant to legislation or through exercise of their powers under the first and second articles, ensure that actual outlays do not exceed the outlays set forth in such statement.

SECTION 2. Total receipts for any fiscal year set forth in the statement adopted pursuant to this article shall not increase by a rate greater than the rate of increase in national income in the year or years ending not less than six months nor more than twelve months before such fiscal year, unless a majority of the whole number of both Houses of Congress shall have passed a bill directed solely to approving specific additional receipts and such bill has become law.

SECTION 3. The Congress may waive the provisions of this article for any fiscal year in which a declaration of war is in effect.

SECTION 4. Total receipts shall include all receipts of the United States except for those derived from borrowing and total outlays shall include all outlays of the United States except those for repayment of debt principal.

SECTION 5. The Congress shall enforce and implement this article by appropriate legislation.

SECTION 6. On and after the date this article takes effect, the amount of Federal public debt limit as of such date shall become permanent and there shall be no increase in such amount unless three-fifths of the whole number of both Houses of Congress shall have passed a bill approving such increase and such bill has become law.

SECTION 7. This article shall take effect for the second fiscal year beginning after its ratification.

This amendment would achieve two related objectives: first, it would increase the likelihood that the federal budget would be brought into balance, not by prohibiting an unbalanced budget but by making it more difficult to enact a budget calling for a deficit; second, it would check the growth of government spending — again, not by prohibiting such growth but by making it more difficult.

The key provisions of this amendment are to be found in the first two sections. The first requires that Congress *plan* for a balanced budget and that the Congress and the President shall make sure that actual spending does not exceed planned spending. Note that nothing is said about assuring that actual *receipts* equal (or exceed) planned receipts. That is deliberate. An Administration can pretty effectively control spending, but it cannot exercise the same degree of control over receipts, which are affected much more by economic conditions. Let a boom develop, actual receipts will exceed planned receipts; let a recession develop, receipts will drop. The first section does not rule out such automatically produced surpluses or deficits. This is one of the important subtleties of the amendment. It avoids a rigidity that would be intolerable and harmful. It requires no year-by-year budget balance, but balance over the length, or course, of business cycles.

By itself, the first section would not directly limit the growth of government. It would simply require that taxes and spending go up together. The second section adds the necessary element. It provides that planned receipts may not increase from one year to the next by a greater percentage than national income. Under Section 1, planned spending must be less than or equal to planned receipts, and actual spending must be less than or equal to planned spending. Hence, limiting receipts limits spending. Moreover, if in any year Congress manages to keep planned receipts and spending below the maximum level, the effect is to lower the maximum level for subsequent years, thus fostering a gradual ratcheting down of spending relative to national income.

Another strength of the amendment is the provision for approving an exceptional increase in planned receipts (hence in planned outlays). Some earlier versions of the amendment called for requiring a two-thirds majority to approve an exceptional increase in spending. The amendment that passed the Senate requires only "a majority of the whole number of both houses of Congress." Nonetheless, we regard this version as stronger than the earlier ones, because the majority must vote for an explicit tax increase. It is harder to get a simple majority of Congress to approve an explicit increase in taxes than to get a two-thirds majority to approve an exceptional increase in spending.

The amendment is very much in the spirit of the Bill of Rights, the first Ten Amendments to the Constitution. Their purpose was to limit the government in order to free the people. Similarly, the purpose of the balanced-budget-and-tax-limitation amendment is to limit the government in order to free the people, in this instance from excessive taxation. Its passage would go a long way to remedy the defect in our budgetary process. By the same token, it would make it more difficult for supporters of ever-bigger government to attain their goals.

It is no surprise that a torrent of criticism has been loosed against the proposed amendment by people who believe that our problems arise not from excessive government but from the failure to give government enough power or enough control over us as individuals. It is no surprise that the Democratic Speaker of the House, Tip O'Neill, and his fellow advocates of big government tried to prevent a vote in the House on the amendment. He and others used all the pressure at their command to prevent its receiving a two-thirds majority.

It is no surprise, either, that when the amendment did come to a vote in the House, a substantial majority voted for it. After all, repeatedly in opinion polls more than three quarters of the public have favored such an amendment. Their representatives do not find it easy to disregard that sentiment in an open vote — which is why Democratic leaders tried to prevent the amendment from coming to a vote. When their hand was forced, they quickly introduced a meaningless substitute that was overwhelmingly defeated (346 to 77), but that gave some representatives an opportunity to cast a recorded vote for a token budget-balancing amendment while at the same time voting against the real thing.

Unfortunately, the criticism of the amendment by believers in big government has been reinforced by skepticism about the amendment's possible effectiveness by persons who otherwise share our basic outlook about the importance of limiting government in order to preserve and expand individual freedom. They say that the Congress and the President could now, without an amendment, reduce government spending and balance the budget. Yet, the fact is, they have not done so and show little sign of doing so. If the same Congress and the same President enact budgets that produce large current deficits and also approve a constitutional amendment to limit future deficits, they are hypocrites. Could such hypocrites be counted on to carry out the amendment if adopted?

Of course, they would be guilty of hypocrisy. We have long believed that Congressional hypocrisy and shortsightedness are the only reasons that there is a ghost of a chance of getting Congress to pass an amendment limiting itself. Most members of Congress will do anything to postpone the problems they face by a couple of years — only Wall Street has a shorter perspective. If the hypocrisy did not exist, if Congress behaved "responsibly," the amendment would not be needed. Congress's irresponsibility is the reason that we need an amendment — and hypocrisy is, ironically, the reason that there is a chance of getting the amendment passed.

Though hypocrisy may eventually lead to the passing of the amendment, hypocrisy will not prevent the amendment from having important effects three or four years down the line — and from casting its shadow on events even sooner. Congress will not violate the Constitution lightly. Members of Congress will wriggle and squirm; they will seek, and no doubt find, subterfuges and evasions. But their actions will be significantly affected by the existence of the amendment. The experience of several states that have passed similar tax-limitation amendments provides ample evidence of this.

No Constitutional provision will be enforced unless it has widespread public support. "Prohibition" (the Volstead Act) certainly demonstrated that. However, if a provision does have widespread support — as public-opinion polls show that this one does — legislators are not inclined to flout it.

Equally important, legislators will find it in their own interest to confer an aura of inviolability on the amendment. This point has been impressed on us by the experience of legislators in states that have adopted amendments limiting state spending. Prior to the enactment of such amendments, they had no effective defense against lobbyists urging spending programs — all of them, of course, for good purposes. Now they do. They can say: "Your program is an excellent one; I would like to support it, but the total amount we can spend is fixed. To get funds for your program, we shall have to cut elsewhere. Where should we cut?" The effect is to force lobbyists to compete against one another rather than, as now, against the amorphous and poorly represented body of taxpayers.

Why are we optimistic that an amendment will be passed? The reason is found in Article 5 in the U.S. Constitution, which requires that "The Congress, . . . on the application of the Legislatures of two-thirds of the several states, shall call a Convention for proposing Amendments." This is the one provision in the Constitution that bypasses Congress. And this provision is being effectively used by the supporters of an amendment. It takes thirty-four states to constitute "two-thirds of the several states." So far, the legislatures of thirty-two states — most recently, Missouri, on May 26, 1983 — have called for a constitutional convention to propose an amendment to balance the budget. It will take only two more to make calling a convention mandatory on Congress. More than two states may so vote fairly soon.

Congress does not want to be bypassed. It will be — as it has been in the past — most unwilling to have to call a convention. To avoid having to do so, it will, we believe, send a consitutional amendment to the states for ratification. When it does so, we have no doubt that the requisite three-quarters of the states will ratify it in short order.

The pressure on Congress offers a danger as well as an opportunity. The danger is that in order to preserve its own flexibility, Congress will try to emasculate the amendment while appearing to satisfy public clamor. The amendment adopted by the Senate in 1982 avoided that danger. The meaningless substitute proposed by the House leadership shows how great the danger is. It will take continued vigilance to ward off this danger.

The opportunity is no less real than the danger. There is every prospect today of an outcome that none of us would have regarded as at all likely as recently as five years ago. We predict that by the mid-1980s, a Constitutional Amendment will have been adopted that will have the effect of limiting federal spending and eliminating deficit financing.

Institutional and Mechanical Control of Federal Spending

BENJAMIN ZYCHER

The Federal budget is too large. That is, resources are more productive (on the margin) in the private sector than in the public sector, so that a shift of resources from the latter to the former would produce a net productivity gain for the economy as a whole. Moreover, taxpayers, like consumers in the private sector, presumably are interested not only in the overall level of Federal spending but also in its composition, that is, in the output mix of the Federal sector. Thus the fundamental public-policy problem is the choice of tax instruments and overall fiscal decision processes likely to lead the political system to choose a public-spending level and output mix consistent with the demands of the taxpayers.

Therefore, the budget deficit per se is not the fundamental problem. This is not to say that the choice of tax instruments (one of which is debt) is not important; on the contrary, various kinds of taxes have sharply differing effects both upon the economy and upon political incentives for public-sector spending growth. The deficit is both a manifestation and a cause of the problem, for reasons much different from those suggested (endlessly) by the conventional wisdom. The thesis here is that constraint of Federal spending in ways consistent with the demands of the taxpayers cannot be achieved through such "mechanical" devices as an item veto or tax "reform," as commonly defined. Instead, we must choose fiscal arrangements that will motivate politicians to make choices consistent with restraint and efficiency in public-sector spending. In short, hope lies in "institutional" reform.

Why the Conventional Wisdom about Deficits Is Wrong

By its very nature, conventional wisdom cannot set anyone free, and it may not even point in the right direction. Nowhere is this clearer than with respect to the ongoing debate over the Federal budget deficit. The conventional wisdom is incorrect, based as it is upon faulty economic analysis and upon a poor understanding of the causes and effects of high real (adjusted for expected inflation) interest rates and a strong dollar.

First, high real interest rates largely have not resulted from large Federal budget deficits. If the Federal budget deficit has driven up interest rates by "soaking up" capital resources, why has fixed business investment grown, until recently, at well over 20 percent per year? Why has the contribution of this investment to GNP growth been more than double that of five other economic recoveries in the postwar period? Why has the ratio of gross investment to GNP recently been greater than that of any other quarter in the postwar period? The answer is that it is *not* Federal borrowing that has driven up interest rates.

In recent years, economists have conducted no fewer than two dozen studies of the causal links between Federal borrowing and interest rates. While no single study by itself is conclusive, this body of empirical investigation taken as a whole offers an unambiguous conclusion: the effect of Federal borrowing upon interest rates is weak. Private-sector investment behavior is such that only small increases in the interest rate are required to release sufficient capital resources for government borrowing needs. Therefore, the present high real interest rates largely cannot be explained by Federal borrowing, particularly in light of the very strong investment growth in the economy.

Interest rates are high not because of Federal borrowing but because the combination of the 1981 tax cuts, accelerated depreciation, and the sharp reduction in the inflation rate has increased the after-tax rate of return on investment very substantially. This increase in the profitability of private-sector investment has expanded such investment activity, thus driving up interest rates. Only this explanation is consistent with the observation of high interest rates, a strong dollar, low inflation, and strong private-sector investment growth. The Federal deficit explanation is not.

Hence, the high real interest rates are not a cause for concern for the economy as a whole but are a *manifestation* of the strong economy. (Two quarters of zero growth in the money stock have produced the current economic slowdown, but that is irrelevant to the issue here.)

Second, while Federal borrowing is "crowding out" private-sector activity, high real interest rates will not "choke off" the recovery. *Any* public sector use of resources "crowds out" some private-sector activity. This is true regardless of whether the government spending is financed with taxation, inflation, or debt. If the deficit is reduced with increased taxes, the "crowding out" problem would not be resolved; it would merely take a different form. Again, the high interest rates, which are the *result* of the strong investment sector, cannot "choke off" the recovery. Moreover, increases in interest rates constitute a "relative" price shift and cannot depress the economy in the aggregate.

Finally, high real interest rates have strengthened the dollar, discouraging exports and encouraging imports, but this does not "destroy jobs." Proponents of tax increases to reduce the deficit argue, in effect, that the strengthening of the dollar caused by high interest rates makes the economy worse off. In other words, they have put themselves in the curious position of arguing that the economy is better off with a weak dollar than with a strong one. That argument is misleading, because a strong dollar hurts some sectors and helps others but in the aggregate makes more goods available to the economy. Thus, jobs are not "destroyed" but are *shifted* among sectors; for the economy as a whole, a strong dollar must increase the number of jobs because a strong dollar makes the economy better off, that is, wealthier. (Despite all the nonsense heard on the evening news, exports are a cost and imports a benefit of United States international trade.) Any economist able to convince policymakers that a weak dollar is preferable to a strong one has fools for clients.

Government borrowing must be repaid sooner or later with interest. The future taxes needed to repay the debt thus are equivalent to the taxes that would be needed if the deficit were to be eliminated immediately without spending cuts. In other words, government borrowing is as much a tax as any other kind of tax, and the true tax burden is the amount that the government spends. It is *not* merely the amount collected as tax revenue.

Therefore, proponents of tax increases as a means of "reducing the deficit" actually are arguing (implicitly) that other taxes are less harmful than debt; that is, the adverse effects of government debt are greater than those of other kinds of taxes. The basis for this implicit assertion is entirely obscure; it is neither obviously correct nor incorrect.

Why Is the Deficit a Problem?

Sound tax policy must be guided by numerous criteria, foremost among them a requirement that citizens be able to see and measure their individual tax burdens and that these varying individual tax burdens be related directly to the varying benefits individual taxpayers derive from Federal spending programs. A tax system embodying such attributes will facilitate (but not guarantee) the implicit provision through voting behavior of information to decision makers about the taxpayers' preferences with respect to the size and composition of the government budget. Just as consumers' choices in the marketplace provide business firms with information about consumer preferences, so Federal tax policy should complement the political process in the provision of such information to Congress. The obvious complexities and ambiguities of real-world political processes preclude great precision in such signals, but tax policy still should strive to avoid taxes that are hidden, that are difficult to measure, or that impose burdens on given groups in order to finance programs bestowing benefits on substantially different groups.

Therein lies the real reason that the large Federal budget deficit constitutes a serious policy problem. The future taxes (or inflation) needed to repay (or retire) the debt will be borne in substantial part by future taxpayers, but much of the spending now financed with debt accrues to the benefit of current voters. Current voters therefore perceive a (partial) "free lunch" and thus have incentives to approve implicitly through their voting behavior a Federal budget that is too large and that is biased too heavily in favor of current consumption as opposed to investment. This is consistent with the stark facts that Federal spending is at a historical peak both absolutely and as a proportion of peacetime GNP and that the truly big spending increase has been in middle-class subsidies.

Moreover, even to the extent that current taxpayers enjoy sufficient longevity to bear these future taxes, the future tax burdens needed to repay the debt are more difficult to measure than the current taxes that would be imposed if current spending were financed with explicit taxation instead of debt. There is some evidence that taxpayers tend to underestimate their tax burdens; consequently, the use of debt leads to a government budget larger than that actually preferred by the taxpayers. Only if debt is used to finance government *investment* can the correct signals be generated. Investment generates a stream of services over time, so that future taxpayers will receive benefits in return for their taxes, and current taxpayers face appropriate choices between future benefits and future taxes. Hence, debt is the appropriate financing mechanism for government investment.

The deficit is a problem further because its size has caused the total (real) indebtedness of the government to increase faster than real GNP, a situation that cannot be sustained indefinitely. To say, however, that the deficit is a problem is not to say that proposed solutions in the form of tax increases or "reforms" would be an improvement.

For example, individual tax burdens under a value-added tax (VAT) would be very difficult to measure, thus obscuring the voting signals that taxpayers send to Congress with respect to the size and composition of the Federal budget. Without an independent spending constraint, a VAT can be expected to result in a substantial (and wasteful) expansion of the government budget, particularly since small increases in the VAT rate would generate big increases in revenue, thus reducing the political penalty imposed upon Congress by major expansions in Federal spending.

The same difficulty applies to proposals to establish a "flat" income tax by eliminating most deductions and other such preferences. Individual tax liabilities would be easier to measure than under a VAT, but again the tax base would be so broad that major expansions in the government budget could be financed with only small increases in the flat tax rate.

It is the nature of democratic processes to subsidize concentrated special interests at the expense of more diffused and "general" interests. Flat tax proposals run counter to this incentive by imposing losses on visible, identifiable, and concentrated interest groups in order to reduce tax rates somewhat for the diffused and unconcentrated mass of general taxpayers. That is only one reason why the Treasury Department proposal is doomed to failure in Congress, whatever its final details when the Reagan administration sends it to the Hill. Major change is possible politically only if the pain is distributed visibly across all interest groups, or if increases in revenue can be used to compensate the losers or to create new concentrated groups favoring the overall package. The administration's forthcoming proposal will fail on both counts, and so its demise in Congress is inevitable.

Nor, again, are such flat tax proposals to be mourned. Tax "simplification" may be attractive, but the hard truth is that those heinous and innumerable "loopholes" serve a crucial function: they constrain the ability of our democratic but avaricious government to overtax the citizenry, that is, to consume too large a slice of national wealth. In the absence of an effective direct constraint on government spending growth, tax loopholes are one of the few such indirect constraints; indeed, with the very broad tax base that would result from the closure of most tax preferences, government could grow enormously with only small increases in tax rates. By magnifying the tax rate boosts needed to finance given increases in the government budget, loopholes create a large concentrated interest group — the taxpayers — opposing government spending growth. *Thus, the administration's ongoing search for ways to reduce both spending and tax preferences is inherently contradictory.* (Loopholes also may render the tax rate hikes self-defeating as the increased rates reduce the tax base further.) Loopholes may indeed distort private-sector decisions, but such effects are a socially useful investment in restraint of that Leviathan ensconced in the nation's capital.

The balanced-budget amendment now under consideration imposes explicit constraints on government spending, but by proscribing Federal borrowing it is likely to result in too *little* government investment. For current voters will tend to look unfavorably upon programs that bestow benefits in part upon future voters but which must be financed entirely with current taxation. Hence, a balanced-budget requirement would create budget composition problems of its own.

The central point here is that such "mechanical" reforms do not change the incentives of decision makers in appropriate directions. Thus they are unlikely to lead to a reduced public-sector (growth rate) or to a more efficient mix of public spending in terms of taxpayer preferences. Nowhere is the prospective futility of such reform efforts more evident than with the "item veto."

Why an Item Veto Will Not Work

Now standing at almost a quarter of GNP, Federal spending shows little hard evidence of reduced growth, let alone actual reduction, despite the presence of Ronald Reagan in the White House and a Republican majority in the Senate. As a purported means of plugging the budgetary dike — and presumably also as a vehicle to shift blame to Congress for the gap between the rhetoric and the reality of recent Federal budget performance — the administration has proposed that the president be given "item veto" power. This allegedly would reduce the ability of Congress to logroll pork-barrel spending past the president, who would be able to veto the pork without rejecting more kosher items included in the same spending package. The Grace Commission report contains examples galore of such profligacy. Indeed, President Reagan and Vice-President Bush have referred to the report in general terms as a blueprint for Federal budget control through an item veto.

Among the myriad recommendations of the Grace Commission is one proposing the sale of Federal electrical power at market prices instead of the heavily subsidized rates now prevailing in most cases. In the summer of 1984, Congress passed a bill extending for thirty years the Hoover Dam contract under which many electricity users in California, Nevada, and Arizona are charged a price for such Federal power far below its market value; indeed, the price is unchanged from that established in the contract fifty years before. Here was a chance for the White House to exercise, in effect, an item veto on a blatant Federal pork barrel arrangement. Here was a chance to demonstrate, as the president has emphasized, that political considerations play no role in policy decisions. And did the White House rise to the occasion, using this bill as an example of how an item veto could be used? Hardly. The administration supported the bill, and the president signed it, accompanied by the loud and conspicuous applause of numerous good Republican burghers and "fiscal conservatives." They proved themselves second to no Democrat in their talent for concocting excuses as to why their part of the porker should be held sacrosanct.

Moreover, the dynamics given impetus by the presidential campaign are revealing. The president felt compelled politically to seek for social-security recipients a special cost-of-living increase not mandated under the current formulas. If there was a dissenting voice in Congress, it was too feeble or too far submerged in the pork barrel to be heard. Furthermore, not only are the benefits of current social-security beneficiaries sacred, but now also those of future recipients, at least for the next four years. And what can we conclude from Vice-President Bush's tireless effort, during his exchange with Ms. Ferraro, to reiterate that various Federal welfare programs have gone up, not down, during the Reagan administration and that, presumably, more of the same can be expected during a second Reagan term? Are the politicians willing to discuss publicly the human havoc wreaked by the Federal welfare apparatus? Can they draw the appropriate conclusions during the course of a campaign? Not if recent experience is a guide: electoral success seemingly is thought to depend upon a perceived level of "compassion" at least equal to that of the New York Times editorial board. If ever a case could be made for unilateral disarmament, Federal domestic spending is it. Unfortunately, the obvious has become unspeakable politically; such is the result when justification of a conservative agenda is attempted on the basis of leftist criteria. To what extent is an item veto really usable in this sort of political climate?

It is in the political self-interest of politicians to bestow benefits that are measurable and to impose costs that are not. The item veto power, in effect, asks the president to swim against this tide by rejecting specific items funded, typically, out of general revenue. This provides interesting incentives for Congress, about which more is to be said below. At this point, an examination of the experience of various states in light of the item veto is instructive. Some form of item veto power is held by forty-three governors. The aggregate data, summarized in table 1, do not support the conclusion that the item veto power constrains government spending effectively.

The states listed in table 1 are those lacking item veto power for the governor. These aggregate data are not conclusive but are highly suggestive: state and combined state/local spending per capita in these states is no higher, and may be lower, than in states with some form of item veto. (Both state and combined state/local

TABLE 1

Per Capita General Expenditure, 1981

State	State Spending		State and Local Spending	
	Amount	Ranking	Amount	Ranking
Indiana	$ 905	45	$1,400	48
Maine	1,081	28	1,533	37
Nevada	1,158	24	2,075	9
New Hampshire	850	46	1,512	38
N. Carolina[1]	1,021	36	1,421	46
Rhode Island	1,373	9	1,941	14
Vermont	1,246	14	1,747	26
Average for states without item veto	$1,091		$1,661	
Average for states with item veto[2]	$1,141		$1,776	

SOURCE: *Statistical Abstract of the United States, 1984.*

[1] North Carolina has neither an item veto nor a whole bill veto.

[2] Excludes Alaska and the District of Columbia, both of which have the item veto and very high per capita spending.

spending are presented because the distribution of functions among government units varies across states.) Experience at the Federal level before and after enactment of the Congressional Budget and Impoundment Control Act of 1974 is consistent with the state experience. The power of the president to impound funds became much more restricted beginning about fiscal 1975. Nonetheless, the growth rate of real Federal spending between fiscal years 1975 and 1984 has been very close to that of the earlier period ending with fiscal 1974, depending upon the choice of the base year. No clear pattern is evident.

Either the item veto is ineffective, presumably for political reasons, or it encourages the state legislatures to behave in ways even more irresponsible than would otherwise be the case. The item veto, in effect, would allow congressmen to boast to their constituents about all the manna from Washington for which they are battling tirelessly, while permitting the president to masquerade as the last barrier between helpless taxpayers and an avaricious Congress, with little net effect upon the budget totals.

The total Federal budget is not the only issue; we must ask also whether an item veto is likely to shift the composition of the budget in appropriate directions. Of the $925 billion in outlays projected for fiscal 1985, about $495 billion, primarily interest and entitlements payments, would be immune from an item veto because they are authorized but not appropriated as line items. Congress could change this, of course, perhaps as a means of allowing the president to take the political heat for doing Congress's dirty work, but the earlier discussion suggests grounds for doubt as to whether presidents systematically will be willing to play that game.

The remaining spending is for defense (primarily) and for discretionary nondefense or, to put it differently, for general-interest programs that presumably benefit everyone more or less, and for special interest programs that benefit particular groups or political coalitions. If the item veto is to be an effective tool for reduction of the budget totals, it is likely also to bias budget composition choices relatively in favor of programs benefiting special interests. For the majority coalition (50 percent plus 1 voter) in Congress can reduce general-interest spending by, say, $1 per voter and thus transfer $2 to each member of the majority coalition. In a simple world, this process continues until $1 of the general-interest program has the same value to members of the majority coalition as $2 of the special-interest program. The real world is more complicated, of course — for example, the "wasteful" practice of dispersing defense facilities geographically is a way to transform defense partially from a general-interest into a special-interest activity — but the present composition of spending subject to an item veto suggests that the item veto may well bias the composition of the budget even more toward special-interest spending.

Another way to view this problem is to ask whether the president or Congress institutionally has a more general set of incentives. While Congress can be viewed as a series of special-interest coalitions, the president is likely to respond, particularly in an era of weakened parties, to special interests in states that are large and competitive in the electoral college. Therefore, the net political effect of an item veto is unclear, but the preponderance of general-interest items, if that is what defense is, in the "discretionary" budget suggests a perverse compositional effect of an item veto; that is, an item veto would shift the composition of the budget inappropriately.

The overall problem, of course, is that the institutional constraints on Federal spending growth have undergone substantial erosion in recent years. If the congressional seniority system and other such traditional sources of spending restraint cannot be resurrected, then the answer is to impose spending restraint directly and institutionally, presumably in the form of a constitutional spending limit — assuming that one can be enforced. Experience suggests strongly that the budget cannot be cut in piecemeal fashion, and the politics of social-security spending suggests that it cannot be cut even in an across-the-board fashion. Therefore, the large absolute size of the Federal sector ought to be written off as equivalent to a one-time reduction in national wealth, and efforts now should concentrate on limiting the growth of Federal spending, particularly relative to GNP. The balanced-budget amendment would impose this kind of spending growth constraint but, by proscribing borrowing under normal circumstances, could result in too little government investment.

What is needed is institutional reform that shifts the basic incentives of Congress and the president toward spending restraint. The item veto would not do that; it would encourage Congress to approve more spending, resting in the final analysis upon a hope that presidents systematically will be willing to bear alone the political costs of fiscal discipline. But any such expectations fly in the face of politicans' self-interest.

Conclusion — and a Caveat

What is needed is a reform that constrains the growth of government by improving the signals passed from the voters to Congress but that allows the use of debt for government investment purposes. This suggestion implies that the Federal budget should be divided into separate operating and investment budgets, a process that would require resolution of important but not overwhelming conceptual difficulties. Borrowing would be used to finance Federal investment, now roughly $100 billion per year. A good deal of Federal investment, such as the ubiquitous Federal water projects, yields a low return and should be cut. The remaining operating budget would be subject to a balance requirement similar to that embodied in the balanced-budget amendment. Some combination of spending reductions and tax increases would be required to balance the operating budget. If the spending limit imposed by the operating-budget balance requirement is effective, then much of the danger of a VAT would be removed, and it could be used for this purpose. However, spending reduction would be better because resources are clearly more productive in the private sector than in the public sector. Such an increase in current taxation could produce a political demand for reductions (or a reduced growth rate) in the operating budget as well.

Further constraint can be generated through federalism, the allocation of functions away from the Federal government to states and localities. These latter governmental entities are much more constrained than the Federal government in their behavior because dissatisfied voters can move among localities and states much more easily than among nations. In this vein, a good first step would be elimination of the revenue-sharing program, which amounts to a cartel arrangement since the Federal government imposes higher taxes than the states could impose if they had to compete with one another.

These are examples of institutional reform, as they shift, at least in principle, the reward-penalty incentive environment within which political decision making proceeds. This is because voters' perceptions of the true tax burden would be sharpened, thus clarifying the signals generated by the political process. The same can be said for a spending limit, however arbitrary. The problem, of course, is that such constraints create incentives for circumvention, and politicians are nothing if not inventive in this regard. What exactly is "investment"? To what kind of "spending" does a limit apply? Can government allocate resources through regulation if the budget is constrained? In short, how can government be made to obey the rules, that is, to serve the general welfare? No answer to that question will be found here, and the seemingly inexorable growth of government does not offer grounds for much optimism.

The President as Manager of
the Federal Government

CHARLES F. BINGMAN

The president of the United States has many roles. He is the chief of state, the commander in chief of the armed forces, and the chief executive officer of the government. He is also the political head of the government and usually the real or at least the presumptive head of his party. As the "leader of the country," he is seen as the person most likely to provide some sense of national objectives or purposes.

The Constitution says that executive power shall be vested in the president, who shall "take care that the laws be faithfully executed." Inherent in this language is the sense that the president would "run" the executive branch of the Federal government, but the framers of the Constitution could not have envisioned — and would probably have resisted — the vast enterprise that the Federal government has become. Indeed, current concepts and practices of management were then known only in rudimentary form. Even today, management is far less understood when applied to the government than to the private sector. It can be argued that, of all of the president's roles, the one that has changed the most involves the management of the Federal establishment. For the present discussion, "management" means:

- How the government conducts its affairs — its systems for deploying authority and administering programs.

- The institutions of government — its organization, human resources, facilities, and equipment.

- How well the government performs — its efficiency and effectiveness, as well as its relevance, reality, equity, and accountability. "Management" therefore means constant deliberation over how to allocate the government's enormous resources of money, talent, and authority.

By any standard, the Federal government is an enormous management undertaking. To quote a recent report: "Last year, the federal government completed 18 million procurement transactions, paying out more than $159 billion to several thousand contractors. . . . Each year more than $935 billion in disbursements go out, and it costs more than $600 million just to print the checks. More than 200,000 employees are needed just to maintain its enormous financial systems of budget, accounting, auditing and fiscal operations. One third of the total land mass of the United States is owned and managed by the federal government. Personnel related cost for its 2.1 million employees is, in itself, a public cost exceeding $65 billion per year."[1]

The growth of large, complex Federal institutions reflects what has happened in the country. Peter Drucker, a respected authority on management, has said: "Our society has become, within an incredibly short fifty years, a society of institutions. It has become a pluralist society in which every major social task has been entrusted to large organizations—from producing economic goods to health care, from social security and welfare to education, from the search for new knowledge to the protection of the natural environment.[2]

Herman Kahn was emphatic and even ominous concerning the role of governments. "With very few exceptions," he said, "the typical pattern in most of the world is a transfer of power from the individual or private corporation to the government. In nations with a federalist system, there is a transfer of power from the lower to the higher elements of government, and a transfer from the legislative to the executive. . . . On the economic level, there is increasing government control over economic activities in almost every nation of the world—and private centralization of economic activities."[3]

Despite these perceptions, it is still argued that the president either cannot or should not exert a truly managerial role. "Cannot" usually centers on the superior importance of, and preoccupation with, the president's role as a political leader. "Should not" addresses the constitutional separation of powers and leads some people to argue that the Federal government was never intended to be "efficient," because disciplined management runs counter to democratic principles. But Drucker has linked the effective performance of institutions (both public and private) to the concepts of democracy: "To make our institutions perform responsibly, autonomously, and on a high level of achievement is the only safeguard of freedom and dignity in a pluralist society of institutions."[4]

There is nothing inconsistent between effective government and truly democratic government. Once the political process has defined what the government should do and the needed checks and balances, it should be possible to deliver better directed and more effective and accountable leadership within that defined framework. But the real issue is whether the political system in the United States makes it *practical* for the president to exercise a managerial role. It would be useless to argue against the overwhelming need for a president who would provide political and policy leadership. But the preoccupation with these demands need not be total. The president can still manage the executive branch. In fact, he has an obligation to do so—an obligation that can work to his political advantage.

What are the president's management obligations? First and foremost, they include an obligation to the American public. This is not meant in the sense that the public necessarily cares about or understands the details of administration, but it does recognize that vast amounts of tax dollars are put in the hands of public leaders. And though the public continues to support the idea of a large government that performs many important functions, it increasingly expects government to perform well. There needs to be greater assurance that the Federal government is doing only what it should be doing; that the resources and institutional apparatus are being well used, with little reason to tolerate waste, obsolescence, and unnecessary structure; and that there are reasonably high levels of performance and achievement. Finally, there appears to be increasing concern that institutions of government may be getting out of hand and that the government has assumed a life of its own and can no longer be constrained by the public will, despite the electoral processes.

The president's second major obligation is to Congress, or perhaps to public law. There are thousands of statutes that hold the president and the chief officials of the executive branch accountable to Congress, and many of these laws address the management of government. Despite the separation-of-powers doctrine, the reality is that there are thousands of hopelessly confusing ways in which Congress and the executive branch are constantly locked together in the task of defining, managing, and sharing the Federal government's powers. While this is a "political" process, it is also, by any definition, intensely managerial. It deals with setting objectives, defining and directing courses of action, laying out rules for implementation, making choices, and allocating resources. In the years since Watergate, Congress has been notably aggressive in penetrating the management of government, all the way from major constraints, such as the War Powers Resolution of 1973 and various forms of the legislative veto, down to "line item" controls exercised through authorizing and appropriating procedures over minor pieces of agency internal activity.

Politics and management are therefore inextricably intertwined. Thus, another of the president's management obligations is to himself, because there are both political advantages and disadvantages in how he handles the managerial role. One of the most compelling of such issues is the public's yearning to see someone at the helm of the ship of state, and if anyone should be seen managing the government, it clearly ought to be the president. But because the public expects the person in charge to get things done, the president cannot merely appear to be in charge. He must actually manage the apparatus of government.

In recent years, the executive branch has lost much ground to Congress in the battle for control of the government. Legislation has been establishing broader mandates for programs but with stipulations that effectively make accountability to Congress paramount, rather than accountability to the president. Whole arenas of Federal activity, such as independent regulatory commissions and "off-budget" programs, virtually exclude presidential authority and are controlled, if at all, only by Congress. Legislation has become far more specific and detailed, passing beyond the establishment of general public policy and deliberately pushing into decisions and processes that might have been left to agency discretion. Agency managers usually find that key congressional subcommittees exert far more real control over them than anybody in the Executive Office of the President or, in many cases, even their own agency front office. The president would gain a real political advantage by reasserting his leadership in those areas where Congress has become the real power, because doing so would give him greater control over the "service delivery" apparatus of government.

Strong, ubiquitous management leadership would also mean fewer gaps and weaknesses into which an entrepreneurial Congress could enter. There are untold instances in which Congress has filled managerial vacuums. Therefore, whenever the president can push Congress out of places where it ought not to be, he gains greater control over the executive-branch apparatus, which must be done if he is to implement his policies. If the public perceives that it is the president — rather than Congress — who manages and produces, his image as a leader is enhanced.

Effective management can also reduce some of the president's vulnerability over issues of government cost, ineffectiveness, or public apathy. These are real concerns. The cost of government has become so enormous at state and local levels that legislated limitations on government taxation and spending have multiplied. As one recent book stated:

> It is remarkable in retrospect how abruptly the historical growth of the state and local sector was halted. With a single exception, in every year since 1976 real total spending in this sector has grown at a slower rate than in any year during the past quarter century. Real per capita spending by state and local governments, which had jumped by 44% between 1965 and 1975, has fallen since then. The share of state and local spending in the GNP declined by two full percentage points between 1975 and 1981, from 15.0 percent to 13.0 percent, and has continued its decline into 1982. The slowdown in state and local spending has been given permanence by state constitutional amendments and other formal measures limiting future spending growth. No fewer than twenty-five states have passed new statewide tax or spending limitations since 1977, the most famous being California's approval of Proposition 13 in June 1978. Most of these measures have been redundant in the short run. Political opposition to taxes and spending has proved stronger than the limits written into state constitutions. However, the limitations have given permanent expression to public preferences on spending matters and made it impossible for elected officials to return to business as usual, even if they had been so inclined.[5]

While the Federal government has not yet been subject to such constitutional or statutory limitations, the president ignores such signals at his peril. Although these signals are mostly about tax policy, they also appear to reflect a strong element of public concern about the size and cost of government. People continue to respond positively to individual public programs but negatively to the total cost of expenditures. If voters are unable to determine how specific program or operating costs should be cut, they can insist that the political leadership do so as quickly as possible. It is within the power of the president to capitalize on this public sentiment. If he is reasonably active and successful, he can reduce some of the vulnerability and friction in this arena that may impair his ability to build a consensus on other policy matters.

One final presidential management obligation is to the people who work in the Federal government. People respond to good leadership, and Federal employees are no different in that respect. And yet, it has become politically fashionable to disparage "the bureaucracy" as a class of employees without really understanding the environment in which they work or how dependent they are on effective top leadership. The success of policies and institutions heavily depends on the motivation of the people involved. Public organizations are officially hierarchial; authority starts at the top and is grudgingly delegated. Most agencies are sensitive to their own leadership, but the recent history of such leadership is a sorry chronicle of suspicion, indifference, and hostility. By taking a strong stance of management leadership and encouraging employee vigor and excellence, the president can benefit as both a manager and a politician.

The magnitude and complexity of the Federal establishment must be recognized as a heavy contributor to the growing concern over the levels and patterns of Federal expenditures. As more programs and subprograms have been enacted, there have been more rallying points around which congressional and client interests can be marshaled. Each program requires its own Federal bureaucracy, which in turn becomes an advocate for its mission and seeks to enhance it. Any given program is easily controllable with the existing political apparatus, but the accumulated total of hundreds of major programs are foundering the system and severely limiting political and managerial control. In his New Federalism proposals, President Reagan argued that one solution to this problem was for the Federal government to reduce its workload by divesting itself of those domestic programs better run at the state and local levels. These New Federalism proposals have made little headway, and future prospects are dim. Equally dim are the prospects for any substantial reduction by legislation of the number and scope of Federal activities by legislation, because no political consensus exists for such flat eliminations on any large scale. What seems to be left is what the Reagan administration has been probing—the extent to which expenditures can be controlled by eliminating some of the marginal elements of programs and by instituting a series of managerial reforms. For example, under one reform effort the civil-service work force was reduced by 75,000 employees. If this reduction can be held, it will represent not only a budget reduction in the short run but also a permanent avoidance of future expenditures, including ultimate retirement costs.

The need for the "president as manager" has never been more dramatically shown than in the report of the President's Private Sector Survey on Cost Control, which was delivered to the president on 12 January 1984, by J. Peter Grace, chairman and chief executive officer of W. R. Grace & Co. By invitation of the president, Grace established a commission of 161 top executives from private-sector corporations. This commission supervised more than 2,000 other senior private-sector executives, managers, and technical experts in the conduct of thirty-six intensive studies of major Federal agencies and crosscutting governmentwide management functions. The work of these task forces resulted in 2,478 recommendations on how the Federal government could cut costs, enhance its cash flow, or improve its management. The total savings from these recommendations could be absolutely staggering—$424.4 billion over three years and a cash acceleration of $66 billion over the same period, as well as hundreds of recommendations about how the Federal government can improve its operations. In his letter of transmittal to President Reagan, Grace stipulated that a dollar saved today accumulates to $34 over twelve years and $71 over seventeen years. He therefore maintained that the $424.4 billion in three-year savings, if achieved and maintained, would mean savings of $1.9 trillion a year by the year 2000.[6]

Grace is using the results of this cost control study to advocate major changes in public policy, especially economic policy. But in fact his commission's report is a set of management initiatives, some of which could be achieved administratively under current law but most of which would require congressional approval. In effect, he proposed that, rather than increase taxes or "cut spending" in the normal manner of budget and expenditure debates, the Federal government can do much to manage its way out of the present fiscal crisis by using his blueprint as the basis for an assault on program definitions, management systems, and the "waste and inefficiency" that his studies have purported to identify.

Major objections have been raised about these reports. To begin with, the Grace Commission was supposed to find opportunities for cost savings, elimination of waste, and improvements in management. The commission was not to evaluate policy or concern itself with political feasibility. Thus, many of the report recommendations strike the Washington cognoscenti as hopelessly naive and politically unreal. In other cases, it is doubtful whether the recommendations deserve implementation. Many of the estimates of dollar savings are suspect, and both the Office of Management and Budget (OMB) and the Congressional Budget Office (CBO) have repudiated them. In some cases, the commission went beyond its charter and proposed unrealistic policy changes.

But even after these substantial discounts are taken against Grace's 2,478 recommendations, there must still be the uncomfortable recognition that these findings cannot and should not be merely brushed off as presidential political maneuvering. Grace himself has acknowledged that many of the findings already existed in the bureaucracy but had been frustrated for lack of support. It is profoundly disturbing to recognize that Grace could identify many hundreds of legitimate management operations or management policy issues in the executive branch that have languished for years because of insufficient leadership or inadequate means to resolve them. Grace stated: "It is, admittedly, a staggering task to manage an organization whose size dwarfs even the largest private sector corporations. . . . It would appear that one Administration after another has simply not been as effective as it should have been. . . . These deficiencies are not the result of lack of competence or enthusiasm on the part of federal employees. Rather, responsibility rests squarely on the Executive Branch and the Congress which in the final analysis are the joint architects of the federal government's management systems, policies, and practices."[7]

One of the most notable conclusions of the report, and one that undoubtedly surprised many in the private sector, was the degree to which Congress, rather than the president, controls executive-branch management. In determining where authority rests, Grace concluded that "Congress has primary authority for 72.5 percent of the PPSS savings, the President has authority over 7.9 percent, and agencies/departments (over which the President obviously exerts considerable influence) have over 19.6 percent."[8]

Most of the recommendations are concerned not with high policy but with the meat-and-potatoes issues of management—overly expensive personnel systems, weak financial management, cash-flow problems, sloppy purchasing, poor facilities management, unwarranted subsidy loans and inadequate revenue collection, poor work-force management, and obsolete computers. In addition, there are attacks on the cost effectiveness of many politically beloved programs and on such issues as the high cost of federally protected labor rates, failure to apply user fees, and the political infeasibility of closing unwanted military bases or other Federal facilities. The opportunities for saving involve "the entire structure of government and concern every major management function, especially human resources, fiscal affairs, procurement, facilities, and organization management."[9]

Finally, the Grace report concluded that there is a critical need for the president to establish a new Office of Federal Management—which would subsume the present OMB, Office of Personnel Management (OPM), and General Services Administration (GSA)—in order to give him a powerful enough organization to establish, modernize, and monitor its management systems.

The dread fascination of these Grace Commission reports is that they are real enough to warrant action. Attempts will be made to repudiate these reports in total, for political motives or because of legitimate concerns about their genuine weaknesses. But most people who read them will agree at least in principle with some of the recommendations. If a potential savings of $424.4 billion over three years is not credible, one suspects that there is some credible level of potential savings that could be substantially achieved if there were the political will to do so. There is no real consensus on what such a credible level is, and it would surely be lower for Democrats than for Republicans, but it is still probably significant. For example, GAO and the CBO have reviewed 396 of the 2,478 recommendations, representing nearly 90 percent of the net three-year cost savings and revenue increases, and 95 percent of the cash accelerations. This review found it difficult to make a valid point-by-point comparison; but where specific budget estimates could be computed and compared, GAO/CBO derived a figure of $98 billion against the Grace Commission's $298 billion three-year projection.

In any event, by its consolidation into one document of almost 2,500 substantial ways to cut Federal expenditures (or enhance revenues) the Grace Commission has highlighted the idea that the Federal government can "manage" itself out of some significant part of its expenditure difficulties. Even if the Grace Commission reports were to be repudiated, it would be unfortunate if many of its specific recommendations were discredited by association and once again disappeared from the agenda of political and management reform.

A Management Reform Strategy for the Next Presidency

Assume that the president is motivated to push for government reform, either for reasons of political self-interest, expenditure control, or a sense of presidential obligation for leadership. Further assume that he has an agenda of management imperatives, gleaned from whatever source, and wants to act quickly. Is there any particular wisdom to offer him about how to proceed? All sorts of mechanisms have been tried from major congressionally chartered commissions to little inter-agency task forces. From past experience, a number of lines of approach stand out as crucial.

1. Plan ahead. Political parties and presidential candidates are becoming more sophisticated in planning what they will do if they enter into (or remain in) office. In the 1980 election, the Republican party, and subsequently the Reagan campaign, showed considerable skill in identifying issues and developing their own positions on them well in advance of the election. A form of "shadow cabinet" existed that drew on Republican members of Congress, former top appointees in the Nixon and Ford administrations, think tanks, and other sources. When Mr. Reagan became the party nominee, these groups became the source of ideas, arguments, and ultimately an agenda of initiatives that would get the Reagan administration off to a fast start and guide its early months in office. The transition team brought all of these efforts into focus and set a large part of this agenda down in writing. As appointees were picked for top political posts, these documents were used to brief them and give them a broad view of overall Reagan strategy and a common starting point for advancing their own part in that strategy.

This is a highly desirable and valuable form of political planning. In fact, most administrations are hard put to sustain equivalent planning efforts once in office. While such planning efforts concentrate on policies or programs, the approach is perfectly valid and equally acceptable for developing what might be called a management agenda as well. In fact, the author was a member of a small group of "organization and management advisers" to the Reagan transition team, functioning as part of the central transition Office of Policy Coordination, headed by Darrell Trent (subsequently deputy secretary of transportation) and Edwin Harper, who became assistant to the president for policy development.

It is unclear what influence this management advice ultimately had, but it does represent a politically vetted device by which a new president can think through the management state of the government and establish plans for action. It also enables the president to formulate policy guidelines for the central management agencies (OMB, GSA, and OPM) and to rectify any inadequacies that had been notable in previous transitions.

2. Start early. Every president in living memory has turned his attention to organization and management matters at some time during his administration. In addition to the Grace Commission, President Reagan initiated the Reform '88 program for management systems, strengthened the role of inspectors general, pressed efforts to cut the Federal work force by 75,000 employees, and moved to reduce fraud, waste, and abuse. Merit pay and performance evaluation have been emphasized, and a substantial program is under way to improve procurement, cash management, debt collection, and many other similar ventures. President Carter mandated a governmentwide "zero-based budget" program (since abandoned), established councils for productivity and for management improvement, and concentrated exceptional attention on organizational assessments, culminating in the creation of two new cabinet departments for Energy and Education. In the Nixon and Ford administrations, there was a similar emphasis on organization schemes for restructuring the entire apparatus of the Federal establishment for domestic affairs. It was proposed that dozens of existing departments and agencies would be reorganized and regrouped by major purpose into four new departments—Natural Resources, Human Resources, Economic Affairs, and Community Development. During these same years, a management-by-objectives system was introduced (and abandoned), and serious efforts were made to realign the Federal field structure and achieve decentralization of management authority. Even in the midst of the Great Society, the Johnson administration pushed a program planning and budgeting system.

But these efforts shared one unfortunate common characteristic—almost all of them began too late in the presidential term. It is not surprising that such initiatives are not early presidential priorities, but much of the effort and good intentions behind them was dissipated because by the time they were reaching a crucial point in their development, the executive-branch leadership had turned its attention to the imperatives of the next presidential election or to shattering events like Watergate or the Iranian hostage crisis. For example, President Nixon received proposals for government reorganization from the Ash Council in November of 1970 and submitted his own legislative proposals in March of 1971, more than halfway through his first term. There was perhaps a year of serious effort to consider these proposals before Watergate doomed such plans. President Reagan's Cabinet Council on Management and Administration was not created until more than two years after all of the other councils. The current Reform '88 program began in late 1982, which left perhaps a year and a half for it to become stabilized before the preoccupations of the 1984 presidential elections.

Without arguing the merits of these specific ideas, it seems clear that the president should start as early as possible on his management initiatives. Even internal management systems have become extraordinarily embedded and resistant to change, and both the Congress and the clientele interests that are affected by Federal management practices tend to want structural and procedural rigidity rather than change. New administrations underestimate this systemic inertia and overestimate their abilities to command change. This problem of inertia exists for changes in policies as well as public programs, and no doubt each president is advised to start everything first. But management reform lacks the regular and focused constituency pressure that normally supports major policy issues or spending programs. This forces the president to create initiatives around which support can build. Past reform efforts have been abandoned in midcourse or have withered for lack of attention. Investments of precious time and commitment have been wasted. By starting early in his administration working for the full four years, the president could markedly improve his chances for real accomplishment.

3. *Recognize the value of long-term persistence.* The Reagan Reform '88 management program was given that name because there was a correct view that fundamental systems reform cannot be accomplished quickly or casually. Reform '88 got started late in 1982 on the premise that approximately six years would be needed to plan and execute its reform objectives. Many feel that even this pace is optimistic. The NAPA report helped to explain why this is true:

> Even where Executive Branch political leadership does support management initiatives, the frequent change in political leadership tenure, averaging roughly 18 months, often means that such support may vanish in midproject, with a high likelihood that the new appointees, once again preoccupied with their own political objectives, will fail to support management projects sufficiently to keep them alive. Soon, another election intervenes, and the cycle of proposals, education, and persuasion begins again. In this manner, months and years may pass, while federal managers struggle to find among political leaders the right combination of interest, motivation, and timing which will actually cause reforms to be carried out, a combination which very rarely occurs.[10]

An unhealthy and unwarranted tradition has emerged around political transitions that apparently requires the abandonment or distrust of all activities from the previous administration that have not been locked into statute. This practice clearly comes from the normal political urge to denigrate the previous administration. But most management issues are relatively nonpartisan and can have equal credibility for either party in responding to the public demand for "good government." There is no reason why this pattern of automatic repudiation needs to be applied to soundly conceived management initiatives that do no violence to the new administration's main themes. The Reagan administration has been the first in many years to break this pattern by quietly continuing a number of Carter administration management programs. These have included procurement systems reform, building on ten years of work that began with the 1972 report of the congressionally mandated Commission on Government Procurement. It has also begun to profit from the debt collection and cash-management programs that President Carter initiated in 1979.

Presidents need not be overly concerned about a paucity of good management ideas. Hundreds of them are available for someone with the will and the guts to implement them. Ideas are generated within the bureaucracy or by such external sources as the GAO, client groups, university scholars, and private think tanks. In fact, appraisal of the government's flaws and foibles is so extensive that it is becoming embarrassingly clear that what is lacking is not the ability to study or evaluate but the ability to take corrective action. This suggests that there are real problems with the tools available to a motivated president.

4. *Sustain interest and reinforcement.* One of the difficulties of management reform is that there is a good deal of cynicism about it, particularly in political circles. Even when the president launches such initiatives and says all of the right

things, his determination is constantly questioned. Further, the political apparatus is notorious for ignoring emerging or long-term issues. Inside the executive branch, people respond to presidential orders, but sometimes they do not respond very much or for very long. In the Carter administration, for example, a President's Productivity Council was created by executive order and chaired by the powerful director of the OMB. One or two meetings were held, and a number of "assignments" were made to various agencies for staff work, but it was obvious from the start that the Carter administration valued this exercise only for the initial public announcement. Within the first few weeks, the practiced observer could conclude that nothing real had been intended and that nothing real was going to happen. This is a perfect case of phony management reform, and it created two types of frustration inside government. It deepened the career managers' cynicism about politicians and "good government," and it preempted the productivity issue. During the remainder of the Carter term, nothing significant was done because the problems and potentials for action were ostentatiously in the hands of a presidential body that, while doing nothing itself, blocked potential initiatives elsewhere.

Outside observers of government were similarly frustrated. To the extent that people believed that a genuine effort to enhance Federal productivity was being made, the subsequent confusion and inaction were further evidence of governmental incompetence. Where the outside cognoscenti recognized the spurious nature of the intent, it simply contributed to their own cynicism about the extreme difficulties of bringing serious political attention to bear on management issues. As a result, the final two years of the Carter administration were wasted, and "productivity" now suffers from an even worse reputation as a potential arena of reform.

Within the executive branch, this sort of callow political machination is viewed with contempt and tends to poison attitudes toward genuine efforts at management improvement. It is undoubtedly better for the president to undertake only those efforts that he genuinely supports and is willing to continue to reinforce, rather than to create such false facades that are predictable failures and inevitably erode public confidence.

In other cases, even sincere White House initiatives are so poorly handled at the next level that they fail, much to the embarrassment of the career managers and political appointees who supported them in their own agencies. This has been the case with perfectly useful management-systems concepts, such as Planning, Programming, and Budgeting System (PPBS), management-by-objectives (MBO), and zero-based budgeting (ZBB), which have been successfully used in the private sector but are now considered failed experiences in the Federal government.

It is also wrong to conclude from these failures that career employees resist the management initiatives and cause them to fail. Although many careerists may have indeed contributed to failures by their resistance or indifference, most are essentially professionals who are not engaged in political policy making but rather draw their personal and professional satisfaction from successfully performing their jobs. Eventually, every management initiative is subject to the attitude of the career work force. If the president makes it clear that he is serious and if he continues to signal sustained interest in his own initiatives, then he will substantially enhance the prospect of engaging the career establishment. Most people realize that the president will not lie awake nights worrying about his management-improvement program, nor can he personally keep track of such ventures. He can, however, develop the necessary tools to provide adequate direction and control for his management role, just as he seeks to do for foreign policy, national security, and domestic affairs.

5. *Strengthen the Executive Office of the President.* Finally, the single most important act in creating the capability for effective management of government will be to strengthen the Executive Office of the President. The 2,478 recommendations of the Grace Commission, even when appropriately discounted, reveal how far the current management capacities of government have fallen behind in coping with management problems. Both the current comptroller general, Charles Bowsher, and his predecessor, Elmer Staats, have been seriously disturbed over the inability or unwillingness of the executive branch to mount adequate measures to correct even the audit findings with which there is essential agreement.

Each president is virtually free to set up his White House staff in any way he chooses and to bring into the staff the skills needed to carry out each element of his job as he sees it. But the president already has a variety of useful mechanisms to implement his management intentions. These are the so-called central agencies of government — OMB, OPM, and GSA. From time to time, commissions, task forces, and working groups have been created to propose courses of action or to help with assessment. Management concerns have been dealt with by mechanisms designed for other purposes, such as the National Security Council, or a White House policy office. A few presidents have had people on their direct staffs with enough management background to serve in this arena. This function has been filled with real sympathy and understanding for President Reagan by Edwin Meese III, counselor to the president, simply because he believed these issues to be important. It was also Meese who finally convinced President Reagan to establish the Cabinet Council on Management and Administration (CCMA) two years after the other cabinet councils had been set up, and it is Meese who serves as the alternate chairman in the president's absence.

GSA has more than 25,000 employees, and it handles both management policy and operations in support areas, such as computers, telephones, buildings, and supplies. OPM, with 5,000 employees, develops personnel policy, directs personnel operations, and manages the Federal government's programs for health insurance and retirement benefits. But very few of the people in these agencies are really involved in broader presidential interests. For more than forty years, the principal arm of the president in the total management world has been OMB and its predecessor, now almost affectionately known as "the old Bureau of the Budget." OMB can and should be the single organization to which the president can turn to help define his intentions and convert them into action.

The embarrassing fact is that the Executive Office resources available to the president are surprisingly weak, and any president who is genuinely zealous about management will first find it necessary to strengthen his Executive Office forces. Because of the complete changes of White House staff that routinely occur even in second terms, the president may not have anyone on his staff who "handles management matters" as Ed Meese has, or who singlemindedly guards the president's interests and tracks whether his orders are being obeyed. In the past, this role has been consigned to the director of OMB, but recent experience has shown that the capacity of OMB has been sadly reduced and its understandable preoccupation with the budget has overwhelmed its leaders to the detriment of management concerns. This has led to a growing concern that the president does not in fact have as powerful a management organization as he may seem to have.

In addition, there are elements of a good organization for management reform that do not even exist in the Executive Office, or are too weak to support the president's needs. For example, when Joseph Wright, Reagan's OMB deputy director, began to develop Reform '88 it was emphasized that the "management side" of OMB lacked the skills to develop a broad reform strategy, to lay out adequate implementation planning, or to supervise more than a handful of reform projects. OMB has shrunk its staff resources, narrowed the range of its interests, and lost relevance with the agencies. Even inside OMB, there seems to be no clear pattern of how management and budget problems should be related, nor is there a well-developed sense of how these respective staffs need to work together. OMB is understaffed for its role, and the management staff in particular has had to rely on "detailees"—people begged and borrowed from agencies to serve on temporary task forces—to carry out its business. These pickup teams have often done excellent work, but this is scarcely the strongest means to serve the president. In fact, OMB's growing dependency on these ad hoc staff arrangements also reflect the long-term congressional unwillingness to allow OMB's staff to grow to any significant degree.

Neither the White House staff nor OMB has developed any really successful ways of evaluating the operations of the Federal establishment. Instead, the evaluation of program necessity or performance has become largely a political activity and often a very partisan one. In such a climate the evaluation of management effectiveness or cost effectiveness becomes more difficult and may even be precluded. Management assessments, which can potentially reduce costs, cut staffs, challenge the need for marginal activities, or change comfortable working relationships, are seen as threats to the program or to the hard-won funding committed to it. There are many interests that do not want their programs to be scrutinized. Clientele groups may fear a loss of funds and assistance. Congress may find itself explaining why it supports questionable activities. Career managers may face embarrassing questions about waste or poor results. In the normal course of events, the dynamics of the political process work best to create or aggrandize programs and to add funds to them. When it comes to close scrutiny of results or to the tough ideas about cutting expenditures, the political process scarcely works at all. Yet this is exactly the syndrome that the taxpayer appears increasingly to challenge. Why is it impossible for the political leadership to eliminate the dross of public programs from the truly valuable substance? Whatever the government does, why is it unable to do it better and cheaper? Career managers are in no position to take on the political arguments, but they can produce the hard evaluations if directed to do so. But the Executive Office must be far more effective and reliable in defining the need for these hard evaluations so that they may become politically actionable. Only presidential leadership seems adequate to initiate the dislodgement of entrenched and stagnant programs.

Presidential transitions are attractive times in which to initiate new actions. Even when an incumbent is continuing in office, there is still the sense that attractive new initiatives are wanted and that some of the failures of the first term can be quietly dropped. An ideal scenario of an incoming president might have the following general features:

• An organized effort would be made on behalf of the president-elect to assess managerial issues in the Federal establishment. This assessment would draw on any number of sources, including the party apparatus, friendly think tanks, experienced party veterans from previous administrations, client groups, and the president's party in Congress. Useful ideas can even be drawn from those in the career civil service who are close to most problems and yearn to be consulted. In many cases, the president himself has had strong beliefs or ideas he wishes to see carried forward. For a Reagan second term, this would probably mean a heavy reliance on the recommendations of the Grace Commission study and a renewed zeal behind the extensive reform agenda launched in his first term.

In any event, it is important that this process culminate either in the transition or in the early days of the new administration so that the full four-year term is available for implementation.

• As the president assumes office, the tools available to him shift. Think tanks and old friends continue to be useful for ideas and advice, but the means must now be found to galvanize the government into action. This directive authority cannot be wielded by nongovernment people. It must be done through formal government channels that can issue orders, compel action, commit funds, and demand accountability. Presidents soon learn that being at the helm of the ship of state does not necessarily mean that the ship will answer the helm even if he turns the wheel. For each initiative a "delivery system" must be found — a means to connect a policy statement or a general intention with some mechanism that has the capacity to engage the necessary gears in the complex machinery of government.

• During the course of the president's term, there must be a person, a group, or an organization capable of assessing the progress of this managerial agenda and of feeding back to the president a combination of political and managerial counsel about how the administration's position may need to be accommodated.

• It would be of great value to the effective management of government if the president would identify those key positions that truly require effective managers. All top positions require political skills, but it is also clear that such top jobs as the administrator of NASA, the commissioner of the Social Security Administration, and the head of the Federal Aviation Administration also require a high order of managerial skill and experience and cannot be filled with some political loyalists.

• There must finally be a recognition that the resources available to the president in the Executive Office are inadequate to provide leadership for these broad-based and sustained management reform efforts that are needed across the entire Federal government. The Grace Commission report advocates the abolishment of the present OMB and the creation of a new and more broadly based Office of Federal Management (OFM), which would subsume GSA and the Office of Personnel Management. The OFM would continue to prepare the president's budget but would add major new staffs for neglected functions, such as financial management and computer systems management. The report of the National Academy of Public Administration also advocates the creation of an Office of Federal Management by breaking the management role out of OMB and setting it up as a separate, larger organization that would report to the president. While these two proposals differ in their structure, they are similar in stressing the need for an executive branch that would be more powerful in planning managerial change.

Conclusion

Future control of Federal expenditures is heavily contingent on the effectiveness and motivation of the people and systems that implement politically defined programs. The current Federal establishment has passed through a generation of role enlargement, power extrapolation, and program and funding proliferation. The machinery of government has been scaled to this pattern of growth and increasing complexity. President Reagan has pressured both Congress and the career establishment through a series of management-reform initiatives, but it is not yet clear how much real political change in Federal programs is possible. The Reagan concept is predicated on the belief that real economies can at least be realized through the elimination of fraud, waste, and mismanagement as well as through more positive measures to upgrade Federal management systems and techniques.

But Federal management is shared management to a degree not often paralleled in the private sector, and change is heavily contingent on the top-down capacity of the president to exert leadership that not only drives action but also motivates a sense of reform and improvement through his political appointees and into the career bureaucracy.

The Congress, which is in conflict with the presidency over so many things, must be persuaded not only that management reform is badly needed but also that it must allow the president to strengthen his Executive Office resources in order to broaden and deepen his managerial impact. The career work force will probably respond better to presidential leadership than to presidential drivership and to a management-reform program that is simple, sensible, and human rather than negative, stultifying, and accusatory.

Notes

1. National Academy of Public Administration, *Revitalizing Federal Management: Managers and Their Overburdened Systems* (Washington, D.C., 1983).

2. Peter Drucker, *Management* (New York: Harper & Row, 1973), ix.

3. Herman Kahn and B. Bruce-Briggs, *Things to Come* (New York: Macmillan Publishing Co., 1972), 13–14.

4. Drucker, ix.

5. John L. Palmer and Isabel Sawhill, eds., *The Reagan Experiment* (Washington, D.C.: Urban Institute Press, 1982), 160–61.

6. See President's Private Sector Survey on Cost Control, *War on Waste* (New York: Macmillan Publishing Co., 1984), v-ix.

7. Ibid., 19.

8. Ibid., 20.

9. Ibid. 15.

10. *Revitalizing Federal Management*, 8.

Revitalizing Federal Management: Managers and Their Overburdened Systems*

One of the important messages which the American public is striving to convey to its leaders at all levels of government is that somehow governments must be less costly and deliver better results.

Many people — especially those running for office — argue that the principal fault must lie with the entrenched bureaucrats who are perceived as slow moving, resistant to new leadership, and more interested in preserving a complex bureaucracy than in streamlining government.

What is bitterly ironic is the fact that Federal managers, both political and career, typically regard themselves as captives of a series of cumbersome internal management "systems" which they do not control. These systems have tended to become so rigid, stultifying, and burdened with red tape that, in the view of these managers, their capacity to serve the public on a responsive and low-cost basis is seriously undermined. The Panel fully agrees with the government managers' assessment of the difficulty of administering programs under current conditions. Managers in the private sector are not so constrained.

Every substantial organization needs systems and procedures to organize and direct its activities. But, over many years, government has become entwined in elaborate management control systems and the accretion of progressively more detailed administrative procedures, often heavily centralized. This development has not produced superior management. Instead, it has produced managerial overburden, barriers to the responsiveness of government, and a tendency to drive

*A panel report of the National Academy of Public Administration, Dwight A. Ink, Chairman, November 1983. The NAPA, founded in 1967, is composed of about 300 practitioners and scholars in the field of public administration. In 1982 it organized a panel of nine members of wide experience to study management in the Federal government. Selections from its final report are reprinted here.

up the cost of government as agencies press for more staff and office space and computers to keep up with this volume of redtape. The individual Federal manager now must cope with thousands of pages of procurement, personnel, fiscal, and other regulations over which he has little or no control.

Many of the restraints and regulatory requirements which now make it so difficult for Federal managers to function have their origin in commendable efforts to prevent or control waste, abuse of authority, or corruption. Others are designed to make management actions and processes also serve government objectives of a social or economic character. Unfortunately the cumulative impact of an ever increasing number of procedures, findings, appeals, and notifications is to jeopardize the effective execution of the basic programs which the managers have been charged with carrying out. Moreover, regulatory requirements, once adopted, tend to be retained long after they have ceased to make any constructive contribution to program management.

As these administrative systems have evolved in the Federal government, they have increasingly been used to control or regulate some piece of the process and have become less useful as tools for the manager on the firing line. And, as the systems have become "locked in" by statute, regulation, and precedent, they have become rigid and very difficult to change. In contrast, far more emphasis has been given in the private sector to the decentralization of responsibility and leadership in combination with central guidelines and evaluation.

When lost in procedural quagmires, the administrative process loses much of its intended meaning. Procedures overwhelm substance. Organizations become discredited, along with their employees.

Another distressing consequence of this overburden is that government managers feel a frustrating loss of relevance and control. Thousands of dedicated men and women who should be the government's greatest resource for excellence and innovation feel they are cogs in some "system" which neglects their true management needs and which they individually cannot change. More and more of their time is spent in coping with the process or defending against criticisms of specific flaws or failures in the execution of thousands of detailed processes. Because there are many times more details than a manager can cope with personally, there has grown up an unhealthy reliance on these systems and the technical experts who operate them.

The Panel believes that the negative impact of this Federal internal redtape on the capacity of managers to manage has reached serious proportions.

The true cost of administrative redtape is impossible to express in dollars and cents. First is the obvious slowing of governmental action. There is the resultant pressure for more staff to keep up with the workload. More and more oversight regulations and mechanisms are put in place to monitor the processes. Professional managers and their employees become frustrated, and the career service has greater difficulty in attracting and retaining able men and women. Accountability for programs and expenditures becomes diffused. The impact of the voter is weakened by this confused accountability and the public is the ultimate loser in this process.

This report addresses a part of the total pattern of the Federal government about which both the political and career leaders agree — that the internal management processes of the Federal government have become so complex and rigid they must be changed. Most of the past studies on deregulation have focused on the Federal burdens imposed on industry, state and local governments, or the citizen. This study concentrates on the perspective of the Federal managers and their agencies which the President and Congress hold accountable for carrying out their goals and their programs.

Reduction in the administrative rules and regulations is clearly necessary to ease the problems confronting the Federal manager. In the view of the Panel this needs to be addressed on a massive scale. The Panel has concluded, however, that the basic problem is far more complex and far reaching.

The most fundamental need is for a philosophy of Federal management which is aimed at enhancing the role and accountability of the manager. The attitude of those who design and administer the rules of budgeting, personnel, procurement, and administrative services must be reoriented from a "control mentality" to one of "how can I help get the mission of this agency accomplished."

The starting point is a genuine commitment by each President and White House staff and Cabinet.

The Cabinet Council of Management and Administration and "Reform '88" led by OMB are positive steps in stressing the importance of good management. GSA has initiated several promising efforts to delegate certain administrative service functions back to the agencies, who are, after all, entrusted with far larger program responsibilities. The Civil Service Reform Act contemplated similar delegations in the field of personnel management.

Although these are very encouraging steps which we applaud, the Panel urges a number of more comprehensive steps.

Since an exhaustive analysis of all administrative systems and procedures is far beyond the scope of any single study, the Panel has focused on those key problem areas which were of greatest concern to the Federal departments and agencies. Generally, these are also areas which, if corrected, would have the greatest potential for fundamental systems reform, particularly if followed by other subsequent actions.

Particular emphasis has been placed on the roles of the Office of Management and Budget, the Office of Personnel Management, and the General Services Administration. To be more effective, the Panel believes the roles of these central agencies require a further shift of emphasis away from the detailed operational controls of the past to a broader and eventually more effective leadership role which is more concerned with broad management policy development and experimentation with innovative management approaches, linked to evaluation and reporting of agency managerial performance. As these central agencies delegate more operational authority to the rest of the Executive Branch, they create the opportunity to redirect their talents into a new form of leadership which places greater emphasis on pressing for innovation, research, the redesign of outdated systems, and the attainment of managerial excellence.

These changes should provide impetus to similar efforts by departments and agencies to further streamline their internal administrative processes.

To be effective, however, most departments and agencies, as well as the Executive Office of the President, must give far higher priority to managerial experience in the recruiting and appointing of political and career leadership to posts with responsibility for operating multimillion dollar programs and supervising many thousands of employees. Otherwise, no amount of administration reform will make much difference.

A series of reforms to meet these needs is proposed in our report, including the strengthening of the President's leadership by the creation of a new Office of Management—tailored in its philosophy and staffing to enhancing the capacity of agencies and their managers to manage.

We propose that these recommendations become an agenda for wide discussion and debate, leading to action on the problems outlined in this report.

Conditions for Sustaining Successful Management Reform

The NAPA Panel has been forced to conclude that the Federal government's pressing needs for broad-based and continuing management reform cannot be achieved through the existing combination of OMB, OPM, and GSA organization and approach. . . .

. . . The current management role of OMB should be transferred to a newly created Office of Federal Management reporting to the President, which would become the organizational framework for providing a more powerful and responsive leadership for management reform and improvement for the entire Federal government. . . .

Since World War II, the pivotal role in Federal management matters has been assigned to the Office of Management and Budget and its predecessor organization, the Bureau of the Budget. BOB/OMB has attempted to maintain a general management capability along with its primary role as the President's budget staff. During several periods of its existence, the management organization has performed exceptionally well. It has successfully carried out management projects of importance to every President and has attempted to maintain a general stewardship over management activities throughout the Federal establishment.

In its earlier years, agencies came to rely on BOB/OMB as a key source of governmentwide initiatives for keeping Federal management modern and up to date. In recent years, however, there has been a growing concern that, even while OMB continues to be capable of occasional excellent performance, it has irretrievably lost its overall effectiveness as governmentwide leader in management matters. Students of BOB and OMB have always recognized that its primary concern on behalf of the President has been the Federal budget process. This has been regarded as both a strength and a weakness in terms of OMB's management role. It is a strength because the budget gives the OMB Director a powerful voice in all government activities, with direct and continuing access to the President, and powerful leverage to deal with agency heads from a position of strength. It has always been hoped and expected that these strengths would be brought equally to bear on the managerial agenda; and from time to time, depending on the President's own interests and the Director's sensitivity to management problems, this has been true. The disabling systemic weakness, however, has been that the budget and related national economic issues have usually proved to be all-consuming. In recent years it has become so intense that it has almost totally preoccupied critical OMB leadership, draining away time, interest, and staff from the managerial initiatives. Further, the annual focus on the budget and the lack of concern with management matters clearly has a chilling effect on many management initiatives. Therefore, even when an Administration such as that of President Reagan seeks to take the initiative for management reform across a broad front, it finds OMB no longer has the talent base nor the recognized capacity for leadership to sustain such major efforts.

Nor does it appear likely that, in the foreseeable future, the budget preoccupation will decline, and therefore proposals and arguments for building up and revitalizing OMB's "management side" seem less hopeful and less realistic.

Meanwhile, the need for strong sustained management reform leadership becomes more pressing. The Reagan Administration's ambitious Reform '88 Project and the recently emerging findings of the President's Private Sector Survey on Cost Control serve only to emphasize the breadth of the management reforms which are needed and the paucity of the resources available to take implementing action. Both of these major reform efforts point out once again the fundamental fact that the Federal government suffers not from a failure to diagnose its management problems, but from a failure to implement the changes which it already knows it requires.

The NAPA Panel has been forced to conclude that the Federal government's pressing needs for broad-based and sustained management reform can best be accomplished by the creation of a new Office of Federal Management in the Executive Office of the President and reporting to the President, which should become the framework for providing a more powerful and responsive leadership for management reform and improvement for the entire Federal government.

What should be the broad role and purposes of the new Office of Federal Management?

• First, to optimize the role of the President as Chief Executive Officer of government.

• Second, to inform the public and the Congress of the imperatives for effective Federal management and to facilitate the relationships between the Congress and Executive Branch with respect to the machinery of government.

• Third, to instigate the development of sound, long-term management planning and policy governmentwide and in all agencies.

• Fourth, to lead the drive for a major improvement in the management capabilities of the government both centrally and in the departments and agencies.

• Fifth, to lead the drive for refurbishment of government management systems.

• Sixth, to take leadership in management innovation through experimentation, test and demonstration programs, and adoption of new management concepts and technology.

The Office of Federal Management should be given Presidential authority and sufficient resources to *implement management change* — either through its own resources or by preparing plans and proposals for Presidential approval which define and mandate the implementation of priority management reforms by other Federal agencies. This authority should include the capacity to establish (and if necessary, fund) task forces, special project offices, advisory groups, consultants, or other resources needed to carry out this implementation role.

The Office of Federal Management would inherit from OMB such important functions as the drafting of nonbudget related Executive Orders, management circulars, and other means for conveying Presidential direction on management subjects. It would include the present Office of Federal Procurement Policy and would coordinate responses to GAO audits of governmentwide applicability. It would also administer the requirements of the Paperwork Reduction Act. It would represent the President in Congress in cooperation with the White House Congressional office on government organization and management matters and would coordinate preparation of Administration management related legislation.

[A second aspect of management reforms is required.] The missions of the central agencies must be rebalanced to strengthen and revitalize the broad governmentwide policy and oversight roles which only they can perform and to deliberately divest themselves to the greatest extent possible of these roles which involve centralized regulation and control. To achieve this second change:

• Central agencies must serve as the agent of the President in his role as Chief Executive Officer, advise the President on management matters, develop governmentwide management policies, and prepare recommendations to the President on crosscutting management policy issues.

• The central agencies should be responsible for Federal systems design, redesign, modernization, and improvement and for directing the use of uniform central systems, but only where a clear need can be demonstrated for such governmentwide systems as opposed to individual agency systems. Even then, the central agencies should mandate only those systems elements necessary to achieve reasonable consistency of purpose and uniform procedures where necessary. Directives should be redesigned to emphasize results or performance objectives and should avoid detailed procedures which attempt to structure the means by which objectives are achieved. This policy closely parallels the objectives of the current Reagan Administration program for regulatory reform. *The NAPA Panel advocates that the Federal government should adopt a policy for its internal operations in which the fullest and most complete delegations of both line and management systems authority not needed for the proper exercise of its redesigned central agency responsibilities should be made to the governmental unit where actual operational management is exercised.*

• The central agencies should build up their capability to provide the President with a full and continuous evaluation of the management systems of government —

to know where they are not being effective and to identify how they must be corrected or improved. In a more decentralized environment, most agency improvements will be the responsibility of agency heads.

• Each of the central agencies must provide far more active leadership in management research, innovation, experimentation, and the introduction of new managerial technology. Each central agency should be given explicit statutory authority *and adequate resources* to conduct such research; to undertake management experiments, tests, or demonstration programs; and to fund such programs through contracts or interagency agreements. Indeed, every Federal agency would benefit from similar experimentation authority through its own enabling legislation.

• With respect to management in the departments and agencies, the central agencies should actively encourage and assist agency management reforms; and particularly in new or smaller agencies, they should provide direct assistance for management needs.

• Particularly for the immediate future, the central agencies should concentrate their efforts on making management systems and techniques more relevant and of greater direct support to Federal managers and on addressing the critical ways in which the managers themselves must be prepared to take on these more demanding roles.

[The Panel devotes five chapters to specific topics. The material on personnel has been selected for inclusion here. It illustrates the approach and in itself constitutes substance of importance.]

New Concepts for Personnel Management

The Federal Personnel Manual (FPM) has eight thousand eight hundred and fourteen pages. If regulations generated good personnel management, the Federal government would have the best personnel system in the world.

But instead, when managers and personnel experts all over government were consulted, they simply reaffirmed what is common knowledge — the frustrations with the system are general and profound. Even experienced personnel officers admit that nobody really understands those 8,814 pages. They certainly are not understood by managers, nor do they describe a personnel system which works for them or for their employees in the workplace where a personnel system should really pay off. In sharp contrast to successful personnel systems elsewhere, Federal managers do not feel that the system is designed to meet their needs, but see it as just another set of obstacles they must overcome in doing their jobs.

In fact, the personnel system doesn't seem to work very well for *anybody*. Because of this, the NAPA Panel was asked to make the personnel systems a central priority in its study.

The reactions of various personnel system users can be summarized as follows:

Executives and line managers feel almost totally divorced from what should be one of their most important systems. They regard themselves as being required to operate under a system which is imposed on them from outside their own agencies, and they feel that they play almost no role in the development of that system, either governmentwide or within their own agencies. They feel they have little or no voice in how the system functions and thus have no sense of responsibility for whether it works well or poorly. They recognize that 8,814 pages of FPM means that the system rests in the hands of the personnel specialists, many of whom have only a tenuous grip on their own processes. Finally, and most significantly, managers have become passive and indifferent. Lacking any sense of relevance in personnel matters, they seldom feel any reward (or penalty) for how they handle personnel situations, spend far too little time on them, and frequently resent the time they do spend because it seems bureaucratic and unproductive. Yet no decisions made by these managers are more important.

Personnel specialists spend far too much time in the mechanical or procedural elements of the system: interpreting the 8,814 pages of the manual, supplementing them with additional hundreds of pages of procedures within their own agency, and administering the paperwork and reporting which the system demands. They believe that they are left with far too little time to consult and work with line managers or employers in positive personnel work, such as recruitment of high quality people, sound employee evaluation and merit pay determinations, and design of intelligent programs for employee development, training, promotion, and transfer. This preoccupation with process also makes more difficult the exploration of cooperation with unions in creative approaches to positive employee incentives.

The Office of Personnel Management operates approximately 70 percent of all examining operations, directly conducts training programs, administers compensation and fringe benefits programs, and runs the Federal retirement system. It also attempts to keep the manual up to date — often unsuccessfully. It relies heavily on standard procedures, preapprovals of agency plans, and audits of individual positions and even individual actions, as system controls. When it develops personnel policy, it is often not able to obtain sufficiently broad inputs from managers and executives in addition to its network of personnel officers. And, it spends minimal time in personnel research and development activities or in exerting its role as the Federal government's personnel system leadership, a role which was intended as an important element of the Civil Service Reform Act.

The Present System

The staff studies on which this report is based makes many specific recommendations for reform of the Federal Personnel Manual. But the NAPA Panel strongly believes that "hacking away at the underbrush" is not a feasible solution to the problem of personnel system ineffectiveness. *A more advanced concept of personnel system value and accountability is needed which goes beyond the advances of the Civil Service Reform Act by placing responsibility for effective personnel management squarely in the hands of the manager, and not in the personnel organization.*

At present, accountability is divided and varies by functional areas within personnel management so that no one is fully accountable. For example:

• Only the agency head has the authority to hire, promote, train, and fire employees, but this must be done following specific procedures laid down by OPM and frequently with OPM approvals of plans or individual actions.

• OPM and agency position classifiers usually have the final say in position classification while the line manager is accountable for determining duties, assignments of duties, and work results.

• Delegations to agencies and within agencies for personnel management vary greatly by functional areas (hiring, promoting, training, separating). Delegation to line managers to act on personnel matters without approval by or formal coordination with others is the rare exception rather than the rule.

These muddied relationships prevail in a government personnel system once highly centralized but in which substantial decentralization took place before and during World War II and again during the Korean War because decentralization was recognized as vital to the success in the war effort. Congress and Presidents have also conceded the need to exempt special government activities from the general civil service: the Tennessee Valley Authority in 1933, the Atomic Energy Commission and the medical functions of the Veterans Administration in 1946, NASA in 1958, the Postal Service in 1970, the U.S. Railway Association in 1973, and the Synthetic Fuels Corporation in 1980. Legislative branch agencies and some security agencies have their own non-civil-service merit systems.

Despite these centrifugal tendencies, there were centralizing forces at work from the 1950's on — notably the recentralization of examining authority in the Civil Service Commission in the 1960's. However, when Congress reconstructed the statutory foundations of the civil service in the Civil Service Reform Act of 1978, it provided authority for the Director of OPM to delegate most of his functions to agency heads.

The basic argument for a centralized, procedurally oriented personnel system is that the Federal government is a single employer, and equity and efficiency demand such a system. However, past decentralizations and exemptions show a clear recognition that the government is *not* a single employer and that flexibility in personnel management delegations to agencies is necessary if they are to administer Federal programs successfully.

On the basis of its overall assessment, the Panel developed several basic assumptions about necessary conditions for further personnel systems reform:

• Effective deregulation is possible only through maximum delegation of authority to agencies with:

— the relinquishing of detailed controls by the central agency and
— the decentralization of operations within agencies.

• To carry out this concept, it is essential to hire, develop, and retain the highest quality of executive and managerial leadership — both political and career.

• Executive leadership should be given full responsibility for personnel management and held strictly accountable for actions and results.

- The central personnel agency (the Office of Personnel Management) should provide positive leadership on behalf of the President by:
  - issuing broad guidelines;
  - carrying out far-reaching research and development efforts directly or in cooperation with agencies;
  - monitoring and evaluating personnel management effectiveness within agencies, and, where necessary, withdrawing delegations of authority;
  - actively enforcing sound personnel management through recommending changes to the President and the heads of agencies when it finds system problems in the agencies; and
  - encouraging and assisting agencies to develop strong positive personnel programs.
- The Merit Systems Protection Board will have to be vigorous in its role and competently staffed, particularly in its merit systems review functions.

A New Conceptual Framework

A new conceptual framework is proposed which is based on consideration of some of the characteristics of successful private sector personnel programs, but, to a surprising degree, it is simply a turnaround of the negative reactions to the Federal personnel system summarized above. In this new framework:

Federal executives and managers must take a more direct and active role in personnel management. (Many of their counterparts in highly successful private companies spend on the average of *more than 50 percent of their time* on the development of people.) The Federal system must delegate more "hands-on" authority to these managers and deliberately draw them more into the design of personnel systems and programs, so that the managerial needs will dominate design rather than procedural concerns. Managers must, within established guidelines, take greater control over critical personnel processes, such as recruitment of talent and the classification of positions as to grade and work content, and ultimately must be held accountable for the success or failure of personnel management.

It must be reemphasized that the basic intent of this concept is to shift the center of gravity for personnel program effectiveness away from the professional personnel organization and into the hands of the managers. The focal point for the personnel program is the workplace. Both managers and employees know how complex and interactive this workplace can be, but it is here that the real utilization of an organization's human resources takes place. People are motivated not by systems but by leadership, the value of the job, the chance to contribute and to achieve, and the sense of being needed and rewarded. Federal supervisors, managers and executives cannot afford to be hampered by their own personnel system, nor can they remain indifferent to and unskilled in personnel matters.

Professional personnel staff must consult more thoroughly and extensively with agency leadership and line managers to give them professional guidance and assistance and to obtain — in fact demand — clearer signals about what management wants from its personnel programs, and they must monitor programs and personnel operations on management's behalf. This is more of a staff function rather than a line function, and it presumes some shifting of personnel operations (notably recruiting, classification, performance evaluation, and merit pay determinations) into line organizations. But it is also a personnel responsibility of a higher quality and ultimately of far greater value to the organization.

The Office of Personnel Management must concentrate less on detailed procedures and focus more on providing directions, leadership, and evaluation. This can be made possible by delegating most operations to the agencies in every feasible way. OPM would continue to design the overall personnel system and give greater emphasis to monitoring and evaluating the conduct of personnel programs throughout the government on behalf of the President. In addition, OPM would continue to guide and review basic compensation and classification systems, and approve certain key individual executive personnel and political appointment actions, as well as labor contracts which are nation- or organizationwide in scope, along with general oversight of labor relations. . . .

Recommendations:

To develop this new concept and and partnership, the Panel recommends that:

• OPM and agencies establish and operate under a clear and consistent set of relationships with each other.

• OPM act for the President in developing and guiding a positive personnel program to be carried out by the agencies, and in sponsoring research and development on useful innovations.

• OPM adopt broad guidelines which permit agencies to have the flexibility to develop and implement personnel programs responsive to their management needs.

• Agencies select and develop career executives and managers who will be competent and willing to exercise the major personnel management responsibilities recommended in this report.

• Executives and Line Managers:
—Take more active roles in personnel, particularly in selection and development of effective employees;
— Help tailor personnel programs to meet their needs;
— Develop a greater sense of personal responsibility for the design and operation of the system;
— Receive rewards based on involvement;
— Be held accountable for effective use of authority delegated to them;
— Participate in developing policies which are approved by the head of their agency or organization.

• Within agencies, personnel offices:
— Provide staff assistance to top management in the formulation of agency personnel policies and standards;
— Serve as consultants to executives and line managers, as well as provide staff help in recruiting, training, and other personnel functions.

One of the unfortunate consequences of past personnel practices is that a significant proportion of Federal managers and first line supervisors move into their jobs without adequate training or preparation to exercise their personnel responsibilities. The recommendations of this report call on managers to upgrade their human resources role and would require more direct attention to personnel processes. If real progress is to be made in bringing about the decentralization concept, it is imperative that special efforts be made to train and motivate managers to fulfill their new role. Such special efforts would be warranted if only to repair past neglect, but it becomes an imperative for the future. No significant improvements can be achieved in human resources utilization, personnel program innovation, or reduction of procedural overregulation until managers are properly prepared to accept their more important roles. This need also represents a significant new challenge as well for OPM and the professional personnel staffs in the departments and agencies. They too must "shift gears" and place themselves in more of a service relationship to line leadership than in the past.

Such changes can't be made overnight. The course laid out in this report will require many years to bring about. OPM continues to be guarded in stating that "OPM favors delegations if these are consistent with law and OPM's mint and fiduciary responsibilities." But clearly the pace at which this change is implemented could be much greater if OPM and agency leadership can be linked together in a partnership to develop plans for achieving these objectives.

Recommendations:

- The NAPA Panel recommends that OPM take the lead in planning and promoting a major program to strengthen the personnel role of Federal managers throughout government by implementing the recommendations of this report.
- It also recommends that agency heads adopt the policies of this report which call for greater delegation of authority for personnel matters and that immediate action be initiated to train and motivate all supervisors and managers to prepare them for the assumption of this stronger personnel role.

Within the framework of the substantial personnel system changes described above, the Panel has developed a series of more complete and specific recommendations for improvement in major parts of the overall personnel system.

The Classification Sytem

Findings:

- A majority of classification standards are out-of-date and inadequate.
- Controls on results of the classification process are outside the authority of line managers.
- The classification process itself is heavy with redtape and invites adversarial relationships.

The classification process, under the Classification Act of 1949, involves the application of governmentwide standards to individual positions in virtually every occupation and pay level within each occupation in the Federal government. The results set both the grade and pay level for each position in the organization and the qualifications required for each position. Yet in today's world, it is virtually impossible to develop and maintain standards that will fit the great diversities found in duties, organizational alignments, and levels of responsibilities found among the 1,500,000 white collar positions in the Federal government. This is illustrated by the fact that for the 430 white collar occupations in government, 40 percent are covered by "new" classification standards using a factor evaluation system started in the 1970's; 60 percent are under old standards. The Panel recommends that OPM concentrate governmentwide standards on the working level or professional level positions in an occupation which represents the predominant numbers of positions in that occupation. (They are frequently referred to as "journeyman" positions and involve the full range of duties in the occupation but do not include any supervisory or special responsibilities.) Broad guideline standards should be issued by OPM which agencies would adapt and apply in classifying positions at all other levels in the occupation. Agencies and line managers within agencies could and should be involved in the development of both governmentwide standards, and line managers should also be involved in the adoption and application of those standards in their agencies.

A second problem is organizational. Managers are not held accountable for grade and salary expenditures, while those who are responsible for grades and salaries (position classifiers and OPM) are not held accountable for the work of employees. This comes about because the Classification Act forces managers to organize and carry out their work through positions, which in turn are assigned a grade and pay range. The first phase is carried out by the line managers and executives; the second by position classifiers in agencies and OPM. Managers decide organizational alignment, distribution of functions, delegations of authority, and duties assigned and degrees of responsibility given to individual positions. The role of the classifier is to put the "price tag" on the result which the manager has determined. By giving the line manager greater authority and responsibility for the final step in the classification process, he or she will consider the results from the total process in terms of (1) the requirement to comply with the basic law (the Classification Act), (2) the impact of costs of salary and fringe benefits, (3) issues of equity in their organizations as well as others, (4) the ability to defend the action with higher levels of management, outside review agencies, and individual employees and groups of employees, and (5) possible alternatives. The classifier, in this situation, becomes more of an adviser to line management, frequently to several levels in the organization, in assisting management in taking into account all of the considerations involved and in monitoring the process for agency executives.

A third problem results from efforts by OMB and Congress to control "grade creep" by discouraging increases in the average grade of an organization (the total of all the grades in the organization divided by the number of jobs). Such a control would be useful only when the organization's work program and number of jobs remain static. Changes in program and staffing are frequent and affect the average grade. Therefore this is an unrealistic form of control and another logical candidate for deregulation. The use of the budget process to set dollar limits on personnel costs linked with stronger workforce planning and control can be far more effective means for curbing grade creep which do not have the same constraining effect on supervisor flexibility. Agency executives should be perfectly capable of enforcing compliance with classification standards through supervisory discipline and internal agency evaluation systems. They can also set and enforce budgetary limits as a means of control. OPM continues to disagree, saying that managerial expediency and pressure must be countered by the classification system. Central agencies such as OPM, GAO, and MSPB have an important role also to evaluate programs and to report results of their evaluations to agency heads, to the President, and to Congress.

Recommendations:

• OPM's role should be changed to that of developing standards for the full performance level positions in occupations and issuing broad guideline standards which agencies would adopt and apply to all other positions in their organizations. Agencies should participate in the development of both these standards and guideline standards.

• Line managers should assume greater responsibility for classification and sound position management; the role of the classifier should be more of an adviser than a control agent.

• OPM should eliminate current methods of classification control, i.e., setting average grades and classifying (certifying) individual positions. Congress and OMB should control classification through overall salary costs and agency heads should exercise organization, position management, and salary controls for their agencies.

• New models of classification systems that meet agency needs should be developed and put in place.

Hiring Quality Personnel

Findings:

• There is a lack of consistent OPM philosophy and practice on delegation of examining authority, and the lack of delegation adversely affects the ability of line managers in their efforts to recruit quality personnel.

• The pipeline for filling professional and administrative career positions essential to effective administration of the executive branch of government has been impaired. No satisfactory temporary or permanent solution is in sight.

Agencies prefer to do their own recruiting and examining for outside hires under delegated authority from OPM, because they find they can do more active recruiting, expedite hiring, increase line management involvement, and achieve better results if they have delegated authority. Yet today, only 30 percent of all outside hires are selected from registers maintained by agencies under delegated authority. OPM has shifted its stance over the years about delegating, recruiting, and examining to agencies, and some current delegations are being withdrawn.

OPM contends that such simplifying delegations are not consistent with the law nor the intent of Congress.

The Federal government has been a major employer of college graduates for professional and administrative positions (normally 7000 per year) hired for careers in all agencies. As an example of their importance, IRS uses college graduates as a primary personnel source. Heretofore, an IRS employing office could go directly to OPM for a certificate of eligibles. Now, OPM delegates "Schedule B" hiring authority to agencies only after obtaining specific approval from OPM for each position to be filled. Requests for approval must be submitted through the Assistant Secretary for Administration for the Treasury. Within Treasury, the request goes from a field office to a region, then to the national office in IRS and then to the Assistant Secretary, who would then submit the request to OPM for approval. This whole process is unreasonably complex and slow. It would be simple and preferable to delegate hiring authority to an appropriate agency manager.

In a serious case of delay in delegating authority to hire college graduates, a Department of the Army request to hire 900 college graduates went to OPM in November 1982, but was not approved until March 1983. This made it extremely difficult for the Army to mount a nationwide recruiting drive for the May 1983 graduates.

The delegation of authority to agencies to recruit and hire is helpful, but there are problems over and above delays. The present process was instituted as a result of a consent decree based upon alleged bias of previous examinations; current procedures are supposed to comply with the consent decree provisions. Agencies have not been given guidance on how to comply with consent decree provisions and therefore may not be in compliance. Finally, new employees are unable to achieve career status and cannot be promoted to levels for which they are being developed. The only out is for them to be selected from a civil service register for that higher grade—an action that may be impossible.

Recommendations:

   • Change OPM policy to one of maximum delegation of examining authority to agencies, including a liberal definition of "common" positions. Delegations should be without a time limitation and should be withdrawn only if the authority has been abused.
   • Assure, by OBM/OPM action, adequate resources for examining.
   • As a short-term solution to the consent decree problem, permit agencies to use schedule B under blanket delegated authority, following decree guidelines, and convert employees hired to career status under an Executive Order upon successful completion of a period of employment.

The Performance Appraisal System

Finding:

   • Basic responsibility for the new performance appraisal systems has been in the hands of agencies. They have produced systems which in many cases demand excessive time and paperwork and do not have the confidence of the workforce. Agencies should be able to solve such problems.

Effective performance appraisal systems improve communications between the supervisor and the employee about expectations and performance and serve as a basis for decisions on training, promotions, transfers, and in some cases, separations.

Prior to 1978, most Federal supervisors could have avoided appraising performance on a regular basis and many did so. Managers generally do not like to appraise performance and Federal managers are no exception. Under the Civil Service Reform Act of 1978, agencies were required to develop new performance appraisal systems for their employees. Further, the appraisals were to relate to the extent of achievement of program objectives. This was a very expensive and time-consuming effort designed to refocus the Federal incentive system from bureaucratic process and assessment of personal traits to the evaluation of how employees are carrying out the missions for which they are being paid by the taxpayers. This major effort still is in progress. Some agencies did their work well; others did not. Most systems went into effect between July 1979 and October 1981; the final evaluation of any of them cannot as yet be made, for industry experience indicates that it takes up to 5 years to fully implement a performance appraisal system.

Agencies have had little initial guidance from OPM and have tackled the effort in many different ways. For example:

• In some agencies, there are three different performance appraisal systems — one each for Senior Executive Service (SES) personnel, Merit Pay employees, and all others.

• Plans for individual employees have varied excessively in quality and lengths.

• Because individual plans are linked to actions which might be appealed, plans can be burdened with paperwork as a defensive mechanism — just in case an employee should appeal.

The only OPM restriction in its regulations was that which precluded forced distribution of ratings. A new OPM proposal to simplify and standardize performance appraisal systems throughout the government indicates that in the OPM effort to correct certain agency problems, the agencies may have lost an opportunity to install effective systems tailored to meet their particular program needs. While every effort should be made to support OPM initiatives to simplify paperwork, it would not be acceptable for OPM to impose a new performance appraisal system in agencies without managerial and employer acceptance.

Recommendations:

• Reduce the excessive paperwork in existing agency systems with attention to the number of systems in an agency, the number and detail of critical elements, and the length of individual plans.

• Eliminate the requirement that OPM approve agencies' performance appraisal plans; instead OPM should conduct the extensive research and experimentation needed to improve appraisal systems and should place emphasis on issuance of broad guidelines and on program evaluation.

• Generally improve and stabilize agency systems, with input from both managers and employees; train managers in the preparation and use of performance standards.

• Request OPM to remove restrictions on forced distribution of ratings and hold agency executives accountable for preventing upward skewing of ratings.

• Evaluate and recognize managers partly on their effectiveness in personnel management, such as employee development and performance appraisal.

Merit Pay

Finding:

• Merit pay for supervisors is one of the most controversial personnel problems resulting from implementation of the Civil Service Reform Act. Few argue with the concept of merit pay but the cost and complexities of administration, the separate and perceived inequitable treatment of supervisors when compared to other employees in the same pay levels, and the meager amount of money involved tend to negate its value as an incentive to better performance.

The law limits use of merit pay to GS-13–15 managers only. All nonmanagerial employees in the same pay range (GS-13–15) and all employees GS-1 through GS-13 continue to receive increases based upon "acceptable" performance and completion of specified waiting periods. Where agencies have dual career ladders, there is a choice of going up via the management route or the purely professional route where the automatic step increase system continues. Top management is concerned about the negative influence merit pay will have on the future career choices of professionals who have the aptitude to become managers.

Employees subject to merit pay are not guaranteed annual comparability increases; one-half their comparability increases go into the merit pay pool which means that the average yearly increase is less than for nonmanagers, contrary to the intent of the civil service reform recommendations. Furthermore, the limitations on the amounts of money available provide meager rewards for the best employees and may preclude "satisfactory" employees from getting their full comparability increases—a point of view which OPM appears to support.

There is no way that a manager or merit pay employee can relate a rating of performance to the specific dollar amount the employee will receive until long after the rating is given. This is due to the fact that the amounts for individual employees are based upon the distribution of ratings in the unit and the funds available—which in 1980 were not known until well after October 24. However, ratings have to be made by October 1.

All these limitations and distinctions are infringements on managers' ability to recognize superior performance with extra compensation—yet another example of the shackling of managerial discretion.

OPM controls on merit pay were imposed after agencies initially developed their systems. These controls discouraged further line management involvement in the development of agencies' programs and precluded the flexibility needed to meet agencies' needs.

The entire process is so complicated that it is difficult for the manager or the merit pay employee to understand it, much less accept the system and its results. These problems point to the need for an intensive interagency review of merit pay under OPM leadership and in consultation with GAO. The objectives should be to solve problems that cause inequities, inefficiencies, and lack of credibility of the system, and there is a need for a careful test and demonstration program to more carefully assess alternative merit pay options. As these objectives are achieved, it will be appropriate to expand the system to levels and types of jobs not now covered.

Recommendations:

• OPM and agencies should change regulations to ensure maximum flexibility in meeting agencies' needs and in making line managers accountable for effective operation of the merit pay system.

• OPM should amend regulations to guarantee comparability increases for merit pay employees if their performance is "satisfactory" or better than "satisfactory."

• Legislation should be sought to authorize agencies to place all GS-13/15 employees under merit pay.

• Funding should be increased for merit pay purposes to a level which assures that amounts paid to employees are sufficient to create real incentives for higher performance. Any merit pay system which is so underfunded that it does not motivate is wasting both effort and money.

• Legislation should be amended to change the merit pay system so that managers and employees will know the effects of a performance rating on merit pay when the rating is given.

Protecting Merit Principles and Protecting Employees

Finding:

• It is possible, though sometimes difficult, for executives and managers to enforce adherence to merit principles, to discourage prohibited personnel practices, to train and direct employees for effective performance, and yet to deal properly with instances of poor performance or conduct.

As is repeatedly emphasized in this report, agency executives and managers must be freed, encouraged, and even trained to practice positive personnel management. They should be held primarily responsible for upholding high standards of employee selection, development, and performance. At the same time they are responsible for assuring that employees are treated fairly, without political or personal favoritism. In cases where executives and managers are deficient in these respects, it was the intent of the CSRA that employees be protected by agency appeal systems and by the processes of the Merit Systems Protection Board and its Special Counsel.

On the other hand, when employees are deficient in their performance, there must be effective tools for managers to seek remedies for these deficiencies. In such cases, the manager is responsible for helping the employee improve or, if that fails, separating the employee. The performance appraisal provisions of the Civil Service Reform Act have resulted in appraisal systems more closely related to agency job requirements. Evaluations completed by MSPB, OPM, and an earlier National Academy of Public Administration Panel on Civil Service Reform verify these improvements. Furthermore, agencies involved in this deregulation study indicate successes in improving performance.

By having and using effective performance appraisal plans, an agency may remove a nonproductive employee within 6 months after action is initiated, according to a study in one department. This is a much shorter time than was required prior to CSRA. Unfortunately, there is little data available to indicate the numbers and disposition of formal actions involving nonproductive employees.

The Civil Service Reform Act reduces the possibility of an agency losing a case on minor technicalities. It does not and should not reduce or change the steps in the process or the fact that management must prove that an employee has not lived up to his or her contract for performance reasons.

The employee's rights to continue in his or her job are formally protected by law and regulation. A manager who starts to take formal action against an employee for failure to perform needs technical assistance to make sure the actions adhere to mandated requirements. This will reduce paperwork and unnecessary delay.

Recommendations:

• Train managers to handle effectively problems of employee conduct or performance. Emphasize use of performance appraisals for setting goals related to organizational objectives, giving employees feedback, and delineating expectations for improvement. Require managers, before formal adverse action becomes necessary, to consult with personnel staff on meeting technical requirements.

• Assure that personnel staffs actively support managers who are experiencing problems with employee performance or conduct, make adverse actions as simple as possible, and reduce technical compliance burdens.

• Require OPM and MSPB to develop, maintain, and distribute data that agencies use to inform managers of the disposition of appeals in adverse action cases.

Equal Employment Opportunity

Finding:

• Executives and managers are frustrated by the overlapping roles of oversight agencies that result in duplicative regulations and requirements. Current regulations and procedures do not relate to the achievement of EEO goals.

One of the merit principles in the Civil Service Reform Act is that "Recruitment should be from qualified individuals from appropriate sources in an endeavor to achieve a work force from all segments of society, and selection and advancement should be determined solely on the basis of relative ability, knowledge, and skills after fair and open competition which assure that all receive equal opportunity." However, this is only one of some 86 different Congressional requirements regarding equal employment. There are numerous special emphasis programs including age discrimination, disabled veterans, upward mobility, and women's programs, each with its own reporting requirement.

The laws and regulations are complex, varied, and fragmented so that agencies are weakened and burdened in their efforts to comply. For example, OPM and EEOC have divided the responsibility for special programs that overlap (OPM is responsible for disabled veterans, EEOC is responsible for handicapped). Agency plans and reports are submitted on different time schedules to OPM and EEOC, even though the objectives of the programs are similar and the same personnel data bases are used. OPM requires collection of data for the Central Personnel Data File, which is the same basic data required by EEOC. However, the system cannot provide appropriate breakouts of data for affirmative action purposes without a major systems redesign.

All these confusing requirements do not motivate managers to constructive action to meet equal employment opportunity goals. Indeed, people tend to pay only lip service to systems that are bogged down in redtape and line managers strive to distance themselves from most of these requirements, thus defeating the very purpose for which they were intended. Furthermore, it is difficult to monitor compliance in such a tangled regulatory situation.

The immensity of the problem is shown by the fact that one agency's multiyear affirmative action plan was 4 feet high when stacked up. The yearly update was eight 3-inch notebooks. The possibility of improvement is exemplified by the fact that another agency, the Department of Education, uses a simple form that managers submit on a monthly basis, which serves as a self-evaluation tool that summarizes the personnel actions or opportunities taken that month, and shows what the managers did with those opportunities.

A governmentwide problem is that no innovative authority exists to depart from normal methods of competitive examination in an organization where underrepresentation clearly exists.

Recommendations:

- Begin an interagency examination by OMB, EEOC, OPM, and Justice of laws, regulations, and reporting requirements with the objective of:
  - recommending, consolidating, and codifying existing laws and repealing of unnecessary requirements;
  - simplifying affirmative action reporting requirements by incorporating affirmative action data into the Central Personnel Data File; and
  - coordinating roles and responsibilities of oversight agencies where they cannot be consolidated.
- Meanwhile initiate collaborative work by agencies with EEOC to initially reduce reporting requirements . . . until the recommendation above is implemented.

• Evaluate managers' performance partly on their use of opportunities to take affirmative action. Place less emphasis on individual affirmative action plans.

• Start development by OPM and operating agencies of innovative programs to achieve improved representativeness of the Federal service. This could include but not be limited to alternative examination procedures where underrepresentation exists. This could be tried under the research and demonstration provisions of the Civil Service Reform Act.

"Redtape" Reforms

Finding:

• The present system of personnel regulations is excessive in length, complexity, and compartmentalization and ill-adapted to use by managers.

The Federal Personnel Manual (FPM) derives authority from Title V of the United States Code. As the requirements of the Code cascade to the Federal Personnel Manual, its 552 pages become 8,814 pages in the FPM. Since agency regulations must parallel the FPM and supplement it in terms of procedure or policy within the agency, two things happen:

• Agency directives become an extension of the FPM and frequently can't be understood without referring to the FPM.

• The compartmentalization of the system and the contents of the regulations make them tools of personnel specialists but undecipherable to executives and managers.

The system is even becoming more complex because proposed regulations are now issued in:

• The Code of Federal Regulations.

• The Federal Personnel Bulletin or the Federal Personnel Letter, which serves as a means of issuing instructions or information on a temporary basis.

• The Federal Personnel Manual, which serves as the vehicle for translating the instruction into a permanent Issuance.

• The Federal Personnel Manual Supplement, which is used to expand on the FPM by providing additional guidance or procedures on a specific subject.

A recent check with OPM indicates that 9 additional chapters and 22 additional subchapters of the FPM are currently in process.

The review resulted in the following number of recommendations for changes in regulations in the FPM:

Rescind all or part of the regulation	2
Increase delegations of authority	25
Delete procedures required	15
Eliminate reporting requirements	10
Reduce prior approvals required	9
Make other changes	16
	77

These recommendations are spelled out in the staff report which supplements this Panel report. Each of the 77 recommended changes will help deregulate the personnel management system of the Federal government. Despite the magnitude of the changes proposed, the Panel believes that the broader changes in OPM recommended in this report would give great impetus to a much deeper and more effective deregulation of the FPM than those proposed here.

Recommendations:

- Develop and issue OPM criteria for regulations with particular concern for delegations of authority, reports approvals, procedures, and program evaluation.
- Require agencies with subordinate organizations to reexamine their criteria in the same areas — particularly delegations of authority.
- Encourage agencies to experiment with issuing essential parts of their manuals in language managers can understand without being bound by the format or the compartmentalization of the FPM.

Delegation of Authority

Finding:

- Executives and line managers feel that delegations in personnel management are inadequate to meet their needs. The result is frustration, time lost, and losses in acquiring and retaining quality people necessary to accomplish mission because the decision authority is held by someone far away from the action and usually not accountable for program results.

If a manager does not have the delegated authority to act, it means that he or she must either request someone else to act or obtain prior approval for his proposed action.

As indicated above, the Panel found in the review of the Federal Personnel Manual that there were:
- 25 types of actions in which agencies should be delegated authority to act and
- 9 types of actions where prior approvals from OPM could be eliminated. . . .

The significance of this is that almost all the actions require prior approval of OPM in Washington, and in many cases under current procedure, by the Director. Agencies tend to follow the practice of central agencies in administering their personnel systems and the problem becomes compounded. The time delays and paper involvement alone are mind-boggling, let alone the hampering of managers in taking action.

Recommendations:

- Expand delegations to agencies from OPM; eliminate delegations with time limitations; withdraw delegations only if there is abuse.
- Encourage agencies to expand delegations to subordinate and field organizations, consistent with delegations for program management.

Concluding Comment

In the opinion of the Panel, the leadership of the Federal government has failed adequately to understand the negative consequences of the cumulative effects of overelaborate and overregulated management systems on the thousands of line and staff executives and managers who are the real strength in the implementation of public programs. In the preoccupation with creating and defending strong central systems, the manager in government has been made less effective and far less motivated to carry his or her organization to high levels of excellence and productivity.

The NAPA Panel concludes that the whole framework of current Federal management policy which emphasizes highly centralized and regulatory management systems is simply pointing in the wrong direction. The best approach to solving the present conditions of managerial overburden and deterioration lies not in further hardening of the central system controls but in a deliberate "turnaround" of this policy to one of finding positive, constructive ways to build up the role and capabilities of its managers. In this way thousands of people all over government can regain a sense of being fully "in charge" and accountable for their own responsibilities and be given positive motivations and assistance to revitalize their own performance and that of the organizations they lead.

Index

Proceedings of
The Academy of
Political Science

ISSN 0065-0684

1983–85
Volume 35